TOMBSTONE
CONFIDENTIAL

TOMBSTONE CONFIDENTIAL

by James Mann

BELL TOWER EDITIONS

SANTA FE, NEW MEXICO

Tombstone Confidential

by James Mann

PUBLISHER:
Bell Tower Editions
2108 Foothill Road
Santa Fe, New Mexico 87505

FIRST EDITION

FIRST PRINTING: 2016

Cataloging data:

Mann, James

Tombstone Confidential / James Mann

Trade paperback, 476 pages
ISBN-13: 978-0-9802278-8-8

1. American Poetry. 2. BISAC: POETRY / American / General
I. Mann, James. II Tombstone Confidential.

LCC: PS301-326
BISAC: POE005010

COVER:
Pieter Brueghel the Elder (c. 1526–1569)
The Triumph of Death (detail), c. 1562
oil on panel
Museo del Prado, Madrid

BACK COVER:
Photo of author by Rachael Walsh

ISBN-TEN: 0-9802278-8-7
ISBN-THIRTEEN: 978-0-9802278-8-8

To the memory of my father,
a public man praised for his eloquence,
and the memory of my mother,
whose joy as the household wordsmith
primed me for poetry

CONTENTS

TOMBSTONE
CONFIDENTIAL

Out of a grave I come to tell you this . . .
— E.A. Robinson

Hypocrite lecteur,—mon semblable,—mon frère!
— Baudelaire

*Brutally honest and confrontational, he
draws attention to the paranoiacal denial
of death that permeates our culture.*
— Virginia Button

*I know not anything which will not
come within the scope of my plan.*
— Wordsworth

CAUTION *Lost World*

No doubt you find yourself a decent sort,
Absent a yardstick of duty or church.
You dream of a home in a trumped-up resort,
Where you savor episodes of *Star Search*.

The past century's savagery undenied,
You deem your instincts civilized enough.
Medicine shunts death's daily threat aside,
And the world is full of entertaining stuff.

You missed boot camp? The harshest words you've heard
Are Dad's the night you totaled his new car.
You'd reckon a monk obsessed by death absurd,
A sergeant mauling your dignity bizarre?

Your paint-by-number brain they shaped in school
Dramatizes a humorless lack of flair.
To save the earth, you round up a car pool;
To save mankind, you mail a check to CARE.

Once your dwelling is climatized and snug,
A burglar alarm is all you guess you need
To ward off evil, keeping you safe and smug,
Content that insurance covers a dirty deed.

Your virtue's condition cause for no concern,
You nurture the common weal with income tax.
No mythic lake where fire and brimstone churn
Persuades you more than debt can dog your tracks.

Plainly your spirit enjoys an easeful ride.
Gleaming appliances help you even think
Goodness is automatic. Feeding such pride?
Garbage ground to bits by the kitchen sink.

Rare the reminders of death, your silent twin,
It shrinks to an odd, lost sequel to life:
No more the hourly present menace to men
For a hundred thousand years of starving strife.

Survival's grim struggle on the frontier;
The wild night's tumultuous choir of shrieks;
Its rumbling hooves and howling wolves; the fear
Prowling in shadows of moonlit mountain peaks;

And the eerie hoot or screech of owls floating
Above the stench of carrion: all unknown
In nowaday's deceptive sugar coating
Of reality's huge, permanent touchstone.

French historian Philippe Ariès
Writes that death's invisible, medicalized,
Unmentionable—a subject to suppress.
Rename it "a future terribly downsized."

The MILTON BRADLEY "CHECKERED GAME OF LIFE"
Had squares for plights galore at any stage,
Cross-sections of living sliced by bread knife—
But no Death, merely a Happy Old Age.

"Youth vanquished age and death itself grew
Unthinkable," according to Jill Lepore,
When new science's progress and worldview
Ushered fatality out the back door.

This is a dream of deep-rooted delusion
Nourished by a secretive shadow soul
Companioning you through a cold fusion
That drops you in a darkness black as coal.

Call the shadow your etheric double:
Etheric as in static electric air;
An unseen presence like a cartoon bubble.
Together you're a gravely bonded pair.

"Even one thing which is ours yet cannot die?
Death," the rhymer Swinburne baits the reader:
"Time's twin-born brother," his tissue bone-dry,
His double a blamed, carnal-craving bleeder.

"All save death can be adjusted: it,
Unto itself exception, is exempt
From change." From SIDS to stroke to your throat slit,
Emily Dickinson sums up death's contempt.

In the 1800's, death was mused about
Constantly, and the preferred manner to die—
Until the Civil War's complete blowout:
No deathbed ringed by loved ones, only sky.

His family photos kept in a pocket case,
A fallen, dying soldier might arrange
These pictures around him. From each tiny face,
Its gaze thus met his for a final exchange.

No bugle playing distant notes of retreat
Soothes the riven heart in this helpless scene:
Sounds undimmed of battle's pounding repeat,
As his fading pulse echoes the war machine.

Death was shared experience everyone had.
"Now it's hidden," says filmmaker Ric Burns:
An absence Civil War Dead would call mad.
Death's a weight no power overturns,

Though taking breath for granted has become
Rife as the Plague in 1349—
While dying's toll still equals the full sum
Of mortals who step past life's starting line.

The Black Death's victims were stacked like cordwood,
Wherever its infected vermin spread.
Killed in a rush that few stricken withstood,
Half of Europe was slain by the fleas it fed.

The Plague claimed tens of millions in three years.
In 1919, the Spanish Flu took more.
Another scourge's onslaught stealthily nears,
Preparing to top pandemic's highest score.

Yet the strange and deep difficulty of death
Finds no relevance in your cool routine.
The simple image of drawing your last breath
Sinks like a psychic depth charge unseen.

Get past your living's fine, complacent state
Of shallow conceit trumping your lone chance
To transcend the time's outdated boilerplate,
Your culture's prison of deadlocked romance.

Your empty approbation of the self,
The overexposed smile of today's dude
Substantial as a disappearing elf,
Has modern ego's vapid attitude.

No wonder you're so cocky, but there's a catch:
You still die, ignore it as late as you please.
You grow so vain, nature demands a rematch,
And liquidates your life with amazing ease.

Pride comes before destruction, *Proverbs* says.
What's more, a haughty spirit precedes a fall:
Whether you sport a silly Shriner's fez,
Or dance with dowagers at a masked ball.

Try turning humble for the MAIN EVENT:
Restore the right proportion to the mix.
Before your being's final effort is spent,
Weigh in at the fight drugs and money can't fix.

As age forms an icicle down your back,
Each moment of life's a step toward the grave.
Nearer every hour to death in black,
You perish, regardless how much time you save.

Watch your face's reflection all your days,
And you'll see death at work like a beehive
Of glass etching craquelure with your gaze,
That deepens every year you stay alive.

Time in its aging overtakes all things:
Golden streaks on a blushing flower bud;
A dickey bird whose heart outlives its wings;
A soldier oozing his last ounce of blood.

Death will play the devil with your dreams,
And knock the living daylights out of you.
A long nightfall ensues which endless beams
Of sun, moon, and starlight can't undo.

The latter days may not be here yet,
But on your lookout they might as well.
The end of the world you know a constant threat,
Its rise is random as an ocean swell.

Tomorrow unlike yesterdays you've known,
Where you're going's like no place you've been:
You hit a wall where hope drops like a stone,
Then terror expels your spirit from your skin.

I YIELD TO NO ONE, death-god Terminus states
On a medal struck in 1524
To honor the sage Erasmus. That predates
This sparkling age yet shuts the same door.

"Our birth is nothing but our death begun,"
Wrote Edward Young in his volume *Night Thoughts*
Of 1742: excepting none,
From Jesus to Jason and the Argonauts.

Death will lurk flush in the midst of your life,
Staking out its ultimate property rights.
It doesn't rely on famine, flood, or strife,
But patient appraisal of your dimming lights.

"The goal of life is death for any man,"
Declared the stony speaker Demosthenes.
None eludes time's all-ruinous plan,
Whether eating manna or black-eyed peas.

"Why should you weep?" Socrates asked his friends.
"Well do you know that since the hour of my birth,
Life sentenced me to death. Who then pretends
By tears and sorrow to break the bonds of earth?

"Death is stronger than birth. Are mine not proof—
As if you required as much? Now dry your eyes.
Admire the hue of the sky's majestical roof
Stage-lighting how an old philosopher dies."

Leveling all distinction, death and dice
Contend in every single second you live.
More life can't be purchased at any price,
And your body leaks its future like a sieve.

What's man, to hope he'll come to a good end?
So asks Anthony Hecht's poem *The Vow*.
Who are you to negate such wisdom, friend,
But rotten fruit still hanging on the bough?

"The finest fate is never to be born.
The second, once born? To die right away,"
Silenus the satyr told King Midas in scorn.
From Plato to Nietzsche, this wit mocks its prey.

The older you get, the closer to the ground,
Gravity pulling your body down like a rock.
The earth will make you pay for every pound,
And undermine it by each tick of the clock.

Sunrise over the hillside, nightlife gone,
The stage it sets isn't a mystery play,
Earth's globe spinning as fast at dusk or dawn,
Its message that you don't have long to stay.

No sudden peeling back the veil of clay,
No angel visitant, no opening skies
Illuminate your steady downward way
To the great darkness no one born defies.

Spurn a punk who riddles the page with blanks,
Or shoots from the hip firing a scatter-gun.
Such talent, better lent to robbing banks,
Leaves the devil's work of wit undone.

Beware a gunman whose holster holds facts,
Who aims for the heart and lets the lead fly
At tedium's parade of lousy acts.
Save the cardboard props? In a pig's eye!

Do you subscribe strictly to wholesome art?
The present tome would try your self-esteem.
Stick to books like *True Love* and *Fresh Start*:
Discard this verse as a villain's ugly scheme.

And do you expect poetry to inspire,
Affirming a grand view of a lost world?
Then toss this awful opus in the fire,
And wash your hands of trash so ably hurled.

The meek inherit the earth. Meanwhile they
Aren't the moving force to make things work.
You protest, like a flower child on May Day?
If a scribbler offends, reject the brazen jerk.

Suppose none of these shortcomings applies?
The book you hold is starkly impolite.
Is yours the sort of flesh that lives and dies?
This story seeks to assess your birthright.

If harder to swallow than a horse pill,
Like a black draught of existential strife—
A remedy none rushes to refill—
Still by and large it's based on real life.

Don't look to encounter tried-and-true taste
Here, or dull concern for how to behave.
Leaving decorum deranged and red-faced,
There's simply the brutal rudeness of the grave.

"Who wishes it were longer than it is?"
Samuel Johnson mused of *Paradise Lost*.
Did poetry ever make your hair frizz?
When have you been completely double-crossed?

Satanic potential vested in the heart
Can bloom at midnight or at noontide fair.
It wants no provocation to jump-start,
No correct moment to lay its nerves bare.

Enough spadework. Reader, please take heed:
Not every poet praises daffodils.
Yet all true bards observe a timeless need:
To harness pain sharp as a dental drill's.

A reader can't avoid a nasty fall
On thoughts recorded with a porcupine quill.
Wallace Stevens writes there's nothing at all
"Like the clashed edges of two words that kill."

Across these pages and across the ages,
Though deep mountains shake the floor of the sea;
Though power's inarticulate pride rages;
Who doesn't like to bash the bourgeoisie?

Hey, wait a minute: won't this clobber you?
Aren't you found amid the madding crowd?
Sorry. Such is what life brings you to—
But give it your best: make your mother proud.

To live beyond the drab, insistent present,
You journey *ad Parnassum* on your own.
No single stage in the trip need be pleasant
To lift you above flesh and marrowbone.

Yet as for reaching a level beyond human,
Recall the suicides of HEAVEN'S GATE,
Who fancied their thirty-nine sterile crewmen
Could ride a comet as a cosmic skate.

Finally, never let it be widely known
To friend or foe that you can't take a joke,
If burdened by a sense as dense as stone,
Obscured in a noxious cloud of black smoke.

PROEM *Skeleton Key*

This is your life to pursue, boom or bust.
With each new step goes time forever lost.
As a spider eats a moth, whose guts are dust,
Breath flees death in your blood like jet exhaust.

If your body bore a warning on it,
DANGER—USE AT OWN RISK, is how it would read.
Your mortal shape is just as God has drawn it—
Except the drawing will wrinkle, bulge, and bleed.

From the wild heart of the jungle, wisdom comes:
You move in a nomad's caravan of dreams.
It's the same for billionaires or stinking bums:
You're born to die, and spend your life on schemes.

Behind the scenes you see are scenes you miss.
Your daily grind's not why the world goes round.
Stags wait in the wings, and back-row couples kiss?
Your spot onstage, like the sun, is westward bound.

A runaway train soon will run out of steam.
All boxcars and no caboose gets deadly dull.
Life's middle and end start in your infant scream,
Before suckling sutures your little skull.

From life your death will lack no exit doors.
There's one way to enter, a thousand to leave.
You breach birth's bone gates, then breath is yours
To reach the close your parents preconceive.

Your life's a spell of being begun at birth,
Your death a future point measured by math.
The gap between them counts your days on earth:
This stretch of dying shades life's only path.

Time's fresh river drags a surface speed,
Whose bright flecks are glints of a skeleton key.
The diamond power of living things is freed
In death by fire, or death deep in the sea.

The river of years only runs one way,
Always rushing to tomorrowland.
EVERYONE HERE'S FLOWN TO THE MOON TODAY,
Say signs that punctuate the Rio Grande.

As the snake a tree drops in your open boat,
Or an unknown bird call too far before dawn,
Earth's impact coins a lonesome cry in your throat.
Once come to terms with flowers and worms, you're gone.

Time frees you as wind cleans scum off a lake.
The way of all flesh expires at ding-dong bell.
The planet's inferno fires a clam bake
That mints fossils where their carcasses fell.

To subdue age's effect but quite in vain,
Superb surgeons labor in perfect light.
What they accomplish helps the body gain
A few odd years of playing with dynamite.

Cruise the fragile cities and desert places,
Bound for your end on a blank sheet of lead.
Noting inroads of silence on strange faces,
Remember: once a tree stops growing, it's dead.

Each morning you last above the grass is good.
Death is the victory over life, indeed.
SAVE THE DAY and CAN'T WIN FOR LOSING should
Jointly convince you life is what you bleed.

A meteor shower shows the far-flung stakes
Stalking your safety: sparks of starshine.
In the future's forest, some day a bough breaks,
Loudly announcing its fall to snap your spine.

Opposite states, life and death are twinned,
Death-in-life your countenance every day.
The second your warm breath departs on the wind,
Death becomes what's left of your molded clay.

You coldly decay into the stink of flesh,
Which yet will dry and blossom into flowers.
Hence the old and the new life perfectly mesh,
With every bloom a beauty time devours.

To reach the beyond, you leave your cage of bone,
Launched by the wreckage of age or a Sunday drive.
There's no official date till it's carved in stone.
Far better to creep towards it than to arrive.

The rock you sit on starts to roll? Jump clear.
Some time to kill remains before you die.
One of two outcomes marks each passing year:
You make it through or you don't, no answer why.

Does death ride from the east, the rising sun?
You're east of Eden; more nobody knows.
Death blindsides you same as anyone,
And thus your infrared no longer glows.

Look at death as a duty-free zone:
No more washing dishes, scrubbing the john.
When company comes, your granite tombstone
Is clean and tidy as Rome's PANTHEON.

In death alone does one have perfect peace.
Whether on country road or city street,
Emaciated or morbidly obese,
That goes for any random soul you meet.

Right on cue are those omens of death—black kites,
Gliding and banking gracefully overhead.
At no cost they provide funeral rites,
Calmly awaiting their hour to be fed.

FIND FLESH ON BONES THAT SOON HAVE NONE their creed,
Kites don't delay a minute once you expire.
Just as the last breath in your body is freed,
They airlift nature's Heraclitean fire.

Each dollar you get you spend, plus a dime?
Hope you're outlived by half your hair and teeth.
No role will pay you posthumous overtime
To play your spectral double underneath.

As you walk the edge of space's dark abyss,
Enjoy the sun and scout the noonday crowd,
Knowing the freshest breeze has a fatal kiss,
And lethal voltage hides in the brightest cloud.

Death visits all; the slayer follows the slain,
Both appointed to wear a wooden suit:
Barreling down the tracks on a midnight train,
Or gridlocked in the afternoon commute.

When lightning flashes miles away, you know
Someone's catching hell, just glad it's not you.
The sky envelops all creatures here below,
Who can't dodge a bolt hurled from the blue.

Detecting the new collapse of a black hole,
Watching the cockeyed spin of Saturn's rings,
Or choked by spewing vapor's fumarole,
You mark the mechanistic nature of things.

Your life barely the shadow of a dream,
Today departs by tomorrow's alarm clock.
A speck of you dies with every solar beam
Piercing the atmospheric sunblock.

You come from nothing; to nothing you return,
Swallowed in the expanding blackness of time.
The dark silence allows no matter to burn
For you beyond your lifespan thin as a dime.

Each page you turn for the latest news and sports
Records hours you've spent and won't get back.
Like timber for pulp to print them, dawn reports
Are dead as a severed head in a croker sack.

Cruising through cyberspace on a crystal screen
Produces the identical results.
Receive what information you can glean:
Nothing immortalizes your heart's pulse.

Where do you think the household garbage goes?
And why do garbage trucks all smell the same?
This vivid globe makes lovely light when it glows,
Yet fire requires the fuel, then the flame.

Imagine you're the fire inside the flame,
Oxidized as fast as the speed of light:
Consider the mass your body overcame
To exit into never-ending night.

From grievous bodily harm or your best lay,
Your eyes wide in a quizzical look perplexed,
Depart this world by any possible way:
You die in the dark about what comes next.

Despite the *Psalms'* wonderful words of life,
And gold all earthbound empires have amassed,
A roast is still served with a carving knife:
There's dawn for every darkness but your last.

How swell does it sound to watch the grass grow
Out of your skull, decades after you died,
Then howl at the comic irony and crow
From glen to glen and down the mountainside?

In only one arc a pendulum swings,
A pound of flesh becomes a puff of smoke,
All the matter around you merely things
The universe can burn when it's flat broke.

A pendulum slices like a knife through time:
The turbulent air in its wake, you don't see.
Yet thus both time and space prevail sublime,
Reigning from Arizona to Galilee.

The wind shifts are swept in sleep each night.
At sunrise vultures circle on slow black wings.
Go crown yourself king, but the buzzards' flight
Zeros in with a funnel's shrinking rings.

Big ideas on bits of paper won't
Halt the mystery's axis humming still.
Weird vessels of war and holy water don't
Help plenipotentiaries drink their fill.

"The emperor's up riding the dragon now,"
Eunuchs from the Forbidden City say.
"He was due to die in the year of the cow,
But cheated us, deciding to die today."

All said and done, you're clad in a vesture of clay.
Either that or you put on a coat of stone,
Darkness enfolding your eyes on Broadway
As you try to escape a NO PARKING zone.

The inconstant hour flees on steady wings.
He that begins to live begins to die.
The angel of death? Not a stripper who sings,
Nor a pilot sent to teach you how to fly.

Mummies emerge from Egypt's drifting sands—
And time's flagrant, sneaking subterfuge.
The sundial's circling shade countermands
The gift of life blessing a newborn stooge.

As ash on a torch creeps over the ember,
Age will steal upon and ravage your bloom.
During that ancient trek, May to December,
For clearing cobwebs use a peacock's plume.

When peace like a river takes your parting soul,
Don the grave's dress for the longest ride.
Thunder dies, the clouds roll back their scroll?
No shining seraph shoulders your stone aside.

EMPTY TOMB, INCORPORATED, has not
Yet opened a branch to serve the common man.
The kingdoms opposed aren't Oz and Camelot,
Once planet Earth completes your living plan.

The rest is silence, chaos, and boundless sky.
Death-dew cold on your brow, stench comes fast.
Aeons' glacial strength, no Troy can deny:
No evidence of your hardest work will last.

"Birth is the beacon of death," observed Plato.
What levels even monumental tombs?
Regard the words of Roman scholar Cato:
"All handiwork long lapse of time consumes."

Santa Ana winds will fan the flames
From gas blasts after a California quake.
Hell on earth will burn away the names
Marking any article man can make.

A twisting vortex of hot air and flame
Instantly turns to a whirlwind of fire,
Consuming a bungalow or an A-frame,
A BAUHAUS box or a soaring church spire.

Lie on a rock's ribbed face—fused ripples of sand—
Like sculpture breathing on a museum shelf.
A diamond's unchanged, traded second-hand
Under the sign: HISTORY REPEATS ITSELF.

Such being as the dead may yet possess
Lingers due to the living's favor alone:
Beyond a barrier none can transgress,
Unreachable by text or telephone.

Does dying impaled by beams of light sound cool?
Stand at a window in neon darkness bright.
The pistol you press to your temple just a tool,
Swim in the splendid motion of starry night.

Go to sleep, a revolver in your mouth?
Split the midnight by a burst of lead?
Just one of many ways to travel south:
Open up the sky with your scattered head.

Maybe open up a fourth dimension,
Where objects all are flipped inside out,
Losing thus reality's surface tension,
Like brain matter sucked up a waterspout.

Is heaven a crown of temples in the sky,
Whose sexless angels sing in coed choirs?
Fly too close to the sun and plunge from on-high,
Trailing infernal fumes of burning tires.

The road to hell goes through your living room,
While hope of paradise goes up in smoke
As trash the hearth consumes in a poison plume,
And your carbon-14 dates a cosmic joke.

Roam as you will, you're bound for one last place.
Whether it's Arizona to decompose,
Or the Land of Midnight Sun's wide open space,
One global rule applies: what time says, goes.

Admit defeat, let the world turn as it must.
You'll find no change to God's original plan.
What other outcome would you consider just?
It's how things are since the moment time began.

Undiscovered country awaits you where
You leave your corpse behind on terra firma.
You crack a new dimension lighter than air,
As death links all from Birmingham to Burma.

Zero is cardinal number of the void set.
Books on the universe need table salt.
Don't bet a savior's luck, flesh-deep in debt,
For buried gold in the San Andreas Fault.

Extending empty, everlasting arms,
Power and glory make the planet burn.
To intercept the world's silent alarms,
Hearts have untold miracles to learn.

Each thing its own unique, divine mistake,
No former angels waltz in Tennessee.
Time journeys towards an eternal daybreak
When time shall cease and Earth's ribs fall free.

Heaven's a secret city of souls unsung,
Their citadel ringed by endless goldenrod,
Where wrapped in fire to rise from life's last rung,
They lift themselves with fond old words of God.

I *Pure Luck*

In every lifetime crucial dramas come:
Battles that storm the flesh and claw the mind.
One sure, central advent sounds the drum
Of a grave Judas-deed told twice combined.

It happens in failing your future's mortal test:
You reach the precise midpoint of your life.
No bell will toll, no star appear in the West,
But chance halves your days like a surgeon's knife.

Nothing will intervene to hold at bay
The rush of spent years that overtakes
You breezing down life's backstretch halfway
Around the track. Time makes no mistakes.

Constant living bleeds your system dry,
While your physical constitution bakes.
Whether you're praying or coming through the rye,
In all weathers, time flies with no brakes.

The more you've been, the less you remain to be:
The roots of this circumstance delve too deep.
The sweep of time over the flashing sea
Doesn't go backwards as you're counting sheep.

Both halves of your earthly passage interface
Across a subatomic spot of time,
A quark of being whose invisible trace
Catches you in a long career of crime.

A time spot like the neck of an hourglass,
Dividing point of its halves' separate flows.
Once all one volume's sliding particles pass,
The other's flying time equally goes.

Like earth piled on either side of a furrow,
Your empty middle fixes a crop of years.
You can't bury your deed in a groundhog burrow,
Or wash away its seed with a couple of beers.

It's well said that destiny turns on a dime,
But your big moment of truth's a slimmer span.
"Fast as an eyelid blinks" is a space-time
Measure gauging how slightly your death began.

Quick as a wink, welcome to life's flip side,
The reverse trip to your overwhelming end:
In pain from a shark attack in a riptide,
Or in quiet sleep, time's kindest dividend.

The world's a forest of symbols, kiddo. Which
Can open its limbs to reveal the shades drawn
On half your life, tripping a hidden switch
That sparks the instant half your days are gone?

A photograph's lone, frozen fairyland
Has no power to picture where time went.
And it takes Einstein's brain to understand
The far-out, future Earth where time gets bent.

Besides, a snapshot steals your precious soul,
Or so one superstitious tribe conceives.
A pendulum in this emblematic role
Is trite, the timing wrong for autumn leaves.

A mirror might work. Assume one waits to frame
Your prime's exact apex. Your steel-capped smile
Glints like a jagged blade etched with your name,
As you ape the dope who eyes your profile.

Dressed and ready to pull off an easy job,
Now cock your hat as anticipation grows.
Grabbing for the world of crime's doorknob,
Look in the mirror: see if your beer gut shows.

In a flash, your raking glance leaps to stab
That half-forgotten brother—your image, Jack.
Like a swap in Dr. Frankenstein's lab,
He's bounced to the glass's Janus glaze of black.

Your sinister sight blindly runs him through.
It's pure luck at least, killing him clean:
Cut to the quick for his double's hit debut;
Killed like a nightmare shot with THORAZINE.

The mirror's depth belies the distance he's gone:
Removed as far as the dark side of the moon;
Sucked into night that never reaches dawn,
Where blazing sun gives only darkness at noon.

Darkness was upon the face of the deep?
More darkness is upon the face of you:
Your double, now swart as a chimney sweep,
Splits with half your soul like smoke up a flue.

II *Blackout Blind*

Hegel called a cultural split "diremption,"
A term perhaps too grand for your divide:
Offering a mere semantic exemption
To your mortality's deadly down side.

"Death is the middle point between two lives,"
Preached the Civil War Reverend George Tate.
He meant when earth departs and heaven arrives,
But your equation is very up-to-date:

The universe coheres by dark matter,
Much as you and your double's halves are held
By an unseen moment free of blood spatter,
In parting paths contrarily paralleled.

A stone-cold killer from a shadow world
Inhabits your psyche's closed carapace.
Sudden as lightning, the killer shadow swirled
Breaks the surface and takes over your face.

The disappearing act you perpetrate,
Miraculous though its upshot backfires,
Leaves Junior no return engagement date,
As death's encroachment wears down your tires.

You snuff your life's first half. Death to the lamb
Is life to the wolf, John Doe, time out of mind.
Your midway vision STAR WARS travelgram
Translates him past a total blackout blind.

You find his Achilles heel as surely as
If clearing his screen by simple point-and-click,
Because your unabiding spirit has
A self-destructive bent like a broken stick.

In postage parlance, you swing a tête-bêche,
Where paired same stamps are printed upside-down
To each other. The second one flips your flesh
Reversed and inverted, doomed to sink and drown.

Now as your story opens *in medias res*,
Shades of your forgotten ancestors stir.
They worry what on earth you'll tell your face,
Once its definition begins to blur.

Picture the sun dropped from a bright blue sky.
Your double's leaving the stage is that stark:
In sunshine and in shadow, from July
To June, BOSTON COMMON to GOLDEN GATE PARK.

Some partners in crime will split their take and part.
Not so with Robert Ford and Jesse James.
The latter tried to reform for a sweetheart,
While Ford's the filthy traitor history shames.

They sever conjoined twins and one dies
To give the other a decent chance at life,
But your crime wears no altruistic guise.
Between your teeth, you clench the killer's knife,

Dripping with sin that stains your rotten soul
Black as a Caribbean buccaneer's.
Cursed by your sorry lack of self-control,
Your critical moment never reappears.

As your Abel splits off in the wink of an eye,
No trumpet sounds to put you wise to the fact,
Which saves you the blame of telling God a lie.
Yet Cain the caveman wasn't caught in the act.

You'd rather blow a hole in his empty head?
You'll want a holster and an overcoat
To carry the bum an overdose of lead.
Stabbing creates a quieter endnote.

Don't risk a collar packing loaded heat.
The sheriff keeps the basement cell of his jail
As an old-fashioned hospitality suite
For a guest without a prayer of making bail.

The jailer's shuffle leading you down below,
He chains you to a sweating limestone wall.
Subterranean dark and your dullness go
Together so well, your numb dungeon sprawl

Is locked where not a solitary ray
Of sun can reach to stoke your lifeless wit.
This chance to feel your brain turn cold as clay
Captures the way your nature is snakebit.

III *High Noon*

You didn't want to do what you just did,
But time has flown that's never coming back:
Gone as fast as the swoosh of a giant squid
Fizzes through frigid depths in oceans of black.

Quicker than the language in God's mind,
Your double dies to seal your stupid fate.
In exchange you spend the years remaining blind
To your victim's ineluctable checkmate.

Joined as killing fingers met by chance,
Eyesight, memory, mirror, moon, and clock,
Slice in half your life's once endless expanse.
The closest no-count kin split their stock.

Your farewell drop of youth goes down the drain.
Don't imagine making self-love last
Between you jokers. Time's earthward strain
Cracks that façade, and the fissure widens fast.

Shy of midway, your vistas advance in light.
Hacked in half, you collide with a stop sign.
Flesh hails high noon to stalk a dim midnight,
Staggering home to a silent finish line.

Felling a tree unhinges the final stroke.
One sawed half through soon falls of its dead weight.
Your milestone shows no harm to man or oak,
Yet harbors the hidden might to annihilate.

You live to kill in a single beat of the heart,
Clueless about it—and his mute reply.
United you stand, but once you hoodlums part,
You're sunk. Dead he's crossed you: now you must die.

Clean a hunting knife by stabbing the ground
Over and over until the blade shines.
But yours is a bloodless kill, and not a sound
Betrays the crime no code of law defines.

Your mirrored specter stares from bulletproof glass?
It's not a bullet that puts his face away.
He dies like murder confessed for midnight mass,
With no sign of the killer or his prey.

What haunt do you head for now, charming Billy?
Iniquity stays, once it invades your bones.
Its progress, helter-skelter or willy-nilly,
Wobbles like carriage wheels on cobblestones.

Divided you fall: treason undoes its own.
No remedy when your double fades to black.
His sole heir is beset by powers unknown:
The puzzle of aging, time's relentless wrack.

The question isn't whether you lost or won.
His death's a crime you never expiate.
Elvis might be alive, but your double's done.
From here on out, watch for your closing date.

Now left in flesh that drifts down to doom,
As bad breaks come and go on the west wind,
You'll see the years' accelerating zoom
Rush the hour your double's death is twinned.

Matching a solar eclipse's double dawn,
Your two nightfalls go for the price of one.
Which of you is the other's unwitting pawn?
The riddle's unsolved, posed by the silent sun.

You're both in the same boat from stem to stern.
He figures first; you lounge in the holding tank.
Shanghaied at birth, the point of no return,
Shove your mate overboard, then walk the plank.

IV *Goose Egg*

In blackjack you can double up or down.
Here either your double gets it or you.
Your soul is cooked to a nice golden brown,
Dead as a duck plucked by FRANK PERDUE.

If D is the dark date of your double's decease,
D times two is the ironclad day of your death.
Your guilty heart is nature's timepiece
To measure your decline's every breath.

Its valves clock your blood as it ebbs and flows.
The chambers void and fill like an hourglass—
Till you flunk, from bald crown to turned-up toes,
The physical Mr. Universe can't pass.

Long-distance lethality seems a good term
For what your double's demise inflicts upon
Your future. Plain arithmetic will confirm
The facts, from Anchorage to the Amazon.

In Vegas they call it "going ace-deuce,"
Named for a bad combination in craps.
And blowing warmth on the dice is no use:
When one and two roll up, your lifeline snaps.

Your balance brought forward then? A goose egg,
And cool acceptance doesn't count as cash.
Scream bloody murder from here to Winnipeg:
Postmortems won't help, once you're lifeless trash.

It's war and the order of battle favors time,
Forever matchless foe of all that lives.
Though nevermore caught at the scene of your crime,
You pocket the payback such transgression gives.

Your double's gone off to another gig.
Will you see him again somewhere somehow?
Against the chance, you'd better wear a wig:
That's one kinship you'll want to disavow.

"'How gross,' says Death to a man with his throat cut,"
Is a Spanish proverb. Always future or past,
Death barely greets you when duty summons him, but
Brief words suffice time's great iconoclast:

"Pleased to meet you. Need I state my name?
I'm afraid I can't tarry, or else I would.
You're puzzled by the point of this little game?
It clears up when your mind goes dark for good.

"Everything that has the breath of life,
From Kennebunkport, Maine, to Bangalore,
Goes as blank as sight destroyed by a knife,
And that's the way you reach the farther shore."

A highly skilled mortician tested by fire,
His actions are one hundred percent legit.
Arriving just when trouble's truly dire,
He solves it quick as space and time permit.

Is one remove from this world very far?
You could be lying dead where you just stood.
In time you've sailed to distant Zanzibar;
In space you've changed to a chunk of driftwood.

"Death meets us everywhere," wrote Jeremy Taylor.
"His presence enters in at many doors"—
Be they doors of the HEART CLINIC at BAYLOR,
Or the rosy scented portals of high-rent whores.

To rid your sentenced soul of one dark blot,
All the earth's beauty must pass away,
And leave you a clotted, gnarled, insensate knot
Of gristle: former flesh becoming clay.

V   *Sex Appeal*

How do you stack up on the mental side?
The label bruited about is *dumbkopf.*
But take the reading public for a ride:
Publish your views with ALFRED A. KNOPF.

Possessing a brain whose blinders interlock,
And thus renowned as a vacant jarhead,
You outstrip even a campus super-jock
In your reason's high concentration of lead.

How do you stack up on the social side?
Your mailing address isn't Royal Road.
Before you point to the well pump with pride,
Its fragrant water makes your bowels explode.

Where you're from is just a dot on the map,
No more than a wide spot of the blacktop.
Open the windows to hear your ears flap,
Driving beyond its crossroads four-way stop.

When the night has come and the land is dark,
And moonrise is the only sight you see,
Think how your body double's vital spark
Dies around the age of—43?

Your center strike will make you lose it all.
Observe your muscle mass begin to shrink.
The copestone crumbled, the rest sure to fall,
Pursue your bliss at an old folks' skating rink.

Your crucial mistake is an appalling goof,
With circumstantial proof: shades of gray
Frame your brow as your sex appcal goes *poof!*
Go sit in the park and play checkers all day.

You're still no dumber than some: those who smoke
Or eat a ton of cheese on fast-food junk.
Is doctors' advice too deep for plain folk
Praising the ice-cream god CHOCOLATE CHUNK?

These Druids' heedless faith is a drastic leap
To take what their diet's fierce god has given.
Each puff or sundae pries at a door to steep
Stairs to the sea, down which the blind are driven.

If you weren't an abject oaf, a perfect simp,
You'd skip the glance that kills like a laser blade.
But skull full of gas as the GOODYEAR blimp,
You're boot-hill-bound, you and your murdered shade.

Your brain's an empty air-pocket enclosed
In a somehow working organism's head,
Where classic pillars of thought are bulldozed
By the provender of motor sports you're fed.

It's scary to assess the awful botch
Your blunder creates, blind as a butcher knife.
Dormant in psychic depths, aged like scotch,
It leaps forth to slash your lease on life.

A convict sneaks a spoon and makes it a knife
By filing the handle down to a dagger blade,
Then terms the result his faithful fishwife
With the sharpest tongue in the stinking stockade.

Suddenly he decides it's time to give
The hag some needed air and settles a score.
Faster than that your double fails to outlive
The judgement by the jailer: NEVERMORE.

This quantum leap wins you the inside track
To Nowheresville, the place you cease to exist.
Doc Feelgood's antidote a shot of smack,
Your dream of life has scenes it simply missed.

As now ensues your long, malignant shame,
One wall transmits your ego's unseen writ
Of summons signed by X, your canceled name,
Your self's pure schizoid second solar-split.

Shocked as Belshazzar? Four verbs framed in fire
Describe you: COUNTED, WEIGHED, DIVIDED, DESTROYED.
Deny their force and label God a liar?
Follow the scripture: tumble down the void.

Mene, mene, tekel, upharsin are
The words transliterated in *King James*.
From there to here, from then to now, how far
Will Jehovah still insist on taking names?

Enthralled by your expression's sullen spell,
You miss a new twitch that ought to seem strange.
Your pinch-hitting mimics your double well,
Yet fine hints in the likeness start to change.

As if a mileage sign were abruptly gone,
You sense something is off, but precise words
Elude you. With an account way overdrawn,
Your math resembles a mush of milk curds.

VI *Copycat Killer*

You're what espionage calls a cleaner,
Whose acid bath makes corpses disappear.
Gauged by your quite unaware demeanor,
Your vanishing act leaves your double CLEAR.

His half-life dispatched to the great beyond,
That phantom face will lurk in a look of scorn
And mar your flesh, waving a sorcerer's wand
To score your skin and mock the day you were born.

In *Three Faces of Eve*, the lady killed
Off two selves and still had one to use.
Your double neatly iced with no blood spilled,
You're stuck as your elder self in the same shoes.

Once death's black curtain sucks your double through,
No Sergeant Friday dusts your place for prints.
No clerk declares in a princess dyed hairdo,
"Boss, this copycat killer ain't got no sense!"

"Brilliant, babe," the copper would tell the skirt.
"We lack the goods to put his neck on the block.
He ages some, we'll hang him by his shirt,
But now he's free to rock around the clock."

Bill Haley died in a Texas border town,
His rocking around the clock come to an end.
Though rock-and-roll brought his name renown,
He died in the skid-row shack of his last friend.

True, Haley didn't really finish that way.
It's some obscure rockabilly who did.
One Spanish DJ tracked him down to play
His "lost tapes" on a station in Madrid.

The victor enjoys the spoils, says the sage,
Your plunder the meager haul of half your days.
Youth's high cotton flecks the dark suit of age,
Ignored as cataracts cloud your fading gaze.

Two dopey dead ringers, your lopped life span
Exactly equals his down to the last
Bad breath in your sunken chest, NASCAR fan.
Tune your dial to time's long-range forecast.

The nexus between you two absolute,
Identity rules or the world is out of whack.
Death's bargain duly sealed in your birthday suit,
Its rabid monkey never gets off your back.

Not two strangers bound by a twist of fate,
Less either of your faces, you're not whole.
Killer within and public buffoon wait
To overturn the order of your soul.

An inextricable intertwining is
Your coefficient of consanguinity's key:
A hundred percent of what you are was his,
In color and UNIVERSAL 3-D.

Flush in the fullness of time you're out of here,
And out of here is worse than out of whack.
You exit from the earth's living sphere,
Life cycles linked in the *Farmer's Almanac*.

Some days can just go wrong, then change is quick.
One sunup you'd bet your boots you're set in spades.
The next your Midas touch has a pinprick,
And pretty soon you're vomiting razor blades.

Another day you know you're rolling in clover,
Visit the TEMPLE OF TRUTH, and feel damn smart.
Without warning your blackboard schemes are over:
From the strain of thought a stroke stops your heart.

No siren's wail proclaims your coming demise.
No trauma team converges like flies on dung.
Expect advance notice? Highly unwise
For a small ballocks cocksure he's heavy hung.

Imagine all mirrors warped, a fun-house game.
You're tall as a pinhead Texan in hip boots,
Or dwarfed in a cowboy hat on a two-foot frame:
Paul Bunyan and a pygmy in cahoots.

As pea-brain Tex your title is Ping Pong.
As shorty the bunkhouse dubs you Tiny O'Toole.
Your fatso moniker? One-Ton "Wild Man" Wong.
Your big-chest alias? Lily Liverpool.

Trick mirrors in life's maze help you pretend
You dodge your vision's double-blind ambush.
Yet doom's proof reflects as glass doors bend
Your shattered face's cracks, PULL or PUSH.

VII *Starry Sky*

You knock off your bodyguard, the sacred cow
Who shields you from false teeth and carrion flies.
His rub-out leaves you locked in time's hoosegow,
The man emerged from the mask through X-ray eyes.

Your heart half left will mortify your flesh,
Steadily breaking down your marrowbone.
You can't stop rot no tonic can refresh,
And constant dripping wears a hole in stone.

Maybe you should quit while you're behind.
There's no percentage in living, win or lose.
Old Man Winter is coming to strike you blind,
Whether you frequent alleys or avenues.

The gaping jaws of *Revelation*'s vision
Aren't what eats up your remaining time.
Sunrise and sunset do it with precision,
The fallen sun repeating its daily climb.

Nothing would do but you had to turn that page
Of the calendar. Now choose your game of chance,
While lost in time's ruins, guilty of age.
Go look for Miss America, ask her to dance.

Don't wash-out trying to win a smoked ham.
You'll win a pig in a poke, gambling with God.
Far wiser to follow the sot Omar Khayyám:
Wear sandals before the judge who's thunder-shod.

Your life spent drinking liquor and telling lies,
That's what people do at a poker table.
Not much rides on a jackpot just your size,
But none cheats the dealer dressed in sable.

No way around it, you meet a tragic end.
It's bluebirds over the mountain, wave good-bye.
You can part the sea and then lasso the wind
Before you can figure out how not to die.

In this your only lifetime, Billy Bob,
The flesh prison won't let you off the hook:
Your sentence death eternal, your prison job
To live by your wits, then die by the book.

Make it up as you go along. —Why not?
You don't eat till you open the tin can;
You can't play till you drop a coin in the slot.
A sure thing? Time always gets his man.

What's not temporary, including you?
That Gaea hasn't finished is naked truth,
And aging's all around you. Says who?
Well try to find bottled ELIXIR OF YOUTH.

STRAWBERRY FIELDS FOREVER, CLAIMS HIPPIE VAN.
Nothing but keeps its season, its DUE DATE.
The earth ensures time totals every plan.
Your clock runs down, yet death is never late.

It's cool news you have a few years left.
Play the ponies to waste some precious time.
Throw fate to the random winds until, bereft
Of life and breath, your corpse sinks into slime.

Connie Stevens sang *Sixteen Reasons* why
She loved her boyfriend. Can you lamely give
A single cause your double has to die
To let a complete yahoo like you live?

From here forward your life's an alibi.
What's your excuse for still sticking around?
So you can paint your name on a starry sky?
Then first cut off your ear without a sound.

Whether you're hanged at midnight or shot at dawn,
The rest of your days are fully death-possessed.
Regardless how the key question is drawn,
You have no chance to pass the mid-term test.

So try to crack how to play the end game.
What gives, once the infusion of life wears off?
Already the devil's doorman has your name.
Meantime better go see about that cough.

VIII *Vandal's Brickbat*

Frank Zappa would succumb to prostate cancer
Before his eyes had watered fifty years.
Why expect a sympathetic answer
From a world that doesn't owe you any tears?

"The pain, I regret, is not arthritis,"
The doctor tells you looking grim. Guess what?
"It's time's necrotizing fasciitis,
That eats your flesh and ties your tongue in a knot.

"Your illness, malignant and incurable,
Has nameless terrors of which I shall not speak,
Except to say the horror's plentiful
And leaves you dead, maimed as a sideshow freak."

Die in daylight while you bathe in the sun:
It need not be a dark and stormy night.
That done, there's no more nothing. No more fun,
No booze, no sex, no dreams, no law, no light.

A snapshot's little frail fragment of time,
A cross-section of anybody's past;
A biographical artifact a dime
Obtained to hold a new memory fast

In the hand, the heart, and in the mind's eye;
Advances the other side of midnight:
The side the mirror no further reckons by,
Where figures buried forever drop from sight.

Most any photo will fade in sunlight.
Darkness alone preserves the image clean.
A depicted instant's disappearing flight
Is only prevented by keeping it unseen.

Digital photography changes that,
As long as the storage file doesn't crash—
By software failure or vandal's brickbat,
The pictures ground to a hopeless mishmash.

What do you see, on the border of darkness?
The glint of a knife, the turn of a doorknob?
Memory is reduced to stunning starkness
Once Satan smells his next grave to rob.

You never died and don't know how it feels?
Tell your double this and have a nice day.
It's not like home where Mama cooks square meals,
Yet count your blessings—before you draw your pay.

Going to hell on a freight train, ride the rails.
Your ethyl breath will stoke the engine awhile.
And wave your flask, passing the small-town jails
Where you slept it off with an idiotic smile.

Ken Palmer, Second Looey, ARMY AIR CORPS,
Met a soldier who looked exactly like him
At a bus station in 1944.
The fellow's name was Palmer also—Jim.

Was this a magic moment or a curse?
On *Unsolved Mysteries* fifty years later,
Trying to locate his image in reverse,
Ken couldn't deem the figure friend or traitor.

"Was Jim that guy, Ken's double, or Jim's ghost?
If any or all, might his face be found
Among the viewership?" inquired the host.
Or had he gone forever underground?

What would this mean either way for Ken?
Did he kill off his double, same as you?
If he's that dumb, five will get you ten
Jim faked this fatal, wartime rendezvous.

"I have a rendezvous with death," he read,
"At some disputed barricade," and laughed.
"I'll make them think a recruit turned up dead,
And use it as a ruse to dodge the draft.

"My twin's a figment of his feeble mind.
We never met, and that's the cold truth.
Leaving his genealogy behind,
He proved the victim of his foolish youth."

And what this means for you is don't assume
You'll ever learn what your status is.
Ask at the CHRISTIAN SCIENCE READING ROOM?
They answer once you flunk the Bible quiz:

"You hardly dreamed of grief in paradise?
Suppose a band of angels all went blind.
Why does death exact its terrible price?
Because God left his blank checks unsigned."

Your past is more and more a matter of faith,
Intensifying your fundamental crime.
Minute by minute your slain silver wraith
Sinks yet farther down the abysm of time.

IX *Crystal Ball*

Life's great mistake, your younger days undone,
Is evil the ghost of youth can't forgive.
Once doubts haunt his killer, he hounds the hun
Every damn day the dog has left to live.

The fatal flash of your ray-gun, robot eyes
Is hard to top, but he'll find a fit reprise;
Waste the withered fruit of Mother's thighs;
And leave you without the blood to nurse your fleas.

He follows you like a monster in a dream,
Whose flaming nostrils burn your future black:
Pursuing his chance to turn your bloodstream
Down in the dust, sticking a blade in your back.

So don't rest easy. You never can really tell
Whether his vengeful nature's gaining ground,
But hurry onward. His breath is hot as hell,
His memory long, his temper tightly wound.

Lonely the vigil you keep as solo drone,
Loudmouth dropout, and highly qualified fool:
Your neck in a noose, a tailor-made millstone
To help you swim down time's black whirlpool.

You've fought the lamb of youth and won a round?
Now report to the lion of age's lair.
Far in the depths of your soul, his roar will sound
A terror freezing you like a frightened hare.

Recall the headline DEWEY DEFEATS TRUMAN.
Wisdom waits till all returns are in.
If war goes well, it's altogether human
That a man decides he's not like other men.

News from the front says little of the rest,
This planet with nothing new under the sun:
The same old constants metaphysics at best
Can overhaul, reloading God's big gun.

For ages Jeremiah was a nut,
Then Jesus sent the prophet's stock sky-high.
Success so rare was sublime—if not clear-cut,
Like CAMEL filters passed through a needle's eye.

"Be wise today, it's madness to defer,"
The prelate says, but what's the point, with you?
No use to talk of frankincense and myrrh
To a mind as empty as a horseshoe.

You die smart as some, dumber than most.
Yet a feeble brain is no sin, for give us all
Our deserts and who'd escape the whipping post?
There's more than whipping in time's crystal ball.

Jesus's flagellation pales compared
To his crucifixion whose goal went haywire.
How otherwise might half the world have fared,
From burning Christ with a cross to feed the fire?

Can any resurrection have occurred,
Lacking a body to breathe the air anew?
Reborn from its ashes, none but a mythic bird
Has pulled off this ultimate switcheroo.

You're batting a thousand so far, twinkle-toes.
Ty Cobb the Georgia jerk would tip his hat.
But you're not privy to all the mirror knows:
Sent to the showers, you've seen your last at-bat.

As you descend in swirling mists of time
To join the congregation of the dead,
There's a cost for your unthinkable crime
That's worse than every nightmare in your head.

What's the doom your youth's death has ordained?
It's not a date you sidestep like a crab.
Long gone, he'd love to see his killer's drained
Cadaver pick up the undertaker's tab.

He's all that keeps you out of the mouth of hell.
No question, you truly chill the wrong guy.
What turn his revenge takes won't fully gel
Till your last sunset splits the western sky.

Your double, now a big apostle of truth,
Tells it how it is in the kingdom of night,
As well as in the kingdom of spent youth,
Advertising his gift of second sight.

Fell sergeant death is strict in his arrest.
Inhale your oxygen, play the man, die game.
Sure as the sun buries its gold in the West,
Your kinsman's curse will set your soul aflame.

Try to picture his fit of seething joy.
Dancing when cold death grabs his old bunkmate,
He'll shriek volcanic curses at Golden Boy
That scald your ears with half a lifetime's hate.

Knife-edged loathing sharp in his bloodshot eyes,
He's long awaited the chance to rip you up,
And here you come for him to terrorize,
As a male wolf will kill a rival's pup.

Emerged from memory's tangled undergrowth's
Virginia creeper into your erstwhile form,
He burns the air you breathe with torrid oaths,
The way lightning forks out of a sudden storm.

The day his stinking blood rots in your veins
Is pleasure he craves with every ounce of will:
To meet you where absolute evil reigns,
A tempest of fire all the oceans can't still.

He'll jeer and taunt, circle like a hyena,
Damning you for the waste of his missing years,
His grievance list as long as Argentina,
Laughing in mad delight through acid tears.

X *Lotus Land*

"It's howdy-doody time! Remember me?
Look real hard at your former mirrored twin.
The man you killed and walked away scot-free?
I'm thrilled to see you, right on time," he'd grin.

"How little on earth carries a guarantee!
Yet each night passed has brought me nearer you.
Now don't I seem happy as I can be
To supervise your entry interview?

"Dawn the day I died broke crisp and clear.
No signs of base betrayal sketched the sky
As dreadful cloud shapes of doubt and fear.
My bowels pushed out dinner's beef potpie

"With breakfast: KRISPY KREME and CRACKER JACKS.
I rinsed my stinking film of sweat and grime,
Then dressed to go: you dropped me in my tracks,
And kept your petty claim of equal time.

"You stabbed me to live while I drowned in flame,
You filthy traitor," his ire would quickly rise.
"At last I can heap livid embers of blame
And sear your foul carcass sparking with flies.

"We were two sides of one unlucky coin,
But you decided to play the phantom of death.
And what the force of nature alone could join,
Your malice separated in half a breath.

"Pop taught us to take the light end of a load.
You beat me to it, you snide son-of-a-bitch.
I've had pure hell now half your life and glowed
Like a man on fire with a radioactive itch.

"My angry heart hard as a baking brick,
From mirrors I've stared at you with granite eyes.
Greetings! Mind if I give your groin a kick—
Or two—or three—in praise of family ties?

"I knew deep down one day we'd meet again.
This merits a scalding cup of blood-red wine.
Here's to the soul of a scoundrel soaked in gin:
Misery now and forevermore be thine!

"I'm grateful every hour that you exist.
Venomous spite has made my spirit soar.
As hate and envy squeeze my heart like a fist,
I jump for joy, now time evens the score.

"Somewhere beyond the grave, there's a land
For any mother's worthless drifter son.
Probably not the place you had planned,
But where to go, with nowhere left to run?

"Muttonhead, have I got blues for you.
And may I remind you: dead men never lie.
The self-improvement program here is through:
No use to chase the elusive butterfly."

He'll stand so close he slobbers in your face,
Dragging you down his roster of done-me-wrongs,
That pounds your skull like a boom box's bass,
And plucks the strings of your soul like red-hot tongs.

"Long time, no see. Welcome to the dead!
Your face is hard to look at. Fancy that!
Somehow I despise the shape of your head:
Recalls a snake, or a wet sewer rat.

"I've practiced my best punches. Let's just see.
I'll knock your jaw back and adapt your nose.
There now, you look a bit less like me—
And even less the more you decompose.

"I was flesh of your flesh, bone of your bone,
But felt like sin and folly fused at the hip.
All those years you weighed me down like a stone.
Now I'm ecstatic over this fellowship.

"It's been a visceral, fitful fever dream,
Visualizing your infernal debut.
My bond of vengeance matured, I'll redeem
It here in eternal damnation's HQ.

"Sure, I could've relied on arithmetic
As certitude to help me sleep at night,
Knowing exactly when your candle's wick
Would fizzle, yet lacked the calm to sit tight.

"Imagine how the fierce anticipation
To see my assassin's self finally fall,
Abandoning his last earthly station,
Kept me awake like a draught of firegall.

"In rapture old acquaintance is renewed!
Fondly have I yearned for your day to die.
You never guessed a welcome quite so rude
Could meet you in the sweet by-and-by?

"You were expecting Dead Man Lotus Land?
A trifle optimistic, I'm afraid.
This scene's all boiling mud and burning sand:
It offers not the smallest spot of shade."

XI *Empty Heart*

"Woe unto the world because of offenses—"
He'd cry with wisdom learned licking up crumbs:
"Remember that day you dropped my cheese blintzes?—
But woe unto him by whom the offense comes.

"You jaybird Johnny-come-lately," he would rant,
"Feature my fate when your mutt chewed the seat
Of the skirt full of your jumbo maiden aunt.
The bitch left my poor butt red as raw meat.

"Two-ton Toni never knew when to quit.
Mama's mammoth sister was one of a kind.
If she got lonely she came to baby-sit,
And the only date she ever had was blind.

"That birthday Grandpa gave me a blue SCHWINN,
Whose red and white reflectors made it glow?
You crashed and bent it up like two tin
Star-spangled snowshoes shooting a crossbow.

"You rotten swindler!" he'd hiss, point, and rave,
"You smashed my piggy bank with a baseball bat;
Spent every dirty penny my paws could save;
And broke my model train on top of that!

"What happened to my oddly missing toes?
Fishing a pond skimmed by skating bugs,
You sank barefooted into a summer doze,
And a turtle snapped three digits off like slugs."

He foams at the mouth and viler words spew
As lava vomited from the heart of hell.
With a wolf's grin he'll flaunt your IOU,
Then gag and retch at your paralyzing smell.

"You birdbrain!" he rambles in savage rage,
"In the school play you grunted like a hog!
Next you puked pink slop on center stage,
And I fell in it fleeing your monologue!

"Consider Tammy's wrath, your first prom date.
You stomped her pumps in a donkey's mating dance.
She howled, 'Take me home!,' at half past eight,
So walking the wench to the car, you wet my pants!

"Don't forget my HARLEY!" he'll fume and rail.
"With SCHLITZ I christened it *Misfit—crash!*—like that!
My legend lives on through its tragic tale.
Who rode it crazed as a drunken wildcat?

"You spun off the cliff, grabbed a hickory limb,
And dangled there like a blind acrobat.
Next day you bragged to the brains at DANNY'S GYM
You'd proven Columbus right, the earth's not flat!

"My *Misfit* was a twisted metal mass:
Nothing left but to sell the mess for scrap.
The fall's rock sparks had torched its leaking gas.
Following that I drove a rattletrap.

"I ought to break this bottle of acid here
To gash your mug like Caravaggio's.
Some Knights of Malta furnished Rome's premier
Painter a highway bandit's cheeks and nose:

"A treatment not inspired for beauty's sake.
(Just think of advancing art's new frontier,
Then seeing your kisser carved as beefsteak,
Scarred by a permanent, predatory sneer.)

"Let's face it, bad boy. What did self-love cost
Between your loser's life and my empty heart,
Your messy flesh and my wasted spirit tossed
Scraps like dogs in a dumpster at WALMART?

"Lowbred moron," he growls and bares his teeth,
"You blew the heist I planned for months on end.
Leaving the station clinging underneath,
You climbed the train's caboose rounding a bend

"To crawl on top, just as the silver *Express*
Shot into a tunnel sheathed in diesel smoke.
You lay there gasping, tapping SOS,
Then dreamed of dollar bills, and finally woke

"To signs that read, GRAND CENTRAL, TRACK 13.
I'd snitch before I'd star in that farce twice.
The horror! I long to relive on morphine
A playback of life without you as paradise.

"In criminology's stern search for truth,
Deny that all this happened, if you dare.
It happened sure as you're born, snaggletooth.
I was the man! I suffered! I was there!

"You dirtbag deadhead, that's how it was then,
Our joint heyday like a bed full of tacks.
These nightmare scenes raised to the power of ten,
My torment's an endless reel of flashbacks."

XII *No Vacancy*

"You gangland scarface," he'd stammer and dissolve
In his flood of rancor—stirred by caustic waves
Of disgust that swirl, as old regrets revolve
In his head, and drown the same revenge he craves—

"About the n-night you swallowed . . . never mind.
I'm not your guide to n-nine circles of hell.
I've come to boil your blood for *auld lang syne*."
Holding his nose, he shouts like a clanging bell:

"You broke our blood bond for spite to destroy
Our role as TV twins for DOUBLEMINT gum!
Sayonara, sport, *Aloha oe.*
Our paths cross but once in this penal slum.

"You're losing time if you wait around for me.
They never heard of daylight savings here.
Eternity's clockwork, under lock and key,
Deems every moment of your punishment dear.

"Ready to put your long black robe on, schmoe?
The scoreboard spelled your end, away or at home.
The clock ticked down to zero, Smokin' Joe.
Welcome tonight to Lucifer's SUPERDOME.

"As white hair wove death's cap upon your brow,
I prayed for this happy meeting's fated time.
Et tu, Brute? Fine words ring hollow now.
Let hell's geysers seethe in your soul like lime.

" 'It's not my fault' are the last words of a fool.
Whose is it then, you skinhead turkey brain?
Death's cosmic voyage spun off the global spool,
The strand you chose led not to the shining plain,

"That gentler place, and none gets there from here.
You're finished. The Pope of Rome can't save your hide,
And instant karma has closed its far frontier.
You'll find no escape on a slave's midnight ride.

"Appear with nail-scarred hands, a spear in your side?
Satan will inspect you like Doubting Thomas,
Dismiss the symptoms, and give you a private guide:
'Summon the outlaw biker, Lorenzo Lamas!'

"One day you woke up dead—just the way
It happened to all the angels' heavenly host—
Yet bypassed Sky City on ROUTE 1-A.
Eternal bliss? There's no prize for ALMOST.

"You'd walk through hell-gate to get there, dear?
That's not an option anymore, you creep.
ALL HOPE ABANDON, YE WHO ENTER HERE,
Is what the sign says, stupid. Read it and weep.

"If any shares the secrets of your soul,
It's me, you indisputable knucklehead.
So don't spout some nonsense rigamarole
About how your inner self was underfed.

"Waken to calm and the peal of golden bells,
Whence rivers of delight shall ever roll?
Perhaps you haven't noticed you're in hell's
Boot camp, where corpses convert to charcoal.

71

"Elysian Fields? An estate you'll never see,
NO VACANCY shining bright: no room at the inn.
As close to God as meant to get, you're free
To begin the trial by fire you'll never win.

"When the roll is called up yonder? You'll be here
In steady meltdown mode with no heat shield,
Busting rocks and dreaming of ice-cold beer.
Prepare to be flogged forever and never healed.

"This nightmare world of unremitting horror
Is where your soul resides from now on in.
Picture a satyr from Sodom and Gomorrah
Peeling patch after patch of your scorched skin."

XIII *Tabasco Smash*

"Hell's a fire that doesn't spare anything.
It burns your bowels all the livelong day.
As your sinews crackle, a million ants sting,
And pterodactyls peck their newest prey.

"Beelzebub will break both tablets' TEN
COMMANDMENTS over your head, after which
Geronimo Bosch paints your portrait when
Babylon's whore dumps you in flaming pitch.

"Hell's kitchen doesn't offer T-bone steaks.
Your diet features cakes of compressed ash,
Accompanied by a thirst nothing slakes
And a bubbling lava red TABASCO smash.

"Your everlasting portion is a dose
Large enough to whet your appetite,
Yet not to let self-pity come too close
To thinking you ever did a damn thing right.

"I bid you adieu, screw, once and for all.
Flogged with scorpions, blinded by DRANO, and
Your branded loins bathed in alcohol,
Go crawl on the brimstone plain of blazing sand.

"A hundred hours of hell only a start,
You're here a hundred million years or more.
This furnace world cooks the oil from your heart,
And burns that too in hellfire's constant roar.

"Your first week here chars your raw flesh black.
Then mocked by a huge choir of howling guffaws,
You're hanged by your testicles' twisting sac,
Your bowed back ripped by a dozen steel claws.

"As a hog roasts on a spit, next you're bound
To a wheel of fire sizzling with your tears
That scald like molten lead, and spinning round
So hard it oozes lava out of your ears.

"Now don't come back whining after a while,
Wailing that you'd rather disappear
Altogether than follow this lifestyle,
Forgetting the very reasons why you're here:

"'Whenever morning comes, I start to cry.
All my days are filled with endless rue,
And when the evening falls, I want to die.
I'm just a lonesome cowboy sad and blue.

"'It's time to move on to the next chapter—
I don't desire to do this anymore—
Whether I'm eaten by velociraptor,
Or pulverized by the Afrika Korps.'

"That's not a penitential choice of yours.
Situational ethics don't apply,
Once you step inside the flaming doors,
And bring your being here to purify.

"You didn't count on me as judge and jury?
I'm glad to disappoint you to the max.
All you'll encounter now is fire and fury,
With sulfur spewing through volcanic cracks.

"You split without so much as a by-your-leave,
You vulgar connoisseur of yo-yos.
And now you turn up, your heart on your sleeve?
Well why not come wearing buttons and bows?!

"Go ahead and cry till your eyeballs bleed.
Any means to increase your suffering's fine.
Given the magnitude of your misdeed,
Your presence here is absolutely divine.

"Me? I've only had one burning desire:
To celebrate the end of my double Dwayne.
This thrill complete, I'll set your flesh on fire,
And watch it melt the tar of Memory Lane."

XIV *Loaded Dice*

Cain was banished straight to the Land of Nod,
But death's slow payoff covers your perfect crime.
No God booms, "On your knees, you cowering clod!"
He merely marks your brow for the march of time.

The wages of sin are yours in spades, alas.
Your surprise showdown jumps the gun on the guy,
Proving your key place in the criminal class,
Your forehead scored as your wrongs multiply.

You scaly sidewinder, a diamondback
By another name remains a rattlesnake.
As cobras hiss, lions' chops go smack,
But your death rattle cancels daybreak.

A paradox, you're both pro and con:
Half of you wants to live, the other half not.
The worm turns like a snake on Laocoön,
And you die foiled by your own counterplot.

The flying jungle snake of Borneo
Can launch itself ninety feet at your throat.
The serpent within you often eats crow,
Yet its poison has no known antidote.

A hundred and two degrees inside your shoes,
Keep them on as long as you're kicking, Hoss.
Death's duel presents pistols and you choose:
Flipping a two-headed coin, you lose the toss.

Your body a temple of the Holy Ghost?
Just balderdash, you All-American clunk.
It's a haunted house hosting a wiener roast
For a bridge-burner caught in a mid-life funk.

Against dullness the gods struggle in vain.
Your grand self-image leads your ego astray.
The weakest link in your being is your brain,
Its thought in an advanced state of decay.

Your business card says, OWNER OUT TO LUNCH.
Gone chasing noonday moonbeams, mastermind?
Looking for Elvis in Anchorage on a hunch?
Look in your head: God knows what you'll find.

Drop this into your in-box, Alley Oop:
The jaws of death are hunting you through time.
Hurry, better hook up with Betty Boop,
Before you dissolve in a pit of quicklime.

Your mental terrain a landscape time forgot,
Not too far from the land where time began,
Your intellectual life's a vacant lot,
A tabula rasa your latest brain scan.

Show off your knowledge, Jimmy, Jacky, Joe.
Kiss your shadow on the walls of the town?
Sorry, wrong as a right-angled rainbow.
Concentrate on your permanent sundown.

Your brain is like a bat cave, Buddy Roe:
A dark cavern of errant, pointless pings.
By day it's eenie, meenie, miney, moe;
By night a mindless chaos of veering wings.

Your cranium little more than a hat rack,
Your mouth's a back channel of empty talk,
A mere echo chamber of yackity-yak,
With now and then an imbecilic squawk.

Your chances once your luck gives out are zero.
Born to lose, you'd run the table twice?
No trick up a sleeve saves our antihero.
This daily planet hands you loaded dice.

Read the music intrinsic in the air
To figure out the tenor of your fate,
But nothing aids escape from Satan's lair,
If disharmony's keys open hell-gate.

You handle what arises, if you can.
It's a mug's game, hopeless as snow in June,
Your days part of a sweeping master plan
With nature's custom dirge in perfect tune.

Don't visit the woods during a windstorm, Sam.
The stroll could leave a tree limb through your head.
A rib of the forest's vault might fall and ram
Your skull to fill its void with oak instead.

Crossing wilderness, always watch your back.
Some hunter could hurl a spear through your liver.
Lightning may strike you, sounding a mighty crack,
As you float on a raft down a lazy river.

Your purchase on life indeed shaky at best,
Enter immortality easy as pie:
Simple as flunking a lie detector test
On whether SUPERMAN's a German spy.

Think how far you are from the grave each day.
A hop, skip, and jump: no more than that.
The devil take tomorrow, you lamely say?
Wait till he calls you down for a little chat.

XV *False Horizon*

Facing eternity in a pinstriped suit,
Or in the tattered clothes of a crusty tramp,
Your ruin is the facts you can't refute,
As Lucifer lights the loser's signal lamp.

Change your name to protect the innocent? Sure.
You fib under someone else's oath, jerkwad?
Don't fail to enroll soon for the sample tour
Of Hades, before consigning your soul to God.

The waters of life are unsafe and ink-black deep.
Churn them, chomp at driftwood, thrash like a shark.
Scavenge oceans of candy and popcorn; sweep
Sludge down your gorge. Is health your bag? Chew bark.

You can go with the flow or buck the mainstream;
Get caught in logjams or sail to distant seas:
Your spine goes slack, time's whiplash snaps life's dream,
And you plunge below like missing a high trapeze.

Davy Jones' locker always holds more room,
And every last landlubber keeps a key,
A warning once you issue wet from the womb:
WHEN WORN OUT, SHIP TO DAVY C.O.D.

Davy Jones, of '60s TV band
The Monkees, died of a massive heart attack
At 66, youthful, fit, and tanned
In 2012. He showed a genuine knack

For winning fans by an engaging smile,
An easy humor of British accent.
Now his career has run its final mile,
All the music and money momentum spent.

So Davy's locker welcomed its namesake,
Although the decedent perished on dry land,
Giving the normal order of things a shake:
The earth divided along the seastrand.

The *Titanic* had smooth sailing through calm seas,
No wave or wake of icebergs ever seen.
The collision caused the captain's blood to freeze,
As if nature just shattered the golden mean.

Thermal conversion's higher horizon made
Super refraction trick the great ship's crew,
The iceberg concealed within a zone of shade
From true to false horizon, a haze of blue.

As icebergs cleave off glaciers and lunge away,
They carry a dense tonnage of moraine rock
Frozen inside them, launched in the ocean spray.
This moderates the universal shock

At the liner's sudden dive into the drink:
It's not a gash that split the hull's thick steel,
And forced the doomed vessel to heave and sink.
The stone-packed iceberg's mass rammed by the keel,

This blow to the hull's overlapped plates would break
Their rivets and bend enough of the ship's length
To open wide the design's huge mistake:
It couldn't withstand an impact of such strength.

The *Titanic*'s fame of luxury and loss,
Despite the latest movie it became,
Remains a source of enormous pathos,
Heroic and tragic import in its name.

What's a king, compared with the open sea?
If death were nothing, breath would be meaningless.
God Save the King or *My Country 'Tis of Thee*,
The band played on in formal evening dress.

Freezing and drowned in midnight icy water
Were fifteen hundred lives, to the world's dismay.
When fathers parted from wife, son, and daughter,
Lifeboats rowed their dearest forever away.

10,000 stars like diamonds in the sky
Could never guide the lost ship back to land.
Instead with a tremendous, expiring sigh,
It foundered, yielding to nature's strict command.

Neither heroic nor tragic is your fate:
A foolish life begets ignoble death,
And a funeral nowhere close to third-rate—
Or so *Leviticus* 29 saith.

Find nice people to die with any time
You board a bus, plane, boat, or ferris wheel.
Yet ask their thoughts, seeking a folk sublime?
The man in the street says, "Death's, like, unreal."

The *Arizona* was sunk by a flying horde.
The Land of the Rising Sun laid down the law
Of averages far too soon for most on board—
Slain by time and flesh, the deepest flaw.

When that law comes for you, what are you worth?
As a soul in steerage trapped by a locked hatch,
Drown with no more value produced on earth.
Before you meet your maker, meet your match.

Bermuda Triangle? Not Mom's groin in shorts,
Bad seed. It's a deep dive at the opposite pole
From bloody birth. Forget *Great Feats in Sports*,
And join the pitch of the dark blue ocean's roll.

Call out the Coast Guard? Won't do any good.
Your crippled ship is well beyond their reach.
Rescue offers zero likelihood:
You'll find land if your bones find the beach.

Bon voyage on the *U.S.S. Unseen*:
Around the world in 80 million years.
Too bad you can't hop the *African Queen*,
So you and Bogy could swap ugly sneers.

Your double? Jetsam dumped riding the storm:
Baggage no further needed, ditched at sea.
But you inhabit his once familiar form,
Accountable to his ghost as sole trustee.

Your rap sheet long as your dragon-draped arm,
Go down dreaming, you blue-tattooed bonehead.
So dumb you think you're smart, you left the farm
To see the world and hit the waves like lead.

You should be centerfold for *Skin and Ink*,
The tattoo artist's trade magazine.
They name their monthly model king of kink,
And you're the craziest case science has seen.

XVI *Grand Slam*

"Yo, ho, ho, and a bottle of rum" is just
About all you have to ease a journey of pain:
The tried and true technique you always trust
To warm your heart and neutralize your brain.

There's more where that was aged, so drink up.
If all the world's a stage, you're the fool.
High life or low, hold onto your baby cup:
Your days begin and end in diapers and drool.

An unknown sweet contentment fills your soul
With bliss obtained from a jug of sour mash,
Like pouring good liquor down a rat hole
To staunch the blood of a stock market crash.

A swift, delirious joy can seize your heart,
Soon as you toss a couple of tumblers back.
Let alcoholic degradation's art
Explain your scene—and help you paint it black.

"The best things in life are free? So are the worst.
There's little pleasure, much to be endured,"
The wise man said the day his bladder burst
From whiskey, all his maladies quickly cured.

You're going but not yet gone. Make the most
Of every breath you have left by staying drunk.
Since time's your main enemy, drink a toast
To sloth. Drag your heels like a brooding monk.

Enjoy life with plenty of magnum force:
An extra-large bottle of cheap red wine.
And always haul the empties back to the source:
Don't miss a purple ounce's fruit of the vine.

It's not a brain swimming in alcohol
That knocks you double dead and out the door.
Suffice it to say, you won't be standing tall
When sound and fury exist for you no more.

"Let's get drunk and be somebody!" is
The thought you framed to see your problems through,
After you failed your first algebra quiz,
And took that odd job at a petting zoo.

No real reason's known to get off the sauce.
The end is forever near, and you die alone.
Show this lost and cruel world who's boss:
Hit the bottle till scripture leaps from stone.

Your buddies JACK DANIEL and JIM BEAM
Can always bail you out on down days.
But never expect BAILEYS Irish Cream:
Much too classy for your rustic ways.

"To one whose life is bitter, give strong drink.
To drown such misery, do provide the wine,"
Reads *Proverbs* 31. Why bother to think?
This makes it a snap to live without a spine.

As among the gifts for numbing pain relief,
Antiquity recommended alcohol.
180-proof or aperitif,
Just place a sofa where you're likely to fall.

Drunken Silenus, a Rubens masterpiece,
Hangs in Munich's *ALTE PINAKOTHEK*:
Stumbling along naked and obese,
He needs assistance not to break his neck.

Dionysus's foster-father indeed,
His nose displays a hearty red glow.
He and you are clearly the same breed,
So open the tap and let the joy flow.

Launch your vessel upon the Cider Sea,
With drunken blood weaving through your flesh.
Some grind might gloss your tale for a Ph.D.,
As a crude crib for the *Epic of Gilgamesh*.

Gilgamesh found the key to lasting life:
A plant he plucked from the bottom of the sea.
But a snake stole it, quick as a naked knife
Sets the captured breath of a body free.

One day the ocean lies in a calm sulk,
Danger circling quiet and shark-finned—
Then heaves in yawning billows of huge bulk,
Which drive the planet wild before the wind.

Counterclockwise a killer cyclone blows,
Yet Neptune can't reverse the hands of time.
Earth's counterclockwise spinning never slows,
Its kill rate even as milling round a dime.

A stretch of railroad's loud clackety-clack,
As the *Silver Streak* hammers every notch,
Unrolls the dime's milled edge as straight track,
Segments of time unwinding a stopwatch.

The rhythm of the rails gets in your blood.
Why do you need a valid mailing address,
That sweeps away in a hundred-year flood?
And you want to join the CENSUS even less.

Awkward as snow in July, reaching your peak,
You skid downslope, ski-poles splayed slapdash
Like swatting flies. Facing a fall so bleak,
Refuse to let it spoil a birthday bash.

Your twi-night doubleheader is whiff against wham.
You win one game on the final out by a drive
To center, but lose to the nightcap's grand slam,
And your season winds up sunk, full fathom five.

Dream a Little Dream is not for the likes
Of you. The future's no magic carpet ride
For double-dealers. A lead balloon with spikes,
It rolls to pierce your ribs in a crimson tide.

XVII *Vulture Vomit*

Your dodo chum, yoked to a buzzard like you,
Will rankle your craw like RED DEVIL LYE—
Or vulture vomit, raw witch's brew,
If you hatched brats to feed in your barren sty.

Stuck in his shadow, you lead a double life,
Then max him out: your dread, impending crime.
Role model gone, future under the knife,
Your death march changes step to double time.

Befriend a dog, you get his fleas to boot.
Every night you sleep in the arms of sin.
A voice cries in a nightmare, "Please, don't shoot!"?
Each time you scratch, its mangy ghost will grin.

You're paired like sculptures on a double-deck tomb.
As *transi* he's the decaying corpse below.
You lord it above, richly defying doom,
Laid out dressed to kill for a fashion show.

Transi means "I've crossed over." So you will:
Trespass beyond self-love's shadow line.
Your pal, like Charon, hands you a poison pill,
His sweet revenge and farewell valentine.

In vampire lore one "crosses over," too.
Once bitten a victim joins the Undead:
A shape-shifting, immortal monster crew,
Its emblematic colors black and red.

Crossing Over, a Cheyenne warrior's name,
Challenged Smoked Shield to a forty-mile race:
They ran a dead heat. Thenceforth the two became
Legends to title ships for outer space.

"Death is only a crossing," wrote Swedenborg,
But keyword "only" buckles under the weight.
Research results at *transcendental.org*:
You'll find no horizontal figure 8.

An antique painting depicts your problem's art,
Battle on a Bridge by Claude Lorrain:
Both sides of a river, peace rules every part,
While combat roils the bridge that joins the plain.

Your Battle of Midway also a pinpoint clash,
Its flash arc bears all the force of the fray.
Foul tracts of living lie as acres of trash,
And flank it on either bank with fetid clay.

So many painters in Rome forged his work,
Claude began a ledger, the *Book of Truth*,
Recording each picture's details like a clerk.
His notes became the incontestable sleuth

When questions of authenticity arose.
Sebastien Bourdon ranked as the fakers' chief
Offender making counterfeit tableaux:
An admired artist who started out a thief.

This here's your own *Book of Truth*, so bad it's banned.
The future always coming, clarity's near:
The past gone and the present poorly planned,
Your blighted years are burning to disappear.

Richmond, Virginia's, MUSEUM OF FINE ARTS
Displays Claude's curious work of war and peace.
War enough to grieve millions of hearts,
Rebellion bloodshed's merciless release:

Richmond stood as capital of its cause.
Nationhood regained in the slaughter's test
Of fault infecting the CONSTITUTION's laws:
Mournful Mr. Lincoln expressed it best.

Then he was murdered by the bitter root
Yanked from the soil of his country's worst sin.
Bred together, the noble and the brute
Forever contend to quell their hated kin.

Both a warning and an awakening here
Are proffered for the intellect to appraise.
Vocabulary, form, and grammar are clear:
The time is yours to fructify your days.

How'd you manage to get a license to live?
Soon you'll reach the point of no concern.
Once you slip your double that homemade shiv,
You change into a dead man walking, Vern.

By any standard your kisser's no prize.
Still the random mirror doesn't crack,
Calmly reflecting death behind your eyes,
Aging's horror glazed with silver shellac.

If aging is oxidation proper's mess,
Its free radicals wearing your body down,
Then run for your life like a king in chess,
Till time and oxygen jointly strip your crown.

Oxygen rules. Lack it, you quickly die,
Yet over the years it eats you alive.
You're damned if you breathe or don't. Knowing why
Is science that won't help a soul survive.

But you can't live off the fizz in soda pop;
Can't exist on the bubbles in champagne.
So spike the punch bowl at the high-school hop,
And drink the harvest of the fruited plain.

Still you must breathe a dozen times a minute,
Or master Houdini's underwater tricks:
Rare as the John Hancock of Button Gwinnett
Since July 4, 1776.

XVIII *Blazing Colt*

Narcissus, trading his will for his stupid gaze,
Turned flower to drink deeper the shallow trance.
Medusa petrified men no fear could faze,
In frozen poses of death's latest dance.

A swell-looking babe in heedless youth,
Her horrid head, hissing with viper hair,
Made a hell of a woman long in the tooth.
She'd turn one peek to a statue's stone stare.

In an old radio show called *Night Beat*,
A geezer named Carver kills his boss Brown.
By concentrating his hatred to white heat,
With a dark glare he brings the fat slob down.

To looks that kill, yours will add one more.
Like a time-delayed lock's on a bank vault,
Its initial effect is easy to ignore.
Lot's lost wife became a pillar of salt,

Stealing a glimpse of Sodom all ablaze.
Eurydice? Vaporized by a backward glance.
Transfixing the goon reflected at hell's crossways,
Your vision short-circuits the laws of chance.

As laser-guided ordnance hits home,
Your sidelong look will launch its lethal bolt
Quick as a flashed frame of KODACHROME,
Faster than hellfire from a blazing COLT.

In old England rural custom would bury
Suicides driving a stake through the heart—
Called "dirty work at the crossroads"—as death's ferry
Bore the poor soul where torment leaves the chart.

Besieged by the hidden power, standard time,
Commit your thoughtless, suicidal act.
Cut your boundless future down in your prime,
Dissolving half your self-survival pact.

Your double's duped gape will leave you possessed
To suck second-hand blood for protein highs.
A vampire stopped by the eye-beam through his chest,
Vanity casts your grave glance and he dies.

Your cheap neck chain's cross can't warn you away
From the hall mirror that frames your brief glory:
Victory absent courage and fair play.
You win, and horror was never less gory.

Body-snatching passé, the concept absurd,
It garners only underground repute.
Your fangs' midnight transfusions are preferred
To drain your waning heart down to the root,

As Heracles killed Hydra. Wait—wrong myth.
Your look-see drives home doom like a rail spike.
A bug impaled on a thorn links you with
Black-masked "butcher bird," the Barbary shrike.

Minus insects, dumb cluck, there'd be few birds.
Your deadly game of chicken is nature's law—
Mutually destructive, in blunt words—
Your mouth a model of time's ravenous maw.

Against the other birds you'd have no chance:
Owls and raptors; ospreys, eagles, and hawks.
They eat their fill and leave the rest to the ants,
Who devour whatever swims, flies, or walks.

A foolish bird fouls its own nest, but then
You never were the spelling-bee whiz kid.
Can't you do more than talk? That hee-haw grin
Only quits your puss when it's stuffed with a quid.

A smile on your face for the whole human race?
Why would you quote such tripe from *Brigadoon*?
Better to throw its score in the fireplace,
And yodel down at the HOLY COW SALOON.

Did you crack your crown in childhood, dynamo?
A rusted exhaust pipe ventilates your car?
Too late to place an order of brains to go,
You're world champion dumbbell. —Have a cigar.

XIX *Midnight Moonlight*

You begin life's second shift without a breach:
Get fat off your former youth like a tick,
And live off the past as a freeloading leech.
Nosferatu loves your scheme, goldbrick.

Since blood is fugitive, pump all you can drink.
And stir in vodka: get some buzz for your bite.
Inflaming a heart black as India ink,
Your chronic blood thirst seals your moral blight.

"Your soul has scarcely started to be bled,"
One blonde says in the vampire film *Near Dark*.
By midnight moonlight, your pink tongue turns red
With blood from crime innate as a birthmark.

A birthmark shaped like a bat's open wings?
Not necessary. Any design will do,
Signifying how both beggars and kings
Die impaled on the future's giant screw.

Chinese syndicates turning a buck on blood
Might provide a fresh but risky source.
Crossing the seas in plasma thick as mud,
Germs can conquer the world without force.

It's not for all tastes, your Bloody Mary mix,
But suits you fine, spud-faced peckerwood.
Tap a steady stream for your nightly fix:
Drink DRACULA brew and prove your manhood.

Beside you, *Dracula*'s just a harmless prank,
A tall tale with Halloween appeal:
Fantasy cooked up by a cockney crank.
Today's most gruesome title is *You're for Real!*

The stillness of the torpid, unflinching look
That zaps your twin rates Richard Speck's esteem,
The pockmarked girl-killer's stare an open book,
Compared to the calm of your eyes' vacant gleam.

Succubi scarred Speck on a bed of nails.
What complex proved yours a cradle accursed?
You plug-ugly, stuck to Satan's coattails,
All his greasers agree: you're their worst.

As for vampires being immortal, well,
Who's to throw the javelin through your heart?
Stay tuned for the next OLYMPICS played in hell,
And don't sink your fangs in a teenage tart.

Even vampires maintain standards and all.
Underage suppliers have been taboo
Since Vlad the Impaler first heard the call.
You're required to resist the groupie crew,

And save your transformational enzyme.
Yet hark to gunshots that unzip the night:
A church bell redoubles a secret crime.
The blood of Abel is sacred, hellkite.

Then there's the simple matter of the mirror:
Some vampires won't show in a looking glass.
But while wasting your double grows nearer,
Your image reveals a perfect horse's ass.

Some vampires don't cast a shadow, either:
Your shadow self is theoretical stuff.
Just as your double tries to take a breather,
Your gaze confirms he's lasted long enough.

These two beliefs emerged in German culture,
Not being universal vampire traits.
Equally well, you could play a vulture,
Clawing carrion even a serpent hates.

You travel in the wilderness of the world,
Lost in America, madly raising Cain.
The sky's the limit, the clouds are all swirled,
But the bottom's hell, and Satan prays for rain.

XX *New Wave*

Your mirror murder is blind mayhem, son:
Domestic too, the common sphere to choose.
So as good as dead, why not have some fun
And head for Hollywood? Sell your soul for booze.

In vino veritas the latest style,
You're wined and dined for rights to the bones in
Your closet—now worth movie millions, while
To you it's worth a nice truckload of gin.

The Best Set of Memoirs Never Written,
The ghosted script is termed at the studio.
With nasty buzz that your mom killed a kitten,
Your character's code-named Malvolio.

Provided the names change yet the facts remain,
Star in your story on the silver screen,
Whose ads will blare: MAN'S LIFE CLEFT IN TWAIN
BY VAMPIRE PSYCHO HIDING IN BETWEEN!

Be grateful you're not written out of the script.
You know how fortunes always rise and fall.
The moneybags producer nearly flipped
And signed up King Creole of Montreal.

Your wardrobe chosen from Dracula's worst dreams,
The pall of your dull presence deepens the gloom.
The director supplies his own tormented screams,
And credits the screenplay to Zane E. Zoom.

JOE BLOW AND SECOND SELF ARE *MONSTER MASH!*
Marquees will blaze in hype's ecstatic tone.
DON'T MISS THIS SUPER CEMETERY SMASH!
DOUBLE FEATURE: *RAMBO MEETS STALLONE!*

You'll hit the big time, hayseed, overnight
Success disguise your secret life of sin.
Then word leaks out an actress died of fright
Tonguing your teeth, touching your scaly skin.

The net result only inflames renown
Your tale attracts, but for your film debut,
To horror add your stature as a clown,
Giving the public yet more cud to chew.

BANNED IN BOSTON? Just helps attendance grow.
The land of bean and cod has zero pull
When TRI-STAR offers a bloodcurdling show
So awful, mockers keep the balconies full.

Your acting earns the critics' great disdain,
But who needs art when Hollywood makes what sells?
You're off to see the wizards of capital gain,
While critics scrounge rent for their private hells.

The taste-shattering blast of cinema you
Bring to the business of film will break the bank
Vault hinges, for a brief ballyhoo
Only attained by bunk of the highest rank.

Avon Ladies of the Amazon,
Along with *Chopper Chicks in Zombietown,*
Built an audience you can draw upon
To turn the movie industry upside down.

And don't forget *I Dismember Mama,*
Which violated all the protocols.
It sparked a new wave of closet drama,
When the hero put her parts in moth balls.

A masterpiece? The brilliant *Spankin' Sisters,*
Based on a book by the Marquis de Sade.
The heroines give each other blood blisters,
Praising their pain as desire's demigod.

Surpassing the epic *Tarzan Learns to Twist,*
You set records with snaking ticket lines.
As tabloids trumpet your latest illicit tryst,
Fans will mob you anywhere Burbank dines.

Fame ignites like tar on COLUMBIA's torch,
Your name in lights big as a cattle barn:
Such a switch from the swing back home's front porch,
Your mind will unwind like a ball of yarn.

Paint the town red, blow a bundle at the track.
You only live twice, death's double domino.
The days of wine and roses don't come back,
So riding high, make temperance your worst foe.

Above all, to thine own self be true:
Stay soused and stagger down the primrose path.
The sword of Damocles is nothing new.
Drown in drink, like Bacchus in a Roman bath.

Trash every joint on Sunset Strip? That's cool.
Your facelift sags and bags? So what? You're rich!
A gossip columnist rates you a B-grade ghoul?
Get crocked at the OSCARS and vomit on the bitch!

Shoot out the lights at the PALOMINO CLUB,
Horsing around with a clutch of whores in tow.
Invade the town's most stylish social hub,
And scatter dandies so fast their tailpipes glow.

Better yet, adopt some mogul's molls,
Squiring them through the garden of delight.
But stay away from the valley of the dolls:
Jackie Susann shoots at gawkers on sight.

LITTLE RICHARD: EVER THE LIVING FLAME,
One palace will boast. How can flesh resist?
Go wild as his Macon magic heals the lame,
And he fires diamond lasers flicking his wrist.

Good Golly, Miss Molly's speed scored a hit,
Then *Tutti Frutti* swept up the charts by storm.
Religious scruples may still give him a fit,
But rock-and-roll keeps his piano warm.

He swore off the devil's music, so he said,
When a blaze crippled his plane. Down on his knees,
"God heard my prayers and spared my pretty head."
For proof he breaks his vow and pounds the keys.

Give bimbos, nymphos, and gold-diggers a whirl;
Drug-trippers, stage strippers, and starlets of smut.
But skip the jaded, flippant valley girl,
And steer clear of the jailbait teenage slut.

The feast of buttocks bouncing around your house
Would plunge Rodeo Drive into gridlock.
Stray cats picked up to amuse your one-eyed mouse,
The pussies will wring him out like a wet sock.

In a red FERRARI, a white BENTLEY or ROLLS,
Impress the natives, except a modest few.
Cruising the canyons to look for tax loopholes,
Ignore the snob who smells a parvenu.

XXI *Dream Machine*

The Hollywood dream machine is hard to shake.
Take Charlton Heston, channeling Moses still.
Adopt a crazy name like "William Blake":
It's the same moldy grave you're born to fill.

The real Blake is buried in BUNHILL FIELDS,
Near the monument raised for Daniel Defoe.
Like your fugitive stardom that soon yields
To truth, mere survival is touch-and-go.

Mad Blake interred to lie in a pauper's grave,
The unmarked spot's forgotten since his time.
Mozart too was buried like a slave,
Broke and dead in his composing prime.

Some claim he yet had ample funds—so now
Explain the stone in the *ZENTRAL FRIEDHOF*.
His marble admits neither he nor his frau
Is resting there. Who'll settle for half a loaf ?

Blake, whose fame grew slowly once he died,
Now has a fierce bust in POETS' CORNER,
By Jacob Epstein: a head of deep-eyed
Vision blazing at the modern mourner.

But noble work isn't what's on your plate.
Although you ride around in a ROLLS-ROYCE,
Your veiled autobiography doesn't rate
Critique in BILLBOARD or THE VILLAGE VOICE.

So be the new fool at an old game, spendthrift:
Frolic in light-pulse rain at the SHANGRI-LA.
Don't slack off: the hangover's hammer is swift,
And every binge could bring your worst faux pas.

In talk-show gigs, play it close to the vest.
Go nuts over classical Greek and dying drunk;
Dwarf-tossing, snuff flicks, and *Father Knows Best*.
Open your mind like a junk dealer's trunk.

What's My Line? changes to *Name That Goon*,
To put your homely countenance on the air.
Then inspired to reverse the lampoon,
They decide to resurrect *The Millionaire*,

And cast you as the character never shown,
The faceless tycoon who gives riches away
To unsuspecting common folk unknown,
Each flabbergasted whether to cry or pray.

Not to be seen or heard, your part fits
The role the invisible magnate desires,
Referred to as a fictitious Mr. Ritz
To shield himself from beggars, cheats, and liars.

The mayor invites you over to present
The key to the city in a front-page flash,
A photo-op of a star's momentum spent,
Just as your image makes its biggest splash.

All stars have edges blurring with their blaze.
Yours is about to collapse in a black hole.
Shortly you'll meet the end of your movie days,
As you peel the last C-note in your bankroll.

Ads promote you as preening Venuses squeeze
Their love-temple pillars in JUDAS jeans.
Alas, your brief celebrity turns to sleaze:
A rival soon ties your favorite scenes

To your TRUE CRIME, revealed in a rumor rag.
Exiled by sundown, slumped on skid row,
You'll slink home to a tarred shack and the skag
You left in the door she bars as scarecrow.

XXII *Gale Force*

Insiders knew you're only tinsel trash,
Yet once the fans learn you live a lie,
Your fall from grace is quick as a plane crash.
In half an hour, kiss your career good-bye.

How do you find the taste of tinsel and ashes,
Their texture, their tactile presence on the tongue?
It's hard to conjure a mix whose mingling gnashes
The teeth worse than your Götterdämmerung.

Nothing retards the instant flight of your fame:
Gone with the wind, and the wind is gale force.
Yet your past remains in place like a freeze-frame,
So rest assured: the skag won't seek a divorce.

D-I-V-O-R-C-E, Tammy Wynette
Wailed to the mike as few besides her could know.
At eight husbands, no bookie would take a bet
Stand by Your Man would stop her bridal show.

Your feature with no future hits the skids,
Its distribution drying up in a week.
The rights are peddled pronto, but no bids
Emerge, from Malibu to Mozambique.

They promised a sequel, *Dagwood Rides Again*,
But that won't halt your plans for heading home
Now, and scratch off *Mighty Ugly Men*,
Plus *Aileen Wuornos Stalking St. Jerome*.

Endangered Feces, filmed in a bat cave?
A down-to-earth progression for vampire lore.
You could've stayed a star, a fright-flick fave;
Instead you'll howl like a washed-up Roman whore.

The Roman brothel was called a "lupanar,"
Its hookers known as "she-wolves," hence the word.
Rarely does etymology reach so far
To confirm a fate as fouled as yours absurd.

The more manure is stirred, the more it stinks.
Your exposé's not California cool.
When newsmen learn your agricultural links,
DISGRACED STAR CAME TO TOWN ON BACK OF MULE,

One headline after your meltdown tells the world,
Wrecking the last of your lost reputation.
With no defense against the charges hurled,
The scandal's shock caroms around the nation.

"An unknown hand, see, stabbed me in the back,"
You try to persuade the public, but who cares?
"I'm the innocent victim, thassa fack,"
But yours is heartache only your agent shares.

Meantime your fortune's going, going, gone.
There's no light without shadow, but your shame,
Proving you had neither brain nor brawn,
Even forfeits any copyright claim.

Your contract mentioned infamy's trapdoors
As grounds to destroy every existing print.
No movie ever fizzled faster than yours:
The backers bury it as a non-event.

"Another star crushed by the tabloid press,"
Justly you might complain, yet it's all true.
How high you could've reached is hard to guess,
But stardom's all over now, Mr. Blue.

The road to ruin taken, there's no way back;
No Hollywood rehabilitation camp.
Lucky you're left no souvenirs to pack:
You're facing a fearsome future to revamp.

XXIII *Poison Recipe*

Revert to the grind of eking a livelihood
From stubborn, red clay: your family spread,
Its hovel leaning where a mansion stood,
And haunted by the harridan you wed.

Now she'll have your butt to barbecue,
Overjoyed at your big break gone bust.
"Don't be cruel to a heart that's true,"
She begged when you left, weeping into the dust—

But kept the home fires burning nevertheless:
Her breath now yields a hundred BTU's.
She's eager to help your ego decompress,
And include a lucid statement of her views.

She didn't nurse a cold vindictive heart
Before you took off, yet sizing up her prey,
Her feelings today resemble a flowchart
Of southbound sewage, down to Mobile Bay.

In case you think you're home from the horror show,
Conditions may prove it wise to think again.
Henceforth, you'll be dancing a do-si-do
With a scowling partner tough as elephant skin.

Welcome back to the mean woman blues,
All her youthful freshness turned to stone.
Of no further import how she screws,
Pray to God she lets you sleep alone.

Be fervent in the hope she ices you out.
For the sex department, that's clearly best:
To watch her frown become a frozen pout
That never will get the grudge off her chest.

Time has changed white sugar to white salt,
John Heywood wrote in 1546.
Pay careful attention when she finds fault
In your wistful praise of California chicks.

A maniac's rage kindles behind her brow,
Where blood rushes in tumult at such talk.
Her eyes fill with fire, as she wonders how
To strangle you: by serpent or beanstalk?

It's nuclear family warfare once you're home.
Surely your heart knew she'd be like this:
So furious her saliva turns to foam;
A woman with a battery-acid kiss.

You can't tell what a girl might do, Joe Cool.
She could serve you meals from the hog trough
To punish you for breaking the golden rule.
Conversely, she could chop your gonads off.

Granted, it's been a good while since her touch
Opened your fly with Cupid's master key.
Drink plenty of brew, but don't eat very much,
To help survive her poison recipe.

Marriage can melt into murder in hot spells,
So exercise extreme caution at home,
Mindful that a strain of violence dwells
Within a deviant, distaff chromosome.

Out for blood, she'll stare as though her eyes
Were night stalkers appraising her wayward pet.
Instead of her stinging words, it's what lies
Behind them that constitutes the true threat.

After a dream of weddings comes a corpse,
John Clarke observed in 1639.
As her new view of marriage rather warps
Her vows, avoid her cornbread valentine.

Shakespeare comedies always end in marriage;
His tragedies always end in blood and guts.
Her killing you might be a slight miscarriage
Of justice, but what goes on in peasant huts

Doesn't appeal to *The Los Angeles Times*,
And other forums refuse to give voice
To such provincial, wholly obscure crimes.
This rundown brings you no cause to rejoice.

Her nails could scratch the sand out of plate glass—
That's if your shack had any windows at all—
Her language now become backtalk and sass,
Accented by a warlike caterwaul.

Revealing a mordant gift for sarcasm,
She paints your character with a tar brush.
Dismissing you as so much protoplasm,
Her curses' filth would make a plumber blush.

Your angry hellhag will hover around,
Assailing your injured psyche tooth and nail.
She'll sniff at your movements like a bloodhound,
And mock her quarry scared as a wounded quail:

"Has big Mr. Monster at last returned
To the cottage of his former Daisy Mae
Grown hard and bony since her bridegroom spurned
The enchantment of her burlap négligée?

"I see it clear: he thought he could escape.
Visions of fancy parties gripped his mind.
Now his taste for French fermented grape
Leaves him gnawing watermelon rind.

"So let me guess: he wants her to forgive
The apple of her eye's brief wanderlust.
Ye gods, this piker don't deserve to live!
What penitence would she consider just?

"I'd order him to serve as my bonded slave
Till the cows come home, but we don't own no cows.
I'll doom his lousy bones to share my grave
For as long as hatred's happiness allows."

XXIV *Mosquito Control*

For a hillbilly, she can be hell on heels,
Yet wishes she were built like a bowling pin,
And spends what she earns by the BLOODMOBILE's
Pint to fill the slack in her sagging skin.

When a wronged woman conceives a desire to kill,
To whip the wicked in all-avenging fire,
Tell her you're glad to dine on hog swill,
If she'll disarm her temper's trip wire.

Perhaps you serenade her with a song
You wrote to defend yourself from her attacks,
Implying that it's she who's done you wrong.
Before you risk it, better hide the ax:

"There's feelin's I gotta say what pains my head.
I think I'm leavin', puzzle from dusk to dawn.
If I want comfort, it ain't in this rusty bed.
Here's warnin' you, I might be gettin' some gone."

Maybe your shot at show biz went astray.
Music instead of movies could have been
The direction in which your true talent lay—
But scrap that when her answer scalds your skin.

Better hide the empty shotgun too,
Just to stay on the safe side of her wrath.
It wouldn't hurt to learn some kung fu,
And every now and then take a bath.

Didn't your pa run a still back in the hills?
Teach his boy to crack corn so liquor flowed?
He saw his bad egg pimping, pushing pills,
And willed you his old DODGE and Thunder Road.

Fulfilling his legacy, cross-eyed second son,
Instead of chasing a star-struck state of mind,
You might have missed the looking-glass stun gun
That put you in a slowly tightening bind.

You never matched Mitchum's daredevil role
Running bootleg to Memphis from Harlan County.
You couldn't even outrun MOSQUITO CONTROL,
Which canceled your birthright to hooch's bounty.

Whiskey pleased Papa, but Mama loved wine,
And both would storm around like a winter gale.
The old man got wasted sipping his moonshine,
While Mama drank to a frog in a fairy tale.

The best bootlegger of all was Jesus Christ,
Changing the banquet water to homemade wine.
He plugged this into a mighty *Welt Geist*
Which still observes its original design.

Your daddy never wanted mirrors around.
He gave no motive; now of course it's clear.
The blood curse explains the day you found
His corpse impaled on a fence post so queer.

Too much bad press is the reason your career
In the vampire brotherhood is cut short.
The ancient hierarchy begins to fear
The fallout, asking if you're the proper sort.

They pronounce you ill-suited to blood work,
To passing its appetite beyond your crime.
Nocturnal athanasy's not a perk
You've earned, so you revert to real time.

There's no effort to keep your story alive,
Unlike the lore of Zara Zavanovic:
A Serbian village helps its natives thrive
By celebrating the blood-sucking bitch.

Your future in revenant roles gone to pot,
Still you could stay in films as a caveman,
One agent swears. Can you tie a square knot?
Enroll now in Satan's retirement plan.

No comeback as a phony funny boy;
No sequel for a flattop anvil head.
A lovely wife your only source of joy,
Plenty of men would just as soon be dead.

XXV *Mad Dog*

You moved to town once you saw the score,
To lie in wait as ingrown psychopath;
Betray the selfsame flesh your mother bore;
And daily deal with time's withering wrath.

A stone-faced cutthroat, flipping a coin non-stop,
You surface as bullyboy at PLUTO'S GRILL.
Cagney's a back-lot gangster stage prop,
Compared to a killer of your silent skill.

Nicknamed Scorpion, you're the underworld's own.
Of evildoers from the annals of crime,
None more baleful, none more accident-prone,
Has a career more saturated in slime.

Yet still a basic dolt, a born blockhead,
You prowl ground the Shadow calls his source:
The crusader in black who loves to throw lead;
The dark marshal of justice by deadly force.

He sees what malice infects the hearts of men,
What foul corruption fills your shiny suit,
And roars with laughter like a lions' den.
The Shadow knows. Crime yields bitter fruit.

In penthouse sanctum, he plots your path by graph—
Ragged but right, each downward blip precise—
Then leads a manhunt by his steel-eyed staff.
Your *Mirror Image Caper* kills you twice.

He puts out a hit on *you* and ups the price.
Of all people, guess who he can't stand.
May fortune be yours, more misty than dry ice,
Chance your shield from the Shadow's black hand.

His voice out of nowhere makes a breeze stir:
"What's the frequency, Mr. Big Round Balls?
Where's the path of the wind, you rabid cur?"
All bets are canceled when the Shadow calls.

Behind twin LÜGERS, his eyes blaze like coal.
His motto NO MERCY, he tracks the truth
To block your air supply for crime control.
An army of agents backs the master sleuth.

The Valley of the Shadow's dangers lurk
Disguised by every random rock and tree.
All over creation, his tireless forces work
To bring you home in shackles, Bobby Lee.

Unseen escort, he vexes lugs on the lam,
And vanishes at will by fogging their sight.
To sounds of KLIK, KACHUNGK, KA*BLAM-BLAM-BLAM!*,
His spitting pistols burn holes in the night.

In *Hidden Avenger*, he flies down to thwart
A Cajun plot to invade El Salvador.
Your stint on his screen? Nasty, brutish, and short.
You learn how fast his guns add up the score.

The pros all say a bullet has no name.
The Shadow's slugs are cast with a spiral mark
To bore through flesh and quench your vital flame,
While blood flows bright as lava in the dark.

This river of living water pouring out
Of inmost being drops you in your tracks.
The Shadow looms: his overwhelming clout
Confiscates your life as usage tax.

Your spurting blood feels nice and warm at first.
The more it spills, the colder feeling gets.
With blood still warm, its exit brings the worst
Sense of chill, which deadening soon offsets.

Your pain is the Shadow's mission, mad dog.
His zeal could drive a pit bull paranoid.
Your mental problem a dense blanket of fog,
The case attracts no Darwin, Darrow, or Freud.

Whether the Shadow helps you to succumb,
Or fault and weakness erect your impasse,
Some inside hangman stuns your muscles numb,
And seals your breath in a bottle, jackass.

Life's a preparation period, so
Settle your mind to follow eternity's plan.
You came to this broad earth a Scorpio,
And leave more star-crossed than the Son of Man.

What's the scene, once you bump off Brother?
They round up suspects, then your ugly mug
Leaps from the lineup like Cain crying "Mother!"—
As jailhouse janitors clamor to pull your plug.

THE GOOD, THE BAD, AND THE UGLY, humanoid:
Your Maker, your double, and you. That's the list.
The fact is you're no kin to Pretty Boy Floyd:
Your fetus sprouted from a uterine cyst.

Reward money gives snipers ants in their pants.
Their cross-hairs itch for a dummy silhouette.
They'd splatter your brains like guano with a chance
To show you the Shadow's sure way to forget.

XXVI *Glass Jaw*

It's tardy to start waving a white flag:
Deadwood's abuzz as you drift like dust to town.
Each kid gunslinger's wild as a stamping stag,
Dying to draw and nail your eyelids down.

Not those punks, but the Furies look you up.
Their ceaseless vitriol blisters your eardrums.
With truth serum, they spike your communion cup
To scorch your lips, crack teeth, and canker your gums.

In short, the test your dullness now must face
Is to hack through jungle, stranded up the creek;
Negate the pull of interstellar space;
And mask your crime with cagey double-speak.

The main obstacle to this plan combats
Your best effort to slash the pythons and vines
Choking your path, while stung by clouds of gnats:
Each way's a trap, a tangle confusion entwines.

The law of the jungle's not mumbo jumbo, flake.
Its raging furnace of nature's bonfire
Consumes, whether you die in your sleep or bake
In the black embrace of a burning rubber tire.

Filled with gasoline, it's placed around
Your torso tight, then someone strikes a match.
The ceremony of innocence is drowned,
The devil's dungeon freed by a broken latch.

"The necklace," this novel, vile revenge is called.
First seen in South Africa, says the NEWS,
Leaving a world audience so appalled,
It can't tell whom to pity, whom accuse.

The whole planet may watch yet stay away,
As a distant people spills its own blood.
When you betray yourself one sunny day,
Cold time will turn on you like a flash flood.

Find a tool the Reaper's ignored to disarm
His clever snares—or sink into a damp,
Uninterrupted dark, where hideous harm
Strips your shape of all familiar stamp.

Machete? Too close to your killing spree.
Chain saw? That's a drive-in picture show.
Bounce like a butterfly, dart like a bee:
Duck hell's haymakers briefly, before you go.

Equipment's no help. Your gloves are EVERLAST,
Yet any champ, even the proud Ali,
Gets TKO'd by the future inching past.
No punches are pulled when time's the referee.

Your eyebrows cut, your back burnt on the ropes,
Life's combination blows pound you to pulp,
And savage bashing clobbers your fondest hopes.
The mouthpiece clogs your windpipe? Cough, don't gulp.

The Heimlich Maneuver stops choking to death,
Not jabs beating your brains like scrambled eggs.
What good is rescue from terror, begging for breath,
To a mind quick as a sprint on wooden legs?

Your sloppy boxing match no magic realm,
The bell won't cancel the count, once you're down.
Dance round the ring till numbers overwhelm:
A split decision leaves a tarnished crown.

Don't lead with your chin or telegraph a punch.
The instant reply will shatter your glass jaw,
Or rock your socks landing a cushioned crunch,
A sound like a mouse squashed by a tiger's paw.

Try one more technique, the rope-a-dope,
Or playing possum: a final, feckless pose
That risks increasing your forehead's severe slope,
As your rebound meets a roundhouse hook to the nose.

A double whammy is your terminal fate,
But roll with the punches, last all twelve rounds.
Go to the dogs too soon, the chance is great
The master death is hot on the heels of his hounds.

After you throw in the towel, no sour grapes;
No falsehood hoarsely crying, "We wuz robbed!"
Take your lumps on this planet of the apes,
And ponder getting out. The place is mobbed.

"A one-punch lucky palooka!" your trainer gripes.
Maybe so, but it stopped your chances cold
For a bigger bout. Yet taking a few swipes
At fate's okay. A loser's allowed to scold.

You can win a fight, then die in the locker room,
Your knockout uppercut a trifle too late,
Your skull pummeled soft as a babe's in the womb.
There's really no reprieve from man's estate.

Nor does a Sugar Ray from anywhere
Feint or head-fake victory out of this.
Every contender collects an equal share
Of pure negation's absolute abyss.

They'll count your carcass down, out, and gone.
You want some news of where you settle next?
There's no less pleasant topic to talk on,
A domain which leaves the mind thoroughly vexed.

Your future awaits you in an empty box.
The cycle of seasons, springtime and fall,
Winter solstice and vernal equinox:
None living can breach oblivion's stone wall.

But where the wall between worlds grows thin,
You see a beast bulge from the other side,
And know this life won't come around again.
The busy monster follows you nationwide.

XXVII *Fingerprint File*

Facing fourth down and five, drop back and punt.
Pass when blocked by a center six-feet-eight.
Sunk in a batting slump? Squeeze out a bunt.
Time's thumb still calls you out at home plate.

Your happiness damned in spirit and in truth,
Out of this world is where your travels bend.
Pursue the path of Lou Gehrig and Babe Ruth:
Rounding the bases, you come to the same end.

Snatch a win from defeat's jaws with a wave,
Abracadabra!, and a quick disguise?
All over the earth, there's nobody to save:
Once a life's begotten and born, it dies.

Nor will you taste the fifteen seconds of fame
A soldier killed in the latest battle receives,
When networks in memoriam flash the name
On-screen, while a watching nation grieves—

After the family hears the knock at the door
To advise them of their loved one's decease
In foreign combat, performing the dread chore
Of stateside noncoms safe on the plains of peace.

Little life to savor, why would you smile?
Your current incarnation a tragic flaw,
An oversight in nature's fingerprint file,
You're slated to come back next as a jackdaw.

How'd you get so many scars on your soul?
What river's narrow rapids have you run?
Has your voyage of life survived some awful shoal,
Leaving you half afraid to greet the sun?

Your spot by a yawning grave understood,
A grave would gladden history's castaways
Fed to the hogs in a dark Bulgarian wood,
As NATO learned of Marx's latter days.

The final insult Balkan secret police
Devised for dissent silenced the songbirds.
To keep the fragile, phony, fascist peace,
They turned their murdered stiffs to swine turds.

Some commie cockroach generalissimo
Improvised this ultimate retribution,
Further trashing bad ideas by Rousseau
With a twist to skew the stats on air pollution.

"All the world's a game of fortune," Defoe
Declares in *Moll Flanders*. The winds of war
Ravage the race from Belgium to Borneo,
While politics proclaims, *"Excelsior!"*

One tenth of Albania's whole population
Was held in prison camps for fifty years,
Because of fixed ideas that brought their nation
Pain whose pity consumes the hope of tears.

"To rest beneath the shade of the Tree of Life,"
One old, forlorn Albanian woman said:
"A lighter thought than this earth lost in strife.
Better to stand and struggle than fall down dead?

"Tell my murdered husband, my maimed son.
Mending their clothes with my own hair for thread,
I know as much of courage as anyone.
Better to stay and suffer than lie down dead?

"Picture a camp where when my daughter died,
To prevent losing her ration's daily bread,
Our family hid her corpse as it putrefied.
Doomed to such hunger, many envy the dead.

"The sun approaches to drive away the night?
In eighty years I've never seen it fail.
Though day returns by its torn curtain of light,
The spirit sickens when half the world's a jail."

XXVIII *Dagger Scabbard*

"A stranger passing through our village of fear,
Peering into defeated faces scored
By decades of malice to those abandoned here,
Appears like an angel with a flaming sword,

"Come from Jerusalem and breathing fire.
A soulless waste, a deep dungeon medieval
Ringed by a circuit of high-voltage wire:
We've been trapped in reason's garden of evil.

"The cloven tongues of flame at Pentecost
Should offer us modern news of ancient joy.
But day by day, each fleeting moment lost
To hope leaves it distant as Helen of Troy.

"A world distinct from this one sounds as far
As Last Judgement from where the sun now stands,
In time's long trek to quench the western star,
Its prospect no more clear than Canaan Land's.

"Granted the means to quit a forsaken place,
This ghetto's denizens would go in droves:
Not needing keys to a kingdom off in space,
We'd settle for sunny Greek olive groves.

"Five hundred miles and fifty years away
Would have us all learning to play the harp.
How long can walking shadows hold at bay
The dark in a dagger scabbard, cold and sharp?

"Do multitudes secure in earthen sleep
Spend two years on every street in hell?
The wrong here done drove its roots so deep,
St. Paul reborn would die an infidel.

"What Cosmic Wisdom allowed into our life
Doesn't guide the forgotten to humble trust.
The sea-hag serving as Satan's midwife
Would ask us to kill for a meager bread crust.

"She's even tricked me into outguessing God,
A fool to question everlasting might.
Shouldn't the witch consider the notion odd,
Of reaching paradise on an empty flight?

"The greatest good for this life's a fresh grave.
Does the state's shining city on a hill
Shower blessings upon dominion's slave,
When her cross of woe falls and she lies still?

"Does anyone ever really escape prison?
Why does man imagine benevolent sky?
The aftermath of every sun that's risen
Should make a gentle creator prefer to die.

"The deep designs of hell are always churning,
Tomorrow promised to no one, angel eyes.
The ship has sailed, and all its youthful yearning,
Which helped me dream edicts of doom were lies.

"While time allows in all its tuneful turning
So few and such morning songs, it's our despair
To live with hunger and pain forever burning
Hope in the heart to ashes that foul the air.

"There aren't as many deaths as there are sorrows.
Who dares say death never arrives too late?
If we could launch our hearts past tomorrow's
Horror, how to purge them of all this hate?

"If the water pump in camp ran black as ink,
There's not enough to write our trials down.
Yet this dark will end in less than a blink,
When I lay down a cross to take up a crown.

"I feel I inhabit time at half past dead.
The manmade world remains the strangest story,
A cyclorama whose turns I need not dread,
After I've taken wing and gone to glory:

"Once I fly to bathe on the shores of light,
Sweetly distilled from the dew and the rain,
Their endless ocean of clouds beyond sight;
After I've lost my final battle with pain.

"The evil I've seen, I would not wish believed.
The grief this heart's withstood cannot be told.
I never want these memories retrieved,
Once I reach my home in the city of gold."

XXIX *Greenwich Time*

Lay down *your* cross to assume glory's crown,
The rest awaiting loyal people of God?
And kick the catechism upside down?
God's rest won't cover your small mound of sod.

The plan says HALLELUJAH! JESUS RAVES!—
Or something of that nature, bright boy.
Ever since men like you emerged from caves,
They've sought a shining cause for lasting joy.

Happiness can't buy money, all of them find,
Before they finish the school of hard knocks.
It's either the IRS robbing them blind,
Or the sands of time wearing holes in their socks.

No drudge from the IRS can have a heart.
Its agents record a blank EKG.
A barren soul's a further vital part
Of their emotional void, sentiment-free.

Tax collectors, since long before Christ,
Have been the hated ogres of the state;
The despised enforcers of the zeitgeist;
The fiendish, fierce exchequers of man's fate.

Martyred St. Matthew was first one of their kind,
A rotten parasite enriching Rome.
But once he'd left his former masters behind,
They dispatched him to his new heavenly home.

April 15th is the Ides of the IRS,
A month from the day Julius Caesar was slain.
All citizens endure the annual stress
Of signing what could drive a saint insane.

Yet "render unto Caesar," Jesus taught,
So every farmhand pays his last thin dime,
Afraid to express his lone subversive thought,
Cowed by the specter of federated crime.

Looking for a foretaste of glory divine?
You're searching around the wrong planet, Chuck.
That's hopeless here since 1789,
And all the rest of your doomed desires suck.

Get the earth's offenses off your back?
You sound like a bureaucrat on a coffee break.
You bear your life's weight as a gunny sack
Of junk so foul, Atlas would cringe and quake.

You're more beef than brains, a telltale fact.
Now heed this warning: you're halfway to hell.
A brain on the blink has ruinous impact
On its host body's empty wishing well.

You sure have all you need to just go crazy:
Bald tires, exhausted funds, a ghastly wife;
Manhood drooping limp as a wilted daisy;
And a torso slowly losing its grip on life.

Your nineteenth nervous breakdown's not your last.
Listen to Dr. Superduck's tapes twice.
Later, play them backwards into the past,
And try to take his transcendental advice.

Two weeks in a rubber room will put you back
Together once your psyche falls apart.
Then televised hypnosis helps to track
Your progress after a shocking new start.

They know your face at every bar in town.
If youth's a course of self-promotion, how
Far have you advanced since named class clown?
What view would your old schoolmates have of you now?

Collapse and die at your class reunion dance:
Nobody bothers calling 9-1-1.
Bury your heart in Hollywood? Fat chance,
Like scarlet slacks on a nymphomaniac nun.

You wash your flesh, the hot sponge soon grows cold.
Your body itself delays longer than that.
The angel of darkness brings death to behold:
He shows up—*snap!*—you're gone in nothing flat.

The angel of death approaching won't regard
Your wishes; sets his watch to Greenwich time.
He'll come as you mow the grass in your front yard,
Or kneel in your pew to pray as the bells chime.

XXX *Shamrock Syndicate*

There was no sword in the hand of David, but
He slew Goliath with a simple stone
Launched from a single strand of catgut—
As a mobster dies from one ring of a phone.

The mafioso "chokes on a chicken wing,"
Abruptly vanishing from his stately home.
Yet sure as mockingbirds return in spring,
His battered car will surface, stripped of chrome.

Suppose he smothers in a plastic bag:
Most mob murders hardly try to be slick,
And many purposely flaunt a red flag.
Sometimes a wiseguy "swallows a toothpick."

Perhaps a don will "buy a black FLEETWOOD,"
The *famiglia* says, meaning a CADILLAC
Hearse's circuit through the neighborhood,
After a crime boss "stalls on a train track."

"Hey, Salvatore, come to hell with us,"
A hitman quips, then blows a hole in your brain,
And one godfather asks what all the fuss
Is about, while the shooter hops a plane.

The contract killer disappears like smoke,
As gangland's old vendetta mode resumes,
Wearing the same blood-soaked and sable cloak
That camouflages evil's eager grooms.

The Irish call the Italians "Al Cologne,"
A tailored and perfumed Sicilian clan.
The shamrock syndicate's Mickey Featherstone
Made John Gotti look mild as Peter Pan.

And Danny Paradiso is a joke,
Pitted against the County Donegal men.
He'll never pass for a black-Irish bloke
To spy on the deadly Dublin kith and kin.

Did Mother Teresa croak on Christmas Day?
If not, she missed a good canonical chance.
The years do indelible harm, come what may—
Just as a dying Pope waters his plants.

You plainly outlive your use, all in all,
Grinding to a halt as the world plows on.
You hang your skates up on the WAILING WALL,
Brain waves end, and—*zip!*—your heartbeat's gone.

The down time once your brain circuits cut off,
And your nervous system's neurons crap out,
Will last so long, even Confucius would scoff
That eternity inspires religious doubt.

If you crashed heaven to find nothing revealed,
In disappointment you'd want your money back.
Jehovah's laws weren't written to be repealed.
Your heaven could be hell, so mind what you pack.

A bag of chips and a bottle of warm beer
Are all the carry-on items you're allowed
When journeying beyond your being here.
You have to travel with your head bowed,

In order not to stray from the twisting path
That draws you through time's lost continent to
Where your soul can take an overdue bath
Of blood and sweat washing what's left of you.

RELIGION TYPES DEBATE WHERE HEAVEN IS:
1. In the sky where clouds and rockets fly;
2. In starry space where comets whiz;
3. Where God resides to glorify.

Just 6% of people believe in hell,
Yet 80% think heaven's a swell place:
A nicer realm by far, it doesn't smell,
And serves as an eternal home base.

The afterlife is spiritual existence
Transcending time-and-space as we know it.
It's not a matter of substance or of distance—
But only unearthly power can bestow it.

XXXI *Jungle Gym*

"How sweet to stand upon the edge of tomorrow,"
One TV evangelist airily said,
Overcoming months of pain and sorrow
Caused by bleeding from a bump on his head.

Mañana thinking's not the right idea
To get the most out of life and die content.
Treat the passage of time as panacea,
And wind up asking where tomorrow went.

Tomorrow's edge could be the end of your days.
What to make of the preacher's comfort then?
Hitting rock bottom, start your final phase.
What will you say on leaving your fellow men?

Will you blow your cool and curse flesh's fate,
As your dying eyes dart around the room?
Why go out of here on a note of hate?
Better be polite to the silent groom

Who ushers you down to the River Styx,
And helps you board Charon's crowded barge.
Best go quietly, clutching a crucifix.
Every passenger pays the standard charge.

The river takes it all, the river of time:
Dead dogs, diamond rings, and murdered men.
It washes away virtue and covers up crime;
Drowns an ox and crushes BARBIE and KEN.

The river of time's a *River of No Return.*
Not Mickey Mantle nor Marilyn Monroe
Sees golden Heraclitean fire burn,
After sinking into its mighty flow.

Time's is the fire in which you evenly burn,
Whether in pestilence, famine, plenty, or joy;
Whether the daily news announcements turn
On a starlet's marriage, or a murdered boy.

Wry clerics call dying the Great Escape.
They look to a world whose sun never sets,
The kind of scene where the soul can just go ape.
But don't get excited yet, cool your jets.

Maybe something splendid is taking place
In heaven, the spotless city built foursquare,
Located somewhere way in outer space,
Yet none like you was ever sighted there.

Leave this dump for good one happy day?
Whom the sun sets free is free indeed.
But grow bright angel wings and fly away?
Sure. Or why not try a wingèd steed?

When We All Get to Heaven isn't a hymn
Embracing you in its optimistic theme.
Relax, play at life on your JUNGLE GYM,
Until your fatal fall from the high beam.

Do angels have minds? What's the difference, hick?
Neither here nor in glory would yours do much.
Yet getting this far with no brains is a neat trick.
Tell the fans the source of your magic touch.

CLIMB ON A CLOUD AND SAIL ALONG THRU LIFE:
That's the way you reached where you are now.
Because of how you treat your whining wifc,
There's no more in-flight time the laws allow.

The Lord won't care if you're living or dead.
The temporal life is nothing special to him.
Often he wants to throw you out on your head,
But always does it under a pseudonym.

The *capo di tutti capi* knows all.
Knows if you're sleeping, knows when you're awake.
Knows whenever you hear an altar call,
And knows you have the black heart of a snake.

None can advise you God's alive and well.
Some things you must figure out on your own.
You feel like there's a gun in your back? Swell.
Heaven can wait; pick up the telephone.

Call 1–900–7–11–SOUL.
Record a threat on Lucifer's voicemail.
Say you heard about hell's opinion poll,
And don't agree it hits the head on the nail.

You wanted him to know you've got his number,
Carry it next to your heart at all times;
That your brain enjoys a constant state of slumber,
And—sorry to cut this short—you're out of rhymes.

The call will cost you twenty bucks a minute,
Yet giving the devil a prime piece of your mind
Beats an earnest speech before the Senate,
Bashing the latest plan to save mankind.

You do what the noise in your skull tells you to?
Including when you wish upon a dream?
A fool defines himself, and raising you,
All your frantic mother could do was scream.

The good you do is greater than the harm?
You really believe that, don't you, scalawag?
Even if good entails the rustic charm
Of making love to a prehistoric hag.

A slave to eternal perdition, you remain
Primitive as a germ in *Jurassic Park*.
JOHN Q. CITIZEN LEAVES HIS PARTNER SLAIN,
While hungry orcas kill a thrashing shark.

A diet of dog-food doughnuts keeps your mind
Free of the interference of fine health,
The bad news blues leaving your brain behind,
As time invades your blood in perfect stealth.

Slipping like a stone, you mumble and jive,
Still pumping up the same old 3–6–9:
A loathsome jackal haunting a backstreet dive,
And flushing your feral heart with poison wine.

The river of no regret you float in,
Aimless as a Sunday afternoon,
Is fed a raging current of BOMBAY gin
You'd ride from Roanoke to Rangoon.

Stand knee-deep in a river and die of thirst,
Unless you know its chemical make-up?
Let LIQUID MAGIC liquor cure the worst
Intestinal tempest in a teacup.

XXXII *Russian Roulette*

Your double's legacy is a heavy debt,
But life won't be complete until you've died.
While the wild world works as Russian roulette,
He deeds you a lingering suicide.

Jim Jones of Jonestown declared a "white night":
He and nine hundred more insanely prayed,
Then swallowed a lethal KOOL-AID plebiscite.
Your own suicide comes in a darker shade.

Waiting for the other shoe to drop,
You're never really hip to how long you have.
Meantime your life's a big belly flop,
Like sticking around for a sperm whale to calve.

Your double's death record, written on water,
May sound poetic, yet it averages out—
Its full import hidden from you, globetrotter,
To save your having the worst to carp about.

Knowledge too prompt could scare you out of your wits.
Kept unawares, you won't drop dead of fright,
Calling longevity's frail balance quits.
This stroke of luck is your basic human right,

A guaranteed lifetime loan, interest-free.
Merely surrender all to settle up.
Take half your life to pay, and no late fee,
Slow as lead in the glaze of your coffee cup.

The lump-sum payment held in your clammy hands,
As more good luck, outlive your odious wife.
Your banker's mum: no harpy's shrill demands—
Till you pay him back with your lousy, stinking life.

The account he oversees goes by the book,
The letter of the law your proper fate.
It's no use trying to brand him a cheap crook.
Besides, you did accept time's prime rate.

Mail him a big fat check, but watch it bounce,
And death's tax man never asks for less.
He trades in pounds of flesh and every ounce
Of you is legal tender for time's redress.

Not worth a cent of tribute beyond that,
A mess of organic matter plus your hair
Is all your fund amounts to, alley cat.
Be glad he takes your corpse and calls it square.

"Your money or your life!" aren't terms he'd use.
He holds you up without an unkind word:
Presents you the bill a body can't refuse,
Like airborne butchers gassing a baby Kurd.

"It's my life, you stay out of it!" thus are not
Words to say to him, on the other hand.
Calling your loan, he has you fill a slot
Somewhere this side of Custer's Last Stand.

Yet living on borrowed time's not so grim,
Though when it runs dry, seers can't foretell.
So don't play dead in a graveyard, Sunny Jim:
Strive as if storming Satan's citadel.

Sit down now and write yourself a letter.
Make believe it's sent by the IRS,
Saying your hope's all wet and getting wetter,
Your refund each year little and getting less.

XXXIII *Oomph Girl*

There's safety having one foot in the grave:
Protects you from dying young by a glitch.
But meet the future squarely, acting brave.
"You look so sallow," make-up salesgirls bitch.

"The fountain of youth transforms your shower tap,"
They smile, pressing a vial of dye in your palm.
"Rinse away gray," declares their damning rap,
"Then treat your face to our latest aging balm."

With a thousand little things to get done,
Until the start of the foregone conclusion,
It's wise to make your grooming number one,
And so maintain life's best-loved illusion.

All is vanity, even in mourning gloom.
Some women bloom anew in black. Do you think
A widow should dress like a witch on a broom,
Or skimp on the coffin, spend the rest on mink?

How soon does her sorrow lead to glad relief?
How long before she sets the memory loose?
Her locks turned resolutely gold with grief,
How swiftly will a gander find her goose?

To remind you: halfway through your mortal days,
You enter the sequence roughly exposed here,
Fumbling forward in a changing maze,
Where much is unjust, and only the end is clear.

Yet a midway's meant for amusement, not despair.
Seek no farther thrills that chill to the quick.
Aren't 40 million minutes enough to bear?
Want less you're timid, more you're lunatic.

Did Methuselah's health, in the ancient scrolls,
Last nine hundred winters' increasing pain,
Like stuldbruggs clogging Luggnagg's welfare rolls?
Living too long will rot the hardiest brain.

In *Nora Prentiss*, Ann Sheridan fell
In love with Dr. Richard Talbot, played
By Kent Smith, casting her usual spell.
He figured he'd ditch his wife and kids to trade

His bourgeois life to enjoy "The *Oomph* Girl"—
As Ann was billed in 1933—
And give the nightclub singer's heart a whirl.
Bypassing divorce to cut his future free,

He tried a risky trick and faked his death:
A fiery crash staged with a corpse in his car.
Yet his plan dissolved like Cawdor's in *Macbeth*,
As he fought to please his pretty singing star.

The stiff, a stranger who just showed up one night
At Talbot's office complaining of chest pains,
Had died right there. Spurred to action and flight,
The doctor seized this chance to break his chains.

The puzzled police thought murder had first occurred,
With the doc's dead body then consumed in flame:
His machinations betrayed the lovebird.
Skipping town and using the stranger's name

Failed to keep the gumshoes off his scent.
When a real accident scarred his hiding face
Past recognition, his jinxed freedom was spent.
The law's tragic irony built a case

Against him as "John Thompson," who had burned
Talbot up in the PACKARD and disappeared.
"Guilty as charged" declaimed the verdict earned,
Which public, press, and his family all cheered.

He went to the chair never baring the truth.
Killing your double, you win the same fate,
Dying because you slew your faded youth,
And find the results in the mirror too late.

XXXIV *Blood Feud*

Your former face is lost and unredeemed,
The clues becoming clearer year by year.
It's not a secret shame you merely dreamed,
But flesh's slow, slackening souvenir.

Your image double-exposed, life's halfway point
Still lets you favor yourself at twenty-one.
At eighty-four, the picture's out of joint.
Your clay mask's glaze cracks when overdone.

Think how repeat xeroxing blurs, compared
To the crisp, original *Ding an sich.*
The same goes for your skin. No spot is spared
As a youthful mien yields to arithmetic.

Like a mirror you forgot was in the room,
Lost youth hides within the old man's skin,
Listening all the while to the voice of doom
Speak from the mouth of its elder, dying twin.

Still hanging onto your looks, relax and ignore
The impact of each new wave of gray hair.
Yet once your face starts falling apart, what more
Proof do you need to go buy a rocking-chair?

A master painting's underdrawing shows
Through in a picture called a reflectogram.
Behind your mirrored features, tracing each pose,
Your youthful double looms to double damn.

Was Dalí right? The mind-bending of time
Melts the mask of your face like candle wax.
The sharper angles youth had in its prime
Are what the elder's used visage lacks.

Handed a high-school snapshot of your youth,
Imagine you're the portrait of Dorian Gray:
The painting conveys the unavoidable truth
That passing time will eat your face away.

As if the painting erodes a bust of clay,
An awkward ugliness replaces flesh
Once smooth yet now in awful disarray,
And keeps your latest degradation fresh.

Live in a world without mirrors, if you wish
To blind the eyes that bring you up to date,
Unconscious of your looks as a crawfish
Crawling in slime to find the perfect mate.

Killing time is all you can manage, Bo.
But time is killing you as you laze around
Half soused, and channel-surfing's undertow
Corrodes your mind by holding it spellbound.

Your manners have never made much headway,
Yet hog heaven beats country-club hell.
It's time to pull out the ELVIS TV tray,
And watch the apes of God you know so well.

Your easy chair becomes pig paradise,
With popcorn, peanuts, and a case of beer.
Although your IQ pays a heavy price,
Enjoy the constant, freely flowing cheer.

Ninety-seven ways to shorten your life,
And you would pick the foremost on the list.
Better to cheat at cards on Mack the Knife
Than cancel your double's reason to exist.

Your ailment? Name it Alpha-Omega 2—
He's dawn, you're dusk—afflicting jocks and mules.
X-rays miss it, blood dye traces no clue.
It's drawn best by poets who vandalize schools.

Another "mule-killer," the praying mantis,
Proves your basic health condition apt.
Hopeless as raising the lost isle Atlantis,
Conception leaves your lifespan handicapped.

Mated, the female mantis eats the male:
What you could term the last turn of the screw.
Creation, whether that small or big as a whale,
Ensures all life a fatal rendezvous.

Your T-shirt's image no Veronica's Veil,
Its eagle decal stares from cold, dead eyes.
Like a bird on a live wire in windblown hail,
Hold on tight to claim your booby prize.

The PSYCHIC NETWORK is sending you a flash:
"To Marblehead of Planet Granite. Log
Onto our nutty FACEBOOK page and crash
When we three friends find you dumb as a dog."

Do golden portals loud with hosannas ring,
Highest archangels in glory wait for thee?
Try 1–800–HEAVEN. See if they sing
At the other end of the line. The call is free.

All plays have understudies backstage,
Stand-ins for any actor indisposed.
Pretend you're the monkey mime, kept in a cage,
Your double paroles once his show has closed.

A dime's worth of difference between you two?
Change your name like Paul of Tarsus? No use.
Your head's the same dim light bulb, stumping you
In thoughts so weak, you can't turn up the juice.

No good will ever come of a blood feud:
Take stock of you two losers' mortal sin.
It can't be phrased without appearing rude,
But which bad apple ruined the other's skin?

XXXV *Holy Ghost*

Feeling faint, with half your life to burn?
A commonplace complaint, condition chronic.
Yet worry is worse. Quit picking scabs and turn
To sterner stuff: the lasting cure is chthonic.

Horde your dough till your soul has hell to pay?
A local quack prescribes TRIPLE-S TONIC.
Sample a vial of his concoction today,
Whose label boasts, BICEPS GO BIONIC.

Why spring for his snake-oil remedy home-brewed?
Who wouldn't pay for a sounder physique, right?
Show the yokel shaman some gratitude.
Illusions help you make it through the night.

Normally, leave your cheer to jingle bells,
And riding in a one-horse open sleigh.
But past what simple, seasonal gloom spells,
You're subject to despair from June to May.

So ADAM'S BOTANIC BALSAM's gentle balm,
More mental, a medicinal make-a-wish,
By some dull opiate works to keep you calm—
Yet twists the liveliest into cold fish.

Say, why not try to find the alchemist's gold?
Rasputin, sly as Lucifer himself,
Charmed the last Czar's ill-fated household;
Could charm the gold off china on the shelf.

Perhaps you're not the actor for that part.
Charm will never become your long suit.
Dress your crocodile skin in wearable art,
Still you'd look chic as a hobnail boot.

No man gets his money's worth in the grave,
Despite how cheap his widow buys his casket.
He leaves and doesn't come back. How can he save
A buck—tight as it makes her look to ask it?

Roots break open the strongest coffin in time,
Insinuate their fingers between the bones:
Tear them apart, rearrange them, and climb
Down to hell-gate sealing damnation's groans.

When you see an old graveyard's cockeyed stones,
The big trees' roots are slowly burrowing through
The peace of both the noted and unknowns
Enduring chaos beneath the cleansing dew.

Your name's on a missile locked on target, one
Not aimlessly sent TO WHOM IT MAY CONCERN,
But fired by a proton blast beyond the sun,
While all your missives to God crash and burn.

Be quick if the Holy Ghost comes to town,
Leaping across treetops like crownfire
To corner your soul in a sudden showdown
Designed to help your hopeless heart expire.

This game's nineteenth hole is six feet deep.
No beer, chips, and peanuts are passed around.
Its putting green requires no close upkeep,
But any score leaves your balls in the ground.

Your double elimination's no golf club
Round robin for look-alike fathers and sons.
It's nature's blunt, uncompromising snub
Of happiness, while the solar system runs.

Nature's a hungry, hectic arms race,
Balance merely a frozen frame of time.
Survival by tooth and claw's wild goose chase
Remains the basic, working paradigm.

A predator takes a life to save its own.
In Gondwanaland millions of years ago,
Or by steel blade that pierces a breastbone,
It's kill or be killed around here, Angelo.

Your turn is clockwork. Tinkers to Evers to Chance,
Your grounder to short triggers a double play.
Who's on first? Hey, drop the song and dance.
Your life has no third option squirreled away.

XXXVI *Vampire's Revenge*

As for *39 and Holding*, what the heck.
When lightning strikes you twice, you mosey on.
Your math must square with waves clearing the deck:
If seen again, you're rain to water the lawn.

No shield deflects the fickle flash of fate
Connecting earth and sky as thunder rolls.
More light than all the gathered stars create,
It dies into darkness new as your dead soul's.

Your caper's fearful symmetry is bound
To bug you, knowing one act is but prelude
To a diamond jubilee, when you're crowned
By a coffin. So to cope, pop a QUAALUDE.

There's no good way to gently break the news.
It cuts like a knife to the stomach when it comes.
But life is full of surprises, tightening screws,
And the final torment hangs you by the thumbs.

Fear and Trembling. The Sickness unto Death.
The first is how you should feel, the second why.
What broke a spirit hard as Lady Macbeth
Will teach you to eat a ton of humble pie.

How to tell you've reached the end of your rope?
It slips and you lose all you ever won.
Examine its tag, sweeping in its scope:
The manufacturer's label, BARR–NUNN.

Accept no less: death on a silver platter.
It's not a fit world to live in anyway.
If life is endless travail, why does it matter,
Since everything stops, come your final day?

You never know, the world being what it is.
You might not know, the world being what it's not.
The latter could make you marvel, "Gee whiz!"
The former's lumpish as a wad of snot.

AJAX cleanser can't scrub from your skin
The stain of being you, and bribes won't work
To change your birthdate and start over again.
"Out, damned spot!" is bull to a registry clerk.

Your birth record, a license to get killed,
Choke on the host and die at Holy Communion,
Is your pass to cross the Jordan and help build
Up time's underground family reunion.

The BUREAU OF VITAL STATISTICS doesn't mind:
Strangle on your dentures or baby spoon.
No matter your progress from the start, they find
Simply that no decease arrives too soon.

You hold a wolf by the ears, chump, and should
You drop him, he chews you up, cracking your bones.
Your scraps get strewn around, like matchwood
Lightning has splintered among random stones.

A color guard tails you, with drumbeat and *Taps*
To measure your forward march as daily dirge.
The guidon, bugler, and drummer shoot craps
To win from your loss in time's complete purge.

They fit you for a pair of cement shoes,
Then drop you off a bridge to watch you swim.
Your body won't rise to make the evening news,
And death squads never sing your favorite hymn.

Scrawl your name all over: KILROY WAS HERE.
Inscribe it on birches, books, and bathroom walls.
Brandish your fragile phallus like a spear:
Your ego comes to naught when Terminus calls.

The talons of time's unhooded falcon rip
Your vitals in clutches that lock, bleed, and shake
Your trembling frame—a nightmare acid trip:
VAMPIRE'S REVENGE—THE DOUBLE'S DEATH REMAKE.

XXXVII *Dark Chambers*

The Lord looks out for drunks and fools, they say,
So you're under his wing on either count.
The price of being born's at last to pay
With your life. The bill's timing is paramount.

Late or soon, you come to a screeching halt.
You're busy breathing, suddenly you're not.
Just that quick your brain enters default,
Earning your corpse a basic burial plot.

What lullaby rocks you in the cradle of death?
Some camper's boom box disturbing the peace?
The trouble is you're totally out of breath,
And have no earthly means to ring the police.

Here one minute, gone the next, is the truth.
When winter sunset slashes red in the sky,
Each day it ends numberless dreams of youth,
Instructing prince or pauper he's bound to die.

To save the day, you have to seize the night.
One evening ballet, another the dog races?
Carpe diem until you lose your sight,
Smell, taste, touch, and hearing time displaces.

Work your way through life, when all else fails.
That's how the permanent waves, says SASSOON.
Your future a snake dance of seven veils,
The last of them lifted, life's a burst balloon.

Salomé told Herod, "Jokanaan's head!"
In your reward the sleep is just as sound.
Her dance of death done, the Baptist bled.
No visions dance in your head underground.

You enter the motionless town of NO PLACE,
Streets eerily empty and devastated:
The home away from home for the human race,
Where leftover life is canceled, not pro-rated.

Below, every day's a DAY OF THE DEAD.
No costume skeletons dance among the tombs,
As festive folk dispel collective dread.
Earth's basement bars noise in its crowded rooms.

No groans from the grave sound in this black and damp
Dungeon those left alive know nothing of.
None this side of its doors can light a lamp
And pierce its dark chambers with beams of love.

No daybreak cracks the quiet world of the grave,
Where few of 90 billion's bones remain;
Where all that beauty or wealth ever gave
Is lost as a lamb on the Serengeti Plain.

Wholly deserting the sphere of sunshine—
Breath surrendering both sorrow and mirth
By transit beyond time's vanishing line—
Multitudes lie sunk in smothering earth.

If life is hardly more than a painted veil,
No prayers can part the gates of darkness here:
Only those finishing time's fairy tale
Silently pass through them and disappear.

You'd rather be in Philly, wonderful one?
You stole that thought off W.C. Fields.
No sooner take your last leave of the sun
Than day can't open the dark's eternal seals.

A renewing fountain, your heart's freshets flood
A veined network of 60,000 miles:
Around the globe twice and halfway back, but blood
Stalls in the Arctic; the pump shuts down its dials.

No double bypass avoids this freezing pole,
Extremity where your world no longer moves;
Still point on the turning earth, your endmost goal:
Arrive whenever the crack of doom approves.

XXXVIII *Daytime Smoke*

In case your arrogant ego acts unruly,
Refusing to fold your lone explorer's tent,
Assert the right to seek your ultima Thule,
Till your lungs hold no further breath unspent.

Make it plain you're reaching your wit's end—
What little you have, of course. Nevertheless,
You bear a burden's message you wish to send
For all humanity to receive and bless:

"'Near sleep, no one is sane,' writes Joseph Tate.
As hypothermia slowly settles in,
If I appear to discombobulate,
The sky is everywhere, and hope wears thin.

"During a dream that all my teeth fall out,
I find a blank key to the portal of time.
As Rainbow Bridge counterfeits rainbow trout,
It breaks another merry pantomime.

"I'm speaking just to hear my head rattle.
Lions are nonplussed by the legs of a stool.
All Gaul divided in three parts, the Battle
Of Belleau Wood made happy face a fool.

"Something that feels like wild horses of fire
Rushes through my heart in a storm of fear.
I'd rather be safe than full of false desire,
Till all the echoed thunder skips a year.

"The hour depends on the force winding your clock,
Or failing to wrest a degree of brain trust.
Maybe it's rolling when it ought to rock,
But chaos anticipates a marble bust.

"When the numbers work, yet the ideas don't,
The element missing to persuade is facts.
Truths that transform either will or won't,
But a precious harvest of blood still attracts.

"Her eyes are bright as diamonds, I believe;
A cool craps player: sixes, sevens, and nines.
If angels from the realms of glory grieve,
A casino sold them cold betting lines.

"I'm startled at the sight of my own shadow,
Found sneaking into camp, silent as light.
He figures to jump my claim on Eldorado,
Which I'll pursue till left replaces right—

"Or right replaces left—try making sense.
A traveler caught between relief and loss,
I realize my rescue is immense,
And owe my soul to a Vegas pit boss.

"Waco Johnny Dean the gambler would,
Helped by his local back-up Daytime Smoke,
Expel impostors from this neighborhood,
Before my shade engages a sun stroke.

"All firebugs fear to venture into the dark
Of death, yet here they'd meet no dark to fear.
Life a drama of pain, constant and stark,
I'll dare to shed a single, frozen tear.

"This icecap looks to be my final address.
Inertia bounces me back to square one:
Terminal solitude in polar chess.
God, what I wouldn't give for a shotgun."

XXXIX *Mission Bell*

"I furnish you fragments of a former mind,
Traces of self unable to cohere:
Featureless as philosophy snow-blind,
Stuck in a brave struggle to disappear.

"I see three crosses and a crown of thorns,
As a numb, peaceful feeling overcomes.
On the big cross is a bull with ten-foot horns,
On the other two a couple of beach bums.

"Mother Mary receives all souls now dead,
The code of the Knights Templar notwithstanding.
Besides, the King of France required the head
Of Jacques de Molay, plus the Knights' disbanding.

"I'm staring at a mansion in the sky,
A black lie that illuminati tell:
Unsolved history swatting a butterfly,
The sounding blow loud as a mission bell.

"Silver wings to a fiery sky ascend,
Doctors, lawyers, and clergy all agree.
That's not a crucial theory to defend
When snoozing under shade of a monkey tree.

"I hanker to dance the Crocodile Rock,
Fondly recalled in an eighties hit song
Written after a season of summer stock,
About a reptile love affair gone wrong.

"Completing the picture raises goosebumps
And spins my head on a disc no sundial ends.
Hobgoblins people my thoughts and tumble jumps
They ought to clear, while victory depends

"Upon skunks patrolling the slopes of Mt. Hood
To close the circles of A–1 Mountain Road.
The sky pilot is shot down dead for good,
With his weird habit of keeping the grass mowed.

"If one sore loser using a sniper scope
On a store-bought gun can stupefy the law,
Think what a dialogue of *yep* and *nope*
Could bring the sovereign state of Arkansas.

"Listen, I guess my talking days are up.
Who yanks the plug on my lousy life-support?
I always wanted to crash the BREEDER'S CUP,
But now abandon the field as a good sport.

"Remember twinkle, twinkle, little star,
The lyric penned by a felonious monk?
Its copyright was sold at a Scout Bazaar,
Fished from a heap of ceremonial junk.

"Use caution at any crossroads you approach,
Or obfuscation at Devil Dog Road.
Fiercely attack a yellow cockroach,
And summon the unicorn in Morse code.

"Dump the spiteful ego in a ditch:
Does the backlash answer an alter call?
Try hoarding stock in CYBERZOMBIE & SWITCH,
To see its rocket value zoom and fall.

"Astro-spirits that guide you to nirvana
Can detour, leaving your body to RESEARCH.
Leap to seize control as a green iguana,
Or stop the madness and raid a jungle church."

XL *Deeper Blue*

"Seal dead letters in flames fed by the wind,
And go to blazes with a hurricane.
Santa Claus was watching you: he grinned
When Liberty Valance ambushed Tom Paine.

"A cursory search indeed is all I get,
Until the film crews scratch me off as lost.
To invigilate the band width I set,
Please be prepared to underwrite the cost.

"The Army mustered me out at FORT ORD.
They didn't admire my sun-damaged brain.
Next I plan to dwell at home in the Lord,
Arriving there as a blue-crested crane.

"Will your great seagull bleed a deeper blue?
Never forget that darkness is for ears.
Long before you were born, nothing was true,
So raise the song of harvest home by tears.

"One item is left to broadcast, ghost to ghost:
I'm sharp enough to catch an arrow in flight;
Or stand in a blizzard, hugging a guidepost
Precise as a long-range rifle's peep sight.

"While snow and freezing rain lash the streets
Of modern memory—all points south of here—
Mark my grave above ground and holy Pete's
Unconcern at my purifying fear.

"I recognize a call to finish now
And demonstrate passing my wisdom on.
Hearing my thoughts is painful anyhow,
Missing the dark to punctuate the dawn.

"For every compass the world has, there's one
Direction for which time is the sole measure,
Its marching beat repeating stun stun stun,
Death its expedition's only treasure.

"I'll die as peacefully as a passing cloud's
Shadow moving over my frozen perch,
Freed forever from the teeming crowds'
Multitudes I'm leaving in the lurch.

"I'm signing off to intersect a dream.
Follow my worst advice, you'll turn out well.
My closing note compels a primal scream,
Then quickly I drift, into a magic spell."

Isn't it hopeless to wrestle against doom?
Resign your soul to wear the garment of earth.
The hours fly around in circles for whom?
Departure's on schedule, saving you a berth.

To know the moment of doom is living death.
It concentrates your thought—and drives it wild.
No need to wonder: rely on crystal meth
To correct every wrong number you dialed.

A sudden dread sweeps over you like the wind,
Rushing through the crevices of your mind,
And whether you're strong-willed or thin-skinned,
Whether your vision's perfect or stone-blind,

Yours is a story ripped from the fabric of life,
The all-consuming battle for existence.
The journey of few is marked by drum and fife,
Detouring to avoid the most resistance.

XLI *Divine Ramrod*

A whipped dog always howls. So will you,
Your prospects wrecked by a brutal bunch of facts.
Bitter comes with sweet, pinprick with tattoo,
Including a raft of underhanded acts.

Bitter comes with sweet, barb with billet-doux.
A dozen dead roses fate leaves at the door
Will make you cast a double-take or two.
Check the vendetta under the kitchen floor.

While singing, "Love letters straight from my heart,"
As Frank in *Blue Velvet*, Dennis Hopper beat
The kid up bad who played the hero's part
Saving the girl who lived on Lincoln Street.

You mustn't assume a losing attitude.
The facts of life are grim, yet don't give in.
Dire straits require a helpless state of feud
With fortune, a long struggle you won't win.

"If you faint in trying times, your strength is small."
(—*Proverbs* 24:10) The weight of the years
Bears heavily upon you? Before you fall,
To suspend the hangman's rope, use sheep shears.

Con man, stop calling your cut-rate crusade
Through life a mistake, disputing the main fault.
What saint could retire your scythe's debt unpaid?
Courage! Swallow all the sorrowful salt.

It's truth, justice, and the American way.
There's no future in talking to a fool.
¡Vaya con Dios, amigo, ándale!
You should've been shown the path in Sunday School.

St. Teresa, speared by an angel of God,
Felt it time and again enter her id.
With a seraph's fire-tipped, divine ramrod,
Could nun deny what heavenly suitor bid?

Rhythmic epiphany's not for every saint:
Convents would fill like brothels on Friday night,
And sisters' earplugs mute a novice's plaint
Of ecstasy quenching her zeal's appetite.

Tired of conflict? Want to lie down and die?
Analyze the error of your ways.
Your heart could explode, you not knowing why
You miss what's between here and the purple haze.

As a headless chicken's scarlet blood will spurt,
Why bare your coward colors, hatchet man,
Feathers flying from circles scratched in the dirt?
No, meet the world in a brazen, beach-boy tan.

Malibu surfers say, "No waves, no ride."
The worse the weather, the higher they hang ten.
Your stunt man tumbles first, so blithely guide
Your board to the last wave, that drowns all men.

You boast as much brains as a shrunken head,
Whose stitched lips reflect your powers of speech.
To prevent your thoughts' becoming widespread,
You'd miss the cut for lifeguard at Muscle Beach.

And forget a role in *Beach Blanket Bingo*.
Not DISNEY nor BLUE STAG FILMS hands you a part.
Old Yeller need a double? You dumb dingo.
Is it taboo for a dog to tup a tart?

Surf City's nowhere that angels grant grace,
As Rhonda yields to Dion's love redeemed,
And you seek breasts in which to bury your face.
There all the bronzed boys and girls get reamed

By time's corkscrew, disemboweled, embalmed,
Then lost beneath the bleached and blowing sands.
While waves roll like cockles or lie becalmed,
You stroll between bosoms and hot-dog stands.

XLII *Dangerous Crackpot*

Emerge as a beachcomber learning the trade.
Let barnacled driftwood be your precious ore.
The shifting tide determines what you're paid:
Entrust your livelihood to the seashore.

A bamboo stalk festooned by coquina shells
Can make a happy stick to smash piñatas.
A broken, hollowed bowling ball sells
For a horror mask face—Mohammed Atta's.

A mass of sargasso, gulfweed hay-baled,
Could feed the starving slaves of west Sudan,
Where hijacked caravans of camels failed
To rescue them with KELLOGG'S raisin bran.

Hammer a tarp to some planks and build a raft,
Then offer wealthy widows a novel cruise:
To sail around in an unseaworthy craft,
And become boat people on the nightly news.

Of course, the visuals here are borrowed from
The Raft of the "Medusa" by Géricault.
To increase your enterprise's income,
Charge the old ladies for brie and merlot.

Then badger the voyagers for their spare change,
Coercing the idle rich to cough up more.
Cross a naval bombardment practice range:
You wouldn't want them branding the trip a bore.

Your cruise line's profit potential looks vast.
For once your gumption meets the initial test.
To culminate, tie yourself to the mast,
Fire off distress flares, and pound your chest.

At last the passengers mutiny, then call
The Coast Guard to seek emergency aid.
Before the uprising turns to a keelhaul,
Your business is closed by harbor blockade.

And the helicopter cameraman damns
Your venture as a crude publicity fraud,
Angrily stows his TV gear, and slams
The station's nose for news as grossly flawed.

Bummer, man, no sense pretending it's not.
You finally had a plan you thought could work,
But word spread you're a dangerous crackpot.
Your one shot now's a job as a soda jerk.

A shock of silver sparks the darkest cloud.
Isn't the sky blue as the deepest funk?
St. Peter grills you, trembling in your shroud,
Dare you say of life, "It bloody well stunk!"?

How should Adam and Eve feel to know
Their progress through this world left a rude
Descendant with the brain of a buffalo,
Long on sin and short on gratitude?

When God's concierge blocks the golden stair,
Asking the password to the golden streets,
Will you curse the day you were born and roundly swear
That death's unfair, the great timekeeper cheats?

Give this slacker a milk-of-magnesia shake!
"Ain't it the truth, there's one in every crowd."
Somebody find a cure for his bellyache
To shut him up, for crying out loud.

Check him into a shelter for special bums
Who don't appear on sympathy's radar screen.
If sundown on a muddy slope of slums
Is your coat of arms, when was it ever clean?

The setting sun's space furnace will cook
Your carcass in subatomic-ticking time.
Locate the facts in any physics book:
The fragile dream of life's a nursery rhyme.

XLIII *True West*

Comes time to go, no matter what you have,
All life's trials are instantly over, but good.
No balm to ease your ills, no Sunday salve,
Once you join the eternal brotherhood.

Death closer by the time this goes to press,
Your life like a tape ending begins to race,
The remainder becoming less and still less
So fast it'll soon annihilate space.

The same from Adelaide to the Zuyder Zee,
In global gloom no St. George parts the mist
To slay the dragon death and set you free.
So dance with a dame you meet on time's hit list:

A tango to match your hair's plastered sheen.
Killer, you need a slinky, black-eyed vamp
To empty your little pistol's magazine—
Till who's upstairs gets bored and snuffs your lamp.

The dance of death's odd pairings make no sense,
So suit yourself, invite whomever you please.
Show her you yet inhabit present tense:
She still dumps you, soon as you start to wheeze.

Your entry paid, now take your prime pick—
But don't stomp her feet, whatever you do.
The price of sweet mortality makes you sick?
Then dance a graveyard waltz with a kangaroo.

Find a new life? No, strictly for VIP's:
Stoolies stuck in a back-stabbing scam.
Besides, for small fry or the biggest cheese,
The years add up to time's farewell *Shazam!*

Down in the dumps, you look surprised, sad sack.
Live happily hereafter? Surely you jest.
With life a death trap, who needs the zodiac?
There's only one fate in the end, one true West.

Read your horoscope and cheat your fate?
Come on, invent a better plan than that.
Lie down in the road and try to levitate,
Before you're flattened and smell like a polecat.

A list of good reasons for all you've done
Must be tucked in your pocket, torn and frayed.
The sentence death for lives of good clean fun,
Figure the price for the devil you've played.

Be mindful of what none will contradict:
Character carries consequence, roughneck.
Malignant habits aren't easily kicked:
They can't be overcome by kiting a check.

All men face an accounting, sweet pea.
Like thunder from distant Sinai, the bell
Summoning you tolls for an S.O.B.
Whose grief here was barely a glimpse of hell.

"What? The flames already?" asked Voltaire,
Mistaking bedside lamp for last reward.
Such wit, as you expire with a clouded stare,
Won't grace your exit when time cuts the cord.

Meteors die in the dark. What's your plan?
The bright and morning star's not your style.
To battle darkness, drink to SUPERMAN.
Why dwell on dope time can't reconcile?

Your brain throbs, a case of infoglut?
Bang pain back with JOHNNIE WALKER RED.
If life's a run of bad luck, take your cut:
Yours till the king of kings calls for your head.

Life insurance steals a poor-boy blind,
Trading on fear the way SEARS sells antifreeze.
Don't pull the panic brake and lose your mind:
Think of death as well-earned, long-term zzz's.

Ice in your armpits? Choose brighter thoughts,
Even if joy's a mask for lifelong pain.
Enter the ranks of nature's astronauts,
Whose atoms pass through aeons of fire and rain.

A top singer says, "Don't worry, be happy."
How do you differ, slouch, from a jellyfish?
A jellyfish whips up an exit real snappy,
But you languish hoping God grants you a wish.

XLIV *Mona Lisa*

The average face smiles fifty times a day,
Claims LISTERINE, and who's to dispute that?
Well, every starving beggar in Bombay,
Or nomads who collect animal scat

As fuel to cook their desert diet. Say,
Try a Mongolian stir-fry barbecue
As a dried dog-turd cookout on Earth Day,
And count the shit-eating smiles that shower you.

But defend yourself: "Let's email LISTERINE
And tell them they're all full of cow manure:
'You're now demoted to cleaning the latrine,
So work till it's 99% pure.'"

What's this? Good-time Charley's got the blues?
For pity sake, you sickly wisenheimer,
If melancholy woos your heart, refuse.
Drown your troubles with Trixie Pickelseimer.

Not her? Then Peggy Sue Studebaker.
She inspired that Buddy Holly tune,
And stoked the passion in *God's Little Acre*,
Making log-cabin love to Dan'l Boone.

Five minutes of fun can earn ten years in jail.
Enjoy today, the worst is yet to come:
A prison house which has no bars, no bail,
And 90 billion inmates, all struck dumb.

Why not get crucified, then rise from the dead?
The chance is small you can stage the second part,
Yet it did happen once, ages have said.
Being already half dead's a good head start.

There oughta be a law, dimwit, but there's not.
Even the postman ignores your resting place,
Though a billboard fibs as X marks the spot:
HERE LIES HILLBILLY GUMP FROM OUTER SPACE.

Marking Dylan Thomas's grave in Laugharne
Is a simple wooden cross painted white.
Often flowers are left for the poet born
With a voice of song distilling starlight.

Pilgrims forgive the sins of Dylan drunk,
And in tribute climb his hillside in Wales,
But none forgives a bellicose bohunk.
Who'd seek your grave, where all compassion fails?

On Heartache Street, stop by THE OASIS.
Rushing headlong, swerve to avoid the brink
Of despair, while booze drowns and beer chases
Truth as brown suds down your mind's slop sink.

Like *Ugolino* by Jean-Baptiste Carpeaux,
Chew your nails, empty your angry lungs.
Then see your ugly anguish only grow,
And horror terrify you to speak in tongues:

"Bamma lamma belladonna no;
Pisa pizza wossamatta you?
Knocka dora lupanario:
Mona lisa gina lola who?

"Arizona hanky panky, sho!
Walla Walla Pascagoula too.
Chattanooga fifty dolla—whoa!
Gonorrhea out the dough skidoo."

They'll say you're cuckoo, not talking to God.
Watch your mouth: the righteous will lock you away.
Remember your spirit's a lumpen clay clod
Of every vice that makes a parson pray.

You're labeled a congenital bedlamite,
Badly flunking the IQ test of life:
"When Satan deploys his armies of the night,
This fink joins up to beat his stupid wife."

XLV *Eternal Flame*

A tough world, it's basically all there is.
Your foothold wobbles on the edge of a knife.
Fallen, hope you die fast as soda fizz—
Or a thunderbolt, the biggest charge of your life.

In World War II, plenty of soldiers went nuts,
Once clear that dying's what they were there for.
More is asked of you: to summon the guts
And see life's battles through to lose the war.

Army math said 270 days
Of combat was all GI Joe could stand,
Before his battered psyche jumped sideways
Into some shocked and shaking nowhere land.

200,000 didn't last that long,
Insanity never a real issue for them.
Whether or not mind and body were strong,
They took up space the war would soon condemn.

When wounds pour forth like holes in tin canteens,
None lives to taste a lemonade refill.
If that's a problem, tell it to the Marines:
Go and test your odds on Hamburger Hill.

Steel yourself—or be quiet as a mouse.
Faint at the sight of blood? Pass out at the sound
Of a smoking gun? Then call the slaughterhouse.
It's treason to spurn death's merry-go-round.

The NRA claims it's part of the game:
People murder people, not loaded guns.
Too bad about JFK's eternal flame,
But the fathers' sins do fall upon the sons:

"Gunfire's a true slice of American pie.
The annual murder rate? Ain't it a shame?
Uncle Sam's nephews really know how to die:
Just give 'em a gun—to defend, kill, or maim.

"GOD, GUTS, AND GUNS made America great."
History by hunters says that's a hard fact.
"Those doubting this trinity," their by-laws state,
"Are never here at the close of the final act."

What better case than yours could they plead?
The right to die from a bullet to the brain
Today invokes a constitutional creed,
Though banning guns won't cancel the mark of Cain.

Yet homicide without firearms lights them up
To argue their heartwarming core belief:
No limit on their weapons' loving cup
To overflow an endless tide of grief.

"You're the proof in the pudding," all clap and sing:
"This yellow JELL-O custard coward kills!"
As sure as sparks fly out and bullets go zing
In the clefts of the rock, you model man's ills.

And JFK? His stricken widow now
Has joined her flesh to his hopeful spring of fire.
Theirs was a doomed dynasty anyhow,
Leaving the world uncertain what to admire.

And next their son has crashed as well, good God.
His ashes swim with sharks and giant squid.
Too near the dangerous curves of Cape Cod?
No, anywhere on the earth's global grid.

The giant squid dwells abysmally deep
In ocean blackness beyond the reach of light:
One of a million mysteries that sleep
In lowest depths of undiscovered night.

Pumping through the deep in a seething plume
Of bubbles, the squid's behavior is unknown:
As human motivation's dressing room
Is guarded by a heavy door of stone.

XLVI *Psychotic Revelations*

History finds no heroes anymore.
Winston Churchill now a racist pig,
Florence Nightingale was fond of gore,
And Bonaparte's a pygmy Mr. Big.

Lincoln displayed suicidal traits.
Were Einstein's theories nurtured by his wife?
Was Joseph Smith inspired by manic states?
He sure engaged a wild fantasy life.

Religious looney tunes are hardly new.
Some may merit now a second look.
Was Jesus merely manic-depressive, too?
Consult Goodwin and Jamison's textbook.

He did exhibit several crucial signs.
Grandiosity seemed his constant theme.
Short of professing you're why the sun shines,
When was egotism more extreme?

Archangel Gabriel played a huge scene,
His wings as drifted snow, his eyes as flame,
Telling Mary the maid of seventeen
The most incredible words he could proclaim.

Sublime providence Jesus was sent to fill.
Who reports he failed to finish the job?
The flesh has tested no more adamant will,
And the grace he avowed always roused a mob.

Did early sense of destiny appear?
Debating with scholars at twelve was one way.
Angry impetuosity? Also clear—
From cleansing the temple's turbulent display.

Charisma, optimism, burning conviction:
All were known to his twelve-disciple staff.
What about his paranoid prediction
Of how and why he'd die? Too true by half?

Self-esteem is one thing. Telling a crowd,
"Believe on me and enjoy eternal bliss,"
Would make an elite audience laugh out loud.
Will the world ever hear the end of this?

Walking on water, raising the dead and all.
Did such marvels prove his promise divine?
Poetic parables are proper to call
A will penned with the quill of a porcupine.

Or was he a mild, master politician,
Finding which buttons to push in Palestine,
Proud to pursue his single-minded mission,
Manipulating any useful design?

His hold on followers mystifies more:
Ecstasy, visions, frenzy, dazed power;
A sense of accessing truth unknown before
In a head ringing like a bell tower.

Quaking, holy rolling, handling snakes,
Psychotic revelations, laughing fits:
Which faithful are truly touched and which are fakes
Says nothing of why they all lose their wits.

The talk was of heroes: not quite your role,
Although you're much the star of this odd tale.
Whoever said, "The grave is not the goal,"
Must have thought you'd seek the Holy Grail.

That doesn't fit the logic of this tract.
You didn't script this strange variety show,
But you've had lots of time to work on your act.
Just call this revue your final rodeo.

XLVII *Southern Comfort*

No wailing or gnashing of teeth, you hellspawn.
Toil and enjoy it, Clyde, come rain or drought.
When the soil is spent and Kronos claims his pawn,
Say your crop of forbidden fruit washed out.

Your veins contain a small bucket of blood,
And human blood is made from human bone.
Plasma, corpuscles, platelets, and sundry crud:
Each helps etch the last date on your tombstone.

Your bucket's got a hole in it, guttersnipe.
Drop by drop, your days descend into dust.
You vacate the brief lease on your blood type,
And lay to rest all trace of Mother's lust.

Since you were cut from the vampire comeback team
In spring tryouts, even the second string
Can't use your tired blood to revive the dream.
Your nightmares' worn-down canines have no sting.

The blood it takes to cleanse your basest sin?
Six lousy pints more bitter than soured wine.
To end up wasted as bombed-out Berlin,
You'd just as well be drinking turpentine.

The death rate on this earth a hundred percent,
Your life's a chronicle of a death foretold.
How they brought the good news from Aix to Ghent
Matters less than a rose in Arctic cold.

WHEN CHANGES OCCUR, hints a funeral fan:
Cardboard cant for change that ends all change.
A grave's not cheap to a broke and wanted man,
But the keys to Hades fit your price range.

If the world is short on heroes, you're no help.
As the beauties of booze and nature flood your soul,
You play dog in the manger, scratch and yelp
When madam decides to plug your peephole.

Will your sodden soul find rest beyond the river,
Or the beast in your gut howl for one more shot?
You've sinned against your long-suffering liver
Like the afterlife's a cruise on Charon's yacht.

A lifetime loser, lamebrain, changing your tune
Wouldn't prevent your joining the multitude
Of creatures missing in time's black lagoon.
Your slice of life is slim as the *Book of Jude*.

Your bellyache growls like a lion? Now,
Throughout the term of your remaining life,
It chews away at your innards. Wonder how
Much it'll hurt? How much do you hate your wife?

Life's first half is more fun, till time cries, "Whoa!"
Then wine, women, and song achieve less good.
Past the midpoint, your afterburners slow,
And yet they keep you flying—knock on wood.

Hold hard to all you have; it won't last long.
"What, me worry?" you drawl and sip champagne.
Age can't ransom what youth gets for a song;
Can't play *Who's Sorry Now?* on a walking cane.

The sweetest songs do tell of saddest thought,
Connie Francis and Percy Shelley concur.
Atheistic Shelley should have taught
That death's a total blank, life but a blur.

In *Adonais* he claims poor dead Keats
Awakes from the dream of life. Tommyrot.
Mick Jagger said Brian Jones walks the streets
Of starland. That's a story without a plot.

Your best song could come on your darkest night,
But you can't carry a tune to the county dump.
Like paratroopers on their maiden flight,
Sing *Get off My Cloud* before you jump:

"Don't you hang around, 'cause two's a crowd!"
Maybe you should make it your party song.
Belt it out when you're completely plowed,
For the fellowship of drunks to sing along.

Old age a desert island, long ago
And far away is the land memory makes
Of youth, when hormones urged you, "Westward ho!"
Marooned in death's wide sea, be glad day breaks.

Getting blotto on bourbon will fog your brain.
Nothing else you attempt relieves the mind
Like pouring SOUTHERN COMFORT down the drain
Of your thirsting throat until you're half blind.

For a lush who'd far rather drink than eat,
The real enemy lies inside yourself.
Your problem is the tavern down the street,
Not whether you're a Ghibelline or a Guelf.

Say you have ten years left. Think it's a lot?
How long do the past ten years feel to you now?
A decade shrinks fast if it's all you've got,
And the question soon becomes less *when?* than *how?*

Suppose you get no older than tomorrow:
The bill comes due, you pay the dearest price.
Will you go hat in hand, in shame and sorrow,
Begging the devil to let you murder twice?

XLVIII *Black Granite*

"The night is long that never finds the day,"
Malcolm cracks, expecting Macbeth's defeat.
The moment your life decides to hit the hay,
It's beside the point if time's a low-down cheat.

THINK OF THE DAY YOU WON'T REACH THE NIGHT—
THINK OF THE NIGHT YOU WON'T REACH THE DAY,
Is carved where the Paris catacombs' lamps light
The bones of millions in grim *égalité*.

Dug up at every graveyard full to the brim,
Seeping a plague of flux into filthy streets,
The bones were readily yanked limb from limb,
Then sorted and stacked, stashed where nice conceits

Like tombstones and epitaphs have no place—
In damp tunnels left by a limestone quarry,
Whose entryway presents this note of grace:
THE CROWD HERE IS SILENT, AND SOLITARY.

Change a name and it's your story, Hank.
THE NAME HERE IS NOTHING, one keystone states.
The roll of the dead fades until it goes blank:
Eternity doesn't give a damn for dates.

If the ranks of skulls inside could raise a shout,
"Shit on the shelter of tombstones!" they'd scoff.
And to build a wall to keep invaders out,
In Athens even the stone was carted off.

Here in a tranquil city for the dead,
Enter the ante-chamber of despair.
What's the preferred method to clear your head?
Run straight home and dye your thinning hair.

A better address for death is PÈRE LACHAISE.
One stumbles onto Wilde, Balzac, Daumier;
Not Synthetic Cubists such as Gleizes;
But Géricault, Molière, Chopin, Musset.

Max Ernst, Marcel Proust, Georges Seurat,
Colette, Nerval, Nadar, Callas, Corot,
Loïe Fuller, Eugène Delacroix,
Rosa Bonheur, Camille Pissarro,

Isadora Duncan, Georges Bizet,
Gertrude Stein, Guillaume Apollinaire,
Ingres, Modigliani, Gustave Doré,
And a million others spend forever there.

Moved to a gothic gazebo all their own
Lie even "Héloïse" and "Abélard."
Extracting their DNA, sealed in stone,
Might prove it's them—but none has gone that far.

The largest tomb's a towering beehive,
A tapered marble column sixty feet high.
The owner died in 1925,
And chose this height for beckoning passers-by:

"I'm here guarding my hoard in expensive earth.
Even my wife never guessed I was rich.
Yet now that I show you mockers my real worth,
My widow can grind her gums like a Breton witch."

Consider the grave of Shirley Goldfarb,
ARTISTE PEINTRE, black granite incised with gold:
A swank if not chic, imposing stone garb
She wears to announce her story untold.

She flanks Picasso's suicide son Paul,
Whose anguish lasted barely forty years,
And now what heartstring sounds for him at all?
Does Shirley Goldfarb still inspire tears?

She rests in the CIMETIÈRE DE MONTPARNASSE.
How many wordless dreams are buried so?
Would-be genius submerged by the chaos
Of time receding into long ago.

Encounter her close cousin in New York,
Who verifies she lived in Paris thus.
Inclined to disbelieve the spacy dork?
Then head for GRANT'S TOMB on an empty bus.

And there the mighty soldier lies ignored,
Nothing present save you and paper trash
Slowly circling the tributes underscored
By history's never-ending culture clash.

The prime commander of the bitterest war
His broken nation's nightmares could conceive,
Today can appear remote as a centaur,
Though but to read his *Memoirs* is to grieve.

The Great Pyramids stand, missing their mummies.
Dead Sicilians fare best: dressed to the nines
In a cold cathedral basement, posed as dummies.
What gives, once the finery rots from their spines?

When glad rags drop from their dry, brittle skins,
And naked at last, they meet revolted stares,
How will they still hold up their bony chins?
No death is perfect, so jump and say your prayers.

XLIX *Atomic Shadows*

Soon you can launch your ashes into space,
Paying for passage on a *Saturn* shot
That puts the earthbound masses in their place,
And buys you an intergalactic grave plot.

The transportation is only one-way.
Here six-feet-under provides the same terms.
Not celluloid journeys to Mandalay,
They raise two choices: with or without worms.

A breathing tube included, the black casket
Of Bela Lugosi took stardom too far.
Yet quite unlike the pharaohs, no fruit basket
Was furnished, nor the vampire's fancy car.

Nearly 200,000 dead in Japan,
All killed in its meat grinder, World War II,
Fill the largest single grave that man
Has dug, their glory silent on Honshu.

The 5,000-year-old man in melting ice,
Preserved in leather duds by a glacial grave,
A Bronze Age hunter from fields of edelweiss:
Who'd exchange fates with this ancient brave?

Now it's decided he was murdered, too:
A sharp instrument entered through his back.
Did he steal a fellow's meal or merely screw
A leopard skin-clad nymphomaniac,

Who happened to have been sired by his chief—
And death is how the top dog repaid him?
He certainly doesn't seem a common thief,
So maybe plain, old-fashioned sex betrayed him.

One tribe in New Guinea cures a body like ham:
Thus warriors are enshrined for noble deeds.
These shriveled sages stare at life as a sham
Spirit state corrupted by bodily needs.

MOUNTAIN MAN'S SLEEP ENDS AT 9,000 YEARS,
Wryly proclaimed the *St. Louis Post-Dispatch.*
Meantime events in Russia lessened fears
Of Kremlin crazies striking the doomsday match.

This oldest human corpse in the USA,
Found deep within a Colorado cave,
Died one ice age before the *Enola Gay*
Brought airborne death in a world-burning wave.

"A roiling mass of ash in smoke and fire,"
Words of one bombardier recalled the sight.
"And as the cloud erupted eight miles higher,
The colors fumed pink to yellow to white."

Weeks later, he noticed a shape on the tile wall
Of a Nagasaki ruin that still stood,
From a man walking down an office hall,
Whose flesh had turned in a flash to firewood,

Carbonized by heat like a dozen suns.
The figure was left, his being's lone mark
After annihilation's kilotons
Unleashed by a minuscule atomic spark.

They called "atomic shadows" such remains,
A term unknown, unneeded elsewhere:
For residue of coal dust blood and brains,
Which couldn't be removed with soap or prayer.

The sky's big bang melted granite and steel
In furious cyclones of fire that fused rails
And railway cars, quenching the iron zeal
Of a nation all prepared to swallow nails.

What's worse, a blinding light or a dark den?
Dead in a cave, or smoked in a mushroom cloud?
The day you die comes once and only when
The dead decide you join their quiet crowd.

They make the final invite none refuse:
"Democracy means always room for more.
All for one means one for all," they muse.
"Equality once you pass our open door."

"Death's a great democracy," John Donne said.
So who are you to stand against the state,
The mighty people's republic of the dead?
Your date of departure, time will designate.

L *Axle Grease*

"A strange illness of sudden, savage changes,"
Described the Spanish Flu in 1920.
Upwards of 50 million the toll ranges,
Death amazed by unimagined plenty.

A Bay State boot camp met the rasping Blue
Death first, its rising tide of terror clear.
Soon victims spreading the dread ocean hue
Totaled no more in Cape Cod than in Cape Fear.

The contagion leapt like lightning everywhere,
Attacking the healthy in lung-foaming waves.
Some died in hours, some in days, with care
Unable to offer any balm that saves.

Hard cases bled from the mouth, nose, and ears:
Same hemorrhagic symptoms as Ebola.
Useless, medicine's pride or impotent tears,
The most comforting drug was COCA-COLA.

The virus killed more Yanks than combat
In wildly optimistic World War I.
To infect half the earth's a chilling stat:
One billion out of two is quite a run.

650,000 died in the States,
Turning busy streets to ghost towns.
The sick and the well, both in survival straits,
Held voluntary, house by house lockdowns.

In 1920, life expectancy fell
A dozen years, by U.S. CENSUS numbers.
As bad as the Black Plague or holy hell,
The aftermath was hardly golden slumbers.

In two quick years the bug burnt itself out,
Finding no further receptive human prey.
But it left defeated medicine no doubt
Of the victor, come the next Armistice Day.

The disease thrust its reach around the globe.
A like pandemic now could shortly claim
60 million, the mighty microbe
Circle the earth before it had a name.

This according to *The Washington Post,*
Reporting a study in 2006.
The planet's poorest nations would suffer most,
Yet every country's covered in the mix.

60 million's twice the yearly take
Death collects from humanity worldwide:
Enough to rival the previous outbreak
That slew so many a groom and swooning bride.

"A strange illness of sudden, savage changes,"
Some might describe *Tombstone Confidential.*
The narrative disorderly arranges
Its progress, meandering or tangential.

No Particular Place to Go could be
An alternate title, yet end up untrue.
Chuck Berry's song does have the pedigree—
If you're sittin' down at a rhythm revue.

Another candidate is *Axle Grease*,
Inspired by Penny Stallings' *Rock-n-Roll*
Existential, to keep your ride in one piece—
But you can't do right to save your doggone soul.

LI *Stratospheric Ice*

Abruptly, as if tapped with a magic wand,
You make the adjustment any duffer must:
Infinite brotherhood's unbreakable bond
Returns you to your element, the dust.

PALE DEATH ARRIVES WITHOUT DISTINCTION AT
HOVELS AND AT THE PALACES OF KINGS.
HAVANA CEMETERY's gate says that,
Where Che Guevara's monument bell rings.

He died in Bolivia, but no drug cartel
Has tried to ship his body back from there.
Since nothing exists that crime lords won't sell,
Che's bones could be nowhere—anywhere.

"Pale death kicks in the door," Horace said,
The poet to whom the gate's quote is due.
Such distant tribute offered one still read
Warrants his judgement's eloquent wisdom true.

Let every lunkhead honor Horace's verse,
Composed with a superbly delicate touch:
To counter vanished classicism's curse
Upon the bereft for whom gearstick and clutch

Imply a complex train of modern thought,
Civilization's cardinal milestone,
With Horace unknown to drivers self-taught
How progress first began with the telephone.

What whispers through the tops of balsam trees?
The Holy Ghost's flames of unquenchable fire?
Listen hard. Sound like a swarm of bees?
It's not the MORMON TABERNACLE CHOIR.

Hell could break loose, suck the life from your lungs,
All while you trust in—what, to be precise?
The ladder to heaven has 10,000 rungs,
The highest coated in stratospheric ice.

Profound as space itself is that great estate.
You can't ascend propelled by a manic high
To reach the human spirit's golden gate.
The best idea? Grow bat wings and fly.

So what if heaven's streets are paved with gold?
Then everyone there must wear asphalt rings.
"Upward for aye on a dove's wings," you're told?
You learn the truth—soon as the *Sphinx* sings.

Vacation in heaven, or holiday in hell?
A grave decision. Death gives no discount,
Whether you die in shining citadel,
Or stalled between Rock Hill and Rocky Mount.

"Old time religion" thrilled Paul and Cyrus,
Yet virtue eludes a deadbeat fly-by-night.
What chance have living tongues or lost papyrus
To drag your darkling spirit to the light?

The characters' names are really Paul and Silas,
Featured in that happy country hymn.
Brand your forehead with a red-hot stylus,
Still you'd carry through your vilest whim.

It's natural then to question where you stand.
Death shocks the unprepared. —Cigarette?
The ground you walk unsure as sinking sand,
Rejoice in how death cancels every debt.

Admitted, you can't tell quite when it'll come.
As said before, knowing would freak you out.
The closer the day, death's martial drum
Grows so loud, you'd tremble, squirm, and shout:

"God save me! An icy grave and hellfire
I've heard of all these years, yet who presumed
The near approach of both could inspire
Such angst in a man's mind so clearly doomed?

"Forgive the times I betrayed my ugly wife!
My hidden income, taxes I left unpaid!
I never knew I lost eternal life
Every time I skimmed the dough to get laid!"

Forgetting something aren't you, terminator?
The crux confessing your sins can't erase.
Take up your double's disappearance later?
Why wait if the crime is written on your face?

Look right, talk right, walk right, act right, do right:
Simple rules for living free of sin.
Don't kid yourself that you found a new right
To duck the charge of killing your double kin.

In black light, luminal glows on blood stains
A cautious killer thinks he washed away.
Your kisser, though it weathers many rains,
Reveals your double's death by clear decay.

Luminal is phenobarbital,
A sedative used for hypnotic effect,
So darkness brings that power to enthrall
Searching out a crime to resurrect.

Cry foul from a mountain top. It's no more use
Than the piercing squeals of a pig stuck and bled.
And, your theology still a little loose,
It's not for a little sex you turn up dead.

It's not for screwing that weasels rip your flesh;
Not for tax evasion that maggots suck
Your blood and flies transport it to Bangladesh.
You die from living, not from a friendly fuck.

Nonetheless, it's only your parents' sex
That brought you here to waste your life and croak.
Look at it either way: the genital hex
Of why you're born is the world's sickest joke.

Sex and death are critical transit points
Of human being, rites of passage which
Have equal claim. The oil of one anoints
A fetus head, the other's a bloody bitch.

LII *Swiss Cheese*

What envy, greed, indolence, folly, or pride
Would cause you to think you won't be crow bait?
If WHOLE FOODS' butcher must flay your rancid hide,
You'll cease and leave your atoms to circulate,

You hissing, black-ringed viper, you poison burr;
You scale-skinned troll, you skunk-striped centipede;
You vice-cult, drug-crazed fiend, you quill-backed cur;
You mouthful of alum, patch of locoweed.

Your smell's horrific, you nauseating disease,
You moss-haired Martian, you last Vandal extant.
Your putrid lungs pollute the swamp breeze
Blowing trash from the dump by the sewage plant.

Your brain not grown big enough for your skull
Gives your family tree a broken limb,
Making your daydreams inconceivably dull,
Your encephalograms ineluctably dim.

Your pet ideas possess the silent strength
Of used bubble gum stuck in your hair.
And sawing wood for a board of any length
Is your endless geometric nightmare.

Your arms hung halfway down your bandy legs,
Your stride bleakly recalls a caveman of old.
Aren't you part of humanity's worst dregs,
Pretending your pedigree is solid gold?

You lost the sense you were born with. Just like that
It dissipated, fast as a plume of smoke.
Even pulling a rabbit out of a hat,
You can't get smart in a head hard as oak.

Your brain's overloaded, bibliophile.
Your ego wants, your front lobe hears, "OBEY,"
And snaps a Klansman's crack salute, "Sieg heil!"
Blazing a trail to the grave till your dying day,

Yours is company anyone would shun.
This side of hell, your reputation reeks
Like unwashed Gurkhas after days of sun
In Calcutta slums, mending sewer leaks.

You're paralyzed from the neck up, Grand Wizard,
Head Dragon of Lost Knights of Dead Horse Point.
As mascot of Bedlam, or the bughouse izzard,
Your brightest days come from smoking a joint.

If light could peek in your Paleolithic skull,
It would find a stony, squirming snake pit
Where thoughts are tied in knots by your mind's dull
Groping, the choke grip of your sluggish wit.

Only a stroke deep inside your brain
Could disentangle the huge confusion there.
Perhaps a ghost of reason might remain,
If you were held in stocks on the town square.

Then the mockers would keep you on your toes,
Trying to answer their vicious insults
Pecking away at your pride like cackling crows:
No other means has garnered good results.

Was your noggin kicked by a horse, Clem, or what?
Your fixed stare says all you see is stars.
To judge from your blunt, brute's face, you got
Beaten senseless by bands of goons on guitars.

That head-banger music warped your mind, hep-cat:
A punch-drunk case all the king's men can't fix.
Hard rockers lose their hearing. Worse than that,
You lost your brain to a bank of hot licks.

Guitar strings snap, sudden as death can strike.
The sound will cease as quick as your heart stops.
Listen loud on headphones riding your bike,
And wind up as roadkill for traffic cops.

Scratch your scalp and wonder, "Where's the catch?"
"Dead, you become lumber," say the leaves.
You're lumber now, you dense backwoods crosspatch:
Smart as a lineman's IQ worn on his sleeves.

Far as the curse of human dullness is found,
You carry its banner: THIS GUN FOR HIRE.
Your feeble brain waves don't get off the ground,
So weak you wouldn't piss if your pants caught fire.

Did TV whack you with a stupid stick?
Young and dumb, you locked your IQ in,
And your brain graph never shows an uptick.
What you are is doomed by what you've been.

You think a marker pen is instant brains?
Where'd you acquire the notion you can think?
You were born free, yet keep your mind in chains,
Trying to choose the right color of ink.

You suffer from Swiss cheese disease of the head,
A condition known in extinct hominids.
Orphaned when your mortified parents fled,
Perhaps a museum will claim you. —Any bids?

LIII *Love Potion*

Supposing you're about as smart as you look
Raises your IQ over 68.
Leastways you're reading this rude poetry book.
Call your empty features a family trait.

Does your right brain decode your left brain's whim?
Are your thoughts and actions synchronized at all?
Inside your skull, the Stygian gloom is so dim,
You're slow as your Lower Appalachian drawl.

You sound like you just hopped off a produce truck.
Mumbling about the savor of turnip greens
And asking for a bushel of corn to shuck,
Your talk is mushy as mashed butter beans.

To sum things up, you're handicapped in the head.
So far no cure's been found to stop the rot:
No smart drug yet devised to take the lead
Out of your manner, when your mind is shot.

This turning world doesn't move that fast.
Pre-human dross still floats in your gene pool.
Nothing changes lineage, whose present is past:
You're fiftieth cousin to every living fool.

Your brain's not plugged in today, half-wit?
The info is short and sweet: once dead, you're done.
You make yourself scarce, you absolutely split,
Taking leave of this earth's barrel of fun.

The COLLEGE OF KNOWLEDGE tossed you in the trash.
Where will you spend eternity—SMOKING or NON-?
What's your drink of choice, a graveyard smash?
Swill it sucking air like a dying swan.

Go down in history: time's amazing man,
Whose sense of direction sought his own heat death.
Liquor in his blood, trouble in mind, he ran
Round and round chasing his dying breath.

Not some Scots bloke alone on a heath,
Give your closest neighbors a decent break.
There's too much moss on your remaining teeth.
Have a heart and brush them, for Christ sake.

Your halitosis of the soul, so rank
It stains your morning newspaper brown,
Would clear out the GARDEN, close CITIBANK,
And shut PENN STATION's air filters down.

You stink worse living than dead, the warm vent
Of your armpits immensely unattractive.
The first whiff of your Brobdingnagian scent
Makes anybody near you hyperactive.

The touch by God that Adam respired becomes
A vapor of foul corruption on your tongue.
Clean up before civility succumbs,
And social harmony's wholly unstrung.

People will belch, fart, sneeze, cough, and blow smoke.
Exhalation's difficult to escape.
Everyone's tied by breath to the same yoke—
Unless you're wearing SUPERMAN's red cape.

And he must brew his own essential smell—
That is, if he's ever standing still.
Wouldn't you love it, locked in a jail cell
With him breaking wind like a paper mill?

Yet how could SUPERMAN be locked up at all?
His little finger can bend the prison bars.
He'd need to be weakened like the *Dying Gaul*,
By Kryptonite launched from sinister stars.

No GOODWILL thrift-store HART SCHAFFNER & MARX
Used-car salesman's suit for you, huh, Zeke?
The jack to reach the grave in a pool shark's
Bowling shirt is your closest shot at chic.

Your double default breaks your sperm bank, Buck.
Your manhood failing, it won't rise an inch,
Languishing in the hands of Lady Luck,
Who buttons her blouse and flees your growing stench.

Forget about LOVE POTION NUMBER NINE.
Did you read the label or just chug the stuff;
Remove your muddy boots to enter her shrine;
Or shrug her off as a dippy bit of fluff?

Once rigor mortis slips into your veins,
One limb stays limp: the wee one she adored.
From now on he can swell up huge when it rains:
She won't touch him, even big as a surfboard.

His conical cap is no Merlin's magic hat.
Its tingle makes you twinkle like Tinkerbell,
But stardust turns to ashes in seconds flat
When death defies the fairy and queers her spell.

The girls did wonder about your gear, Clint.
Talk spread down the holler, demon lover.
"It comes to smarts," their vicious gossip went,
"God said 'brain,' he heard 'rain,' and run for cover."

No cretin was ever duller, stumblebum.
What gal would run her fingers through your hair,
Call you sugar pie, quiver, and hum—
And be caught dead washing your underwear?

There's nowhere to hide, lacking enough spunk,
So stand and take your lumps, it's the Lord's plan—
Or drift around desperate, lost as space junk.
Death is the same, by bullet or bedpan.

Your mule done balked on Broad Street, brother Dave.
He knows the ground can't wait to swallow you whole,
And the harbor wall can't stem time's tidal wave.
Plus he's not on the coroner's payroll.

LIV *Necktie Party*

Your bubble bursts like a blimp in the Andes,
Landing your expedition, deep in debt,
To descend slopes of 65 degrees.
You walk the earth's tightrope without a net.

What goes up comes down: fundamental physics.
Living draws a bell-curve from playground to pain.
You start, an impish, pigtail-pulling Skeezix,
And end looney and bent as a whooping crane.

Life's zenith caps the crazy climb to the top
Of your test flight from Mother's breast. Your nadir?
Your flying contraption's wings break and you drop
To swing by the neck like a midnight raider.

A midnight raider hanged at Andersonville.
Take a history lesson for once in your life.
The world's all new and modern now, but still,
Learn to whittle while you sharpen your knife.

The Raiders were thieving, homicidal dregs,
Yankee trash in Johnny Reb's stockade,
Where penned like swine and watched like powder kegs,
Sixty battalions had only their shirts for shade.

Men froze in frost, then baked in Georgia sun;
Teeth fell out of their scurvy-swollen gums;
And their gangrene hatched maggots fed by its run
Of pus. Disease and hunger's atrocious sums

Left 13,000 soldiers feeding flowers
Girls should've worn to welcome heroes home.
Screened by night from rifles in sentry towers,
The Raiders ravened with Satan's fine-tooth comb

To stab and strangle for money, clothes, or food.
Traitors down to the blood cells in their bones,
Their deeds bespoke their evil's magnitude.
Undone, they soon outdid their victims' groans.

Their captive comrades tried the felons for tricks
From mugging to murder. Crime put some in chains,
A lucky hundred ran the gauntlet, and six
Swung spinning at rope's end like weather vanes.

In silence the six were marched beneath clear sky.
10,000 wretches ringed the scaffold, and twice
That number covered a slope to watch them die.
This army stood hushed; the dead men broke the ice.

Appalled, they begged for mercy like bleating goats
To mud's mosaic of faces, hell's tableau,
Till anger opened 30,000 throats—
And wave upon wave of vengeance thundered, "NO!"

"NO!" in thunder, boomed the starving throng:
Unanimous condemnation had its say.
The gallows floor fell through, the drop was long:
A jury of 30,000 gets its way.

Six guests at the necktie party danced on air.
The outraged breath of the dead demanded blood.
They bought the farm, paid for it fair and square,
But while their history lasts, these names are mud:

Sarsfield, Sullivan, Curtis, Delaney, Muir,
And Collins made six. You twist in the wind alone.
None volunteered for this earth's mystery tour,
Yet all were born in time's danger zone.

You're snatched by time's riptide, which won't depend
On judgement shouted by 30,000 strong,
But your leaving this scarred world without end
Is just as final, its aftermath just as long.

Once the war was over, Captain Wirtz,
The prison's commandant, was duly hanged.
The march of history celebrates and subverts:
The power of his position boomeranged.

Life's a trial and nobody's innocent, Fats.
Walt Whitman wrote, "Life's a suck and a sell."
From filthy crusted bum to the king of cats,
Man's pecking order goes up in smoke, in hell.

LV *Oral Sects*

"Your dying day is better than your birth
(—*Ecclesiastes*), and you won't break this rule.
If the law measures what a life is worth,
You rate as time's two-headed toadstool.

But breeze on, Jethro. Hell's barely half full.
The Doppler effect deceives when time's freight train
Hits Holy Cross like a megaton bull,
Halfway from Genesis Gorge to Dark Domain.

No whistle blares as the cowcatcher's wedge
Cleaves you. Crushed for the scrap-yard's iron jaws,
You salvage less than a Wall Street window ledge
To sidestep the fall such a crash will cause.

Born either side of the tracks, this wreck leaves men
All equal. Taste liberty and the pursuit
Of pleasure, far from the shade of BIG BEN—
Until the ageless Bunnies give you the boot.

"Liberty or death!" you want? It's both you get.
In the workaday world's concentration camp,
Roam as free as an aimless, shell-shocked vet:
You're stopped by a wrong turn up time's off-ramp.

Such error's danger doubles for a dunce,
Yet duty calls: wear your stripes like a man.
In mansion or madhouse, you're only born once.
At least you weren't choked and chucked in a trash can.

Hired as Gemini stars of a zodiac game—
Your alter ego sired by rapist Zeus—
One twin's myth zapped, the second's stellar frame
Fails as Cerberus bays like a rutting moose.

Jump from the frying pan into hellfire.
Don't think Lucifer ever calls off his dogs.
Your whole life long, those flames keep getting higher,
Their fumes fouler than Mexico City smog's.

As bad-boy tag team of ALL-STAR WRESTLING, Hulk,
Replace your partner, prance and paw at the mat.
The ideal weapon your skull's mammoth bulk,
Try butting heads with the world till it's beaten flat.

Your agent calls you Bighorn Banzai, chawbacon,
Paired with flat-foot fatso, Hammerhead Huge:
Opposing Elmer Overwhelmer from Macon,
And the Reverend Oral Sects from Baton Rouge.

Those two knocked off Joe "Bananas" O'Bane
And Mississippi bigmouth Brain-Wave Dave,
Who had defeated beanpole "Corn Pone" Payne
And Hambone Slewfoot, son of Bugs the Brave.

Bumstead and Bugs licked Sonny Braggadocious
And backward plowman Turkey "Buzzard" Beeks,
Who triumphed over Engelbert Atrocious,
Coupled with the King of Football Freaks.

The Dixie Chicks vs. the Tricky Dicks?
A wish-fulfilling, fight promoter's dream.
A perfect match-up no payoff could fix:
A clash no man considers peaches and cream.

The fans dub you "Big Daddy" Brickwall Bash,
Teamed with "Muleskinner Mauler," Freddy Fudd.
Big Daddy batters his brains for petty cash,
But Freddy's forehead bombs, encasing a dud.

Your adversaries christen you Junkyard Dog,
For cuspids you plant in their balloon biceps.
They name your back-up Hermès the Human Hog,
After his fine diet of truffles and crêpes.

"In red tights, from Waycross and parts unknown,
The dumbest double-clutchers on the east coast!"
The crowd will boo till it wilts your backbone,
Tasting blood like wolves at a wiener roast.

Your foes will focus their force on kicks to the crotch,
Then jab your eyes and karate-chop your throats:
Inspired by the mob's cheers for the chance to watch
A pair of blowhards squirm and squeal like shoats.

Your twin bill a sell-out, you wimps tank the match,
So rotten your double dives like a bullfrog.
Back in the ring alone, you fidget and scratch:
Time grabs your groin, and you fall like a split log.

LVI *Vanishing Point*

Defeat will tender no peace dividend,
You two-time loser. But shrinks welcome trouble:
Your death-struggles fan a suicide trend;
Your deconstruction helps their incomes double.

You bad example, when bookworms feed the fad;
When teens drop like knights in a pageant play;
And moms brand you a villain in nylon plaid;
Network drama casts you as malice per se.

One crime chronicle paints your portrait in mud,
Your profile a smear of soot in *Gumshoe Gazette*.
One sherlock swears homicide runs in your blood,
And MADD rates you a grave security threat.

You're tuned to the wrong channel, no-neck,
If you think death's rerun isn't COMING SOON:
By terrorist bomb, innocent auto wreck,
Or brain clot in bed on your honeymoon.

COMING SOON: NOTHING is the premiere
You'll attend, and it's not a happy choice.
Absent will be a festive atmosphere,
Whether you ride in rickshaw or ROLLS-ROYCE.

Tokyo Rose's mockery failed to work,
Razzing GI Joe with radio flak.
Your bull's-eye kill, no torment's crazy quirk,
Stars you in time's kamikaze attack.

The essence of *kamikaze*? Divine Wind.
Death on the wings of ZEROS born of God.
Finding a target meant a life could end
In fire, instead of before a firing squad.

Slingshot precision fells the giant, your past.
You split the apple with capital crossbow.
Yet in such savior roles, you're badly miscast:
They want Bugs Bunny, not Edgar Allan Poe.

The Masque of the Red Death is more your speed,
Where aristocrats gather against the Plague.
What party-crasher pays their care no heed?
Who waits, as your vigor slowly grows more vague?

Your *Descent into the Maelstrom* is real art.
Its balanced vision on time's cataract's rim
Would help a simple suspense writer look smart,
Whose hope of higher style is horribly grim.

Your kill in *William Wilson*? Even better.
Four words on your flophouse wall square that score.
What legend is stamped upon your *Purloined Letter*?
UNKNOWN, NAMELESS HERE FOREVERMORE.

Poor Wilson, cursed from birth to look like you,
A flaw which earns him embers of hate in your breast,
Quenched at last by your sword. The man you slew?
Stigmata that copy his wounds gash your chest.

His slaying lands you in hell's hall of fame.
SACRIFICED HIS YOUTH, they word your plaque;
HIS BRAIN A TOTAL WASTE OF SPACE, as the blame
On a million tongues burns your eyeballs black.

The killer instinct proves too strong to suppress.
Your parents' brave attempts to tame you flop,
And soon their savage offspring makes a mess,
The self-ruin he lacks the sense to stop.

Your tombstone could be worded, MAMA TRIED.
The countdown to killing time is right on track.
Half your life spent standing at graveside,
The other half is spent watching your back.

SICK VENTRILOQUIST THROTTLES DUMMY. Now
Explain his empty suitcase to the cops.
Perhaps you believe, portraying I and thou,
You'll cover up through doubletalk psy-ops.

The soul train left the station in clouds of steam.
CELESTIAL RAILROAD's never a minute late.
It strands you in Last Chance Flat by a dry stream
And, far as the eye can see, on doom's estate.

The train gone down the tracks leaves you to stare
At the rails' gleaming steel's vanishing point.
The bright horizon of unbreathable air
Lies beyond reach as you wait to blow this joint.

Lost on a checkerboard of parching mud,
You cross life's wilderness just to die of thirst,
Without so much as a single cactus bud
Commemorating that your blood was cursed.

The distant, undiscovered savannas of
The future open after a little hill
Six feet long and one foot high above
Your grave: a prospect felt as the big chill.

LVII *Action Heroes*

You can try offering incense to the moon—
Preferred to blowing smoke rings in the dark—
Then roll your eyes around and loudly swoon:
Your effort fails to grind a single spark

Of insight to decode eternity's keys.
Wrap yourself in electromagnetic fields,
Or memorize the blocks of an antique frieze:
More puzzlement is what the process yields.

Once howling storms of doubt and fear assail,
Sweeping in from distant summer thunder,
Pastures that shone with promise fill with hail
Your scattered nest of thought is buried under.

Dumber than pulse's beat is spirit's speech,
When woe and anguish lie too deep for words.
No mute, unfounded testament can teach
A heavy heart new songs light as a bird's.

If alarm begins boiling up toward terror,
Should you encounter a large litter of bones,
Successfully avoid the karmic error
Of gray rodents who scuttle among the stones.

In sunlight smashing off steep canyon walls,
And an organ sound of wind through the pines,
Don't hide where a hungry owl's wisdom calls
To enforce nature's NO TRESPASSING signs.

Dropped in the sacred forest's dark heart,
As sustenance, you must forage for ferns.
Drinking the blood of a snake is a lost art,
Yet progress can lead to prison and rope burns.

The wild night is swinging high in the trees,
The skin-destroying sun fallen away.
Here you may follow any route you please,
A journey bound back of beyond today.

What if a whale decides to rock your boat,
So now you inhale a belch of his last meal?
Does your life lack the weight of a cork float—
Or right itself with a sturdy, even keel?

By which all advent plunges into the past,
Present happenstance is gone in a flash.
Neither will tomorrow's emblems last.
Thus the flight out of time is windblown ash.

"Right to the end, put off the evil hour,"
Wrote Jonathan Swift in 1738.
Two years later he rocked the bell tower,
Quickly slipping through breath's terminal gate.

"Good-bye, everybody," says Harold Hart Crane,
Then sheds his stylish topcoat and leaps
Overboard to obliterate the pain
Of waking, just as Melville's shadow sleeps.

Crane concludes his poem *At Melville's Tomb*,
"This fabulous shadow only the sea keeps."
Hart held death as his closely watched groom,
To sink his lost verse in the ocean deeps.

"Ah, Bartleby! Ah, humanity!" writes
Melville ending the tale of a quiet clerk
Who furtively sleeps at his desk overnights.
Does the strange bird absurdly love his work?

No, he often refuses a new task,
Responding simply, "I would prefer not."
No sway can peel away his passive mask—
As most ignore the drift of their mortal lot.

Bonnie and Clyde died in love by the gun:
That's happy ending number eighty-nine.
Six-feet-under is destiny number one;
The D-word death is Venus on the vine.

The horses racing underneath your hood
Will make you wish the captive herd could fly,
But action heroes reign in Hollywood.
Uncover earthly guidance from the sky.

Your fingers, groping for the heart of the world,
Disturb the glint of saint-seducing gold.
Your sterling pistol's handle may be pearled,
Yet where the blacktop ends, the lots are sold.

An ordinary, rock revival speech,
The prince of glory offers on demand.
What spirit poles the psyche fails to teach,
The eyes of Texas fix in a burning brand.

Magic peaches of immortality taste
Like any ancient, alabaster peach.
Their intercepted sunbeams fully waste
The emptiness connecting each to each.

Echoing down the corridors of time—
Every one piled high with dead men's bones,
The future that didn't occur sunk in lime—
The citadel of silence breaks its stones.

The temple of time has Doric columns and
Reliefs of long-abandoned fables and forms—
From above the Arctic Circle or Zululand—
All scrambled by backlash winds and sandstorms.

Get out of town with a hurricane on your heels,
For great mountains incline beneath the ocean.
Few stars fall as the tumbling firmament reels,
The pinholed vault of night's abiding motion.

Not senseless heads of a lost civilization—
From the body of their people severed in stone—
But portraits on money by a bankrupt nation,
Suspended in space, all value will disown.

LVIII *Abundant Rain*

You're nobody now, a zero bank account.
Stop at a crossroads, abruptly changing course.
Minutes tick into history and mount:
A steady march of overwhelming force.

From deep inside the earth, destiny comes,
Your journey via shadows of the night,
The odds against you astronomical sums
To enter paradise at the speed of light.

Allow yourself a spell to cogitate.
Let snares grow with the wheat till harvest time.
Right turns to nowhere foil the interstate,
And reaping busy blood is fiction's crime.

Captain Midnight, Sword of Justice, strikes
Terror in the hearts of evil-doers,
Wielding a mace studded by poison spikes
To clean house from City Hall to the sewers.

Can silk sheets form a noose around your neck?
As easily as a roll of barbwire.
You can die by bare hands or by high tech,
Remote control or old-fashioned gunfire.

A forbiddingly dark aura hobbles your mind?
The black cloak of memory drapes your pain.
Your westward gaze will blur and could go blind,
As imagination's absence cracks your brain.

If you see it rain flames from a perfect sky,
This indicates your vision is half alive.
A natural-born killer will catch a fly
And lose it before the scientists arrive.

A doorway to another world for the Celts,
Water is liquid life diluted down.
Every spring, when the icing of snow melts,
Gives ample water for every soul to drown.

Yet water in baptism brings rebirth:
So hordes of true believers all have claimed.
The medium's not the message found on earth,
But only matter, without a heart inflamed.

Does salt hurt nothing save an open wound?
All is vanity, chasing after the wind.
Your autobiography's dish is fine-tuned
To silence, and your wit has never sinned.

Back at the SHADY REST MOTEL again;
Looking for a better spot to get killed;
Wait till the wind dies down first and then
Drink your lethal spirits partly chilled.

To cease upon the midnight with no pain?
An easeful death, if you're lucky enough.
Suffering goes against the modern grain,
But a pleasant voyage ends, the waves turn rough.

Free and clear on this terrestrial ball?
Death underscores the smell of abundant rain.
A condor ascends, then an eagle's fall
Suddenly banks to still a weather vane.

What word is wound in the spiral roar of shells
Washing ashore from beneath the sea's skin?
A waterspout, riding the rolling swells,
Springs up, spun off a circling shark fin.

Will the end of time come in stealth by night,
Or when dancing flames surround your living room?
Emptiness being its own seal, the flight
Of time's a long, accelerating zoom.

You don't have the time, the time has you,
As stellar mystery hides Shelley's heart.
Of all the evidence here, none is more true,
Yet a major question beckons: is it art?

The right environs nurse the wildest fangs:
The Bengal tiger crouches in spiced groves;
Rattlesnakes sun on rock-ledge overhangs;
And Paris's promenades formed the Fauves.

The hour is always now and nevermore,
No less pronounced when roots invade your skull.
The quiet family dead beneath the floor
Traces creation newborn gods annul.

This queer bequest comes off without a sound.
The brain emerges in open-ended fog.
Driving your future down in the cold ground,
Live like a king, until you die like a dog.

You sense it when the headsman's eyes turn dark,
To telegraph you that the king is dead.
Considering life a burden or a lark,
Choose your funeral garment, black or red?

As thunder stumbles, lightning flashes by.
The king is dead, then what? Long live the king.
While souls rejoice that hangmen also die,
Step into the shadows, where hosannas ring.

The king can now go forth among the stars,
Johnny Angel and Tommy Gunn agree.
And living stones will bury burning cars,
As soon as the planets enter phase three.

You drop this robe of flesh and either rise
Sublimely in a shower of clouds, or fall
Through centuries of storms that crystallize
Columns of carrion into a rock wall.

LIX *Cotton Candy*

It's checkmate in DRY GULCH SALOON, Bronco Bill.
Holsters all empty, palms hold mother-of-pearl.
Six-guns will total your fare to Powdersville:
You make it there before their smoke can uncurl.

Staccato shots and a one-way ticket to hell:
The gents are jealous of their drinking space.
Allege some kind of mix-up? They wish you well—
Until they blast you back to your birthplace.

"Hands up!" won't preface their blazing fusillade,
And pleading for time begets a crisp "No dice!"
No warning volley prepares you to meet God,
But lead blows to the body soon suffice.

Those hammer blows aren't like throwing rice.
Nothing to glorify when they pound your flesh.
Not even the fiery trip to paradise
That iced the Waco prophet David Koresh.

Like a clock's hands up in a closing V,
Embracing your end means you reach for the sky.
Your number comes up at 12:53?
Simple. At five and a half past one, you die.

Not pausing to ask questions, Billy Boy,
They pick you off from twenty angles at once.
No Western movie, this is the real McCoy,
With snipers assigned to roofs and storefronts.

Tie up your steed, step inside for a drink:
Firewater, rotgut, or grain alcohol.
The barkeep loves a silver dollar's clink,
So smile and gulp your ammo, back to the wall.

A bottle of courage lifts your spirits some,
And fortifies your soul to no avail.
When bar lamps throb like a fatalistic drum,
For silence guzzle enough to drown a whale.

Yet don't stand if the walls start moving: just
Keep your seat, watching the objects swim.
Try to forget the customers' blood lust,
But doff your hat, should the lights go dim.

Upstairs or down, sample the dance-hall whores.
Spread and explore their lively legs laid bare,
Ignoring a presence inside the swinging doors:
The proof of death, a girl with golden hair—

The painting of Diamond Lil as odalisque
Above the bar, prize of a happier day.
She's now a crone, slowed by a ruptured disc
From breaking beds with boys from the CIRCLE K.

Queen of the velvet virtues, born to please,
Bit by bit she slipped in standing until
She's not far from scrubbing floors on her knees—
Soon the last means of paying her bar bill.

At least she knows the posture pretty well,
After decades working her steady gig.
Yet age can transfigure a blonde bombshell
To a cabbage head in a cotton candy wig.

For years she reigned, the night's unchallenged champ.
Now only art suggests what she was then.
Golden hair turns gray, her little red lamp
Of lust quenched in the hearts of a world of men.

Once over the hill, a whore sees naked truth
Trump Eros every time a wrangler forsakes
Her flaccid arms for the leaner clasp of youth.
An old tart never wins desire's sweepstakes.

The loveliest rose in Texas sparkled like dew,
Home on the range where ranchers and cowpokes play.
Now creased and blotched, she buries her face in goo,
Her beauty restored smooth as liver paté.

The bloom goes off the rose, a pitiful sight,
And rouge is silly, cracked like dried red mud:
Such dark shadows furrowing flesh so white;
Such wilted petals grown from a firm rosebud.

When white hair littered her love-bed, then she knew
Her rhythm was marking time till trade went bad.
Though LADY CLAIROL saves her a john or two,
The older a heart, the harder to make it glad.

LX *Quiet Rage*

Thoughts of her comforted drifters at night,
Whose cosmos linked her to Mom and apple pie.
One wakes beside her today in dawn's new light
And, skin crawling like spiders, zips his fly.

They're all Mae West in the dark, but come daybreak,
Time's assault and battery reconvenes.
Her restless old heart fights a familiar ache
To watch his disgust, brushing dust from his jeans.

Joy in the morning? Quite the opposite here.
Her sunlit countenance like a relief map,
She looks so broken it nearly brings a tear
To his eye. Then she farts a thunderclap.

He pays her, biting his tongue until it bleeds,
Straps on his guns and gathers his saddlebags.
The wooden nickel she flips him as change reads:
BEWARE OF WOLVES, WAR WHOOPS, AND WITHERED HAGS.

Observe her gnarled feet and lumpy legs:
Think how sexy those are on a bright new day.
For business the poor soul bargains, even begs.
Not long now, she'll have to give it away:

"Is that a hole in your pocket, or are you glad
To screw me? Buddy, can you square a dime?"
Her memory's worse, if her looks are bad.
"Why don't you drop dead and ditch me sometime?"

The girls get prettier toward closing time?
Pitch-black dark can't smooth her checkerboard cheeks.
It almost makes you wish there weren't a rhyme
To say her padded PULL-UPS diaper leaks.

"Old women should not seek to be perfumed,"
Archilochus wrote in 600 B.C.
A long way from Texas, yet beauty bloomed
And faded won't attract a honeybee.

Centuries later Horace penned an ode:
"Her wrinkles, yellow teeth, and snowy locks
Leave Cupid cold as a hibernating toad."
Her fallen looks move no hands but a clock's.

Often nature needs a little aid,
Yet after the age of—after a certain age—
Why try to disguise the skin by masquerade?
Better protest against time with quiet rage.

Time transfixes the flourish set on youth
And delves the parallels in beauty's brow,
As aggravating as an abscessed tooth—
Or horrid as Halloween, anyhow.

"Love's Progress" is page one of *Death's Jest Book*,
Providing plenty of fuel for hellfire.
Some comic moments of lust is all it took
For Adam and Eve to found MURDER FOR HIRE.

It's lucky that Eve didn't leave her purse
Behind on a tree limb in paradise.
To pump the blood of life through the universe,
Could man survive expulsion from Eden twice?

She'd go retrieve the snakeskin bag, of course,
Unwisely getting impatient Adam's goat.
He'd gripe at God to grant a quickie divorce,
Thus ending mankind on a sour note.

That is, before Cain and Abel and all:
The sons laying the daughters to reproduce,
10 trillion more trespasses since the fall . . .
These things weren't caused by sipping apple juice.

A premature demise for the human race
Might not have been a bad idea back then,
Giving Jehovah the chance to save face,
And cancel a world already living in sin.

So deeply steeped in sin, this rotten world
Isn't what God imagined or conceived.
Keeping old paradise's banner furled
Could let him down enormously relieved.

But the horses left the stable long ago.
Impossible now to close the barn door,
Considering all the science people know,
And all that art to pay the people's whore.

LXI *Royal Flush*

You and that hail of bullets? A great way to go.
Many a grifter eats lead for his last meal.
As gunpowder conquers your status quo,
Just hope God or the devil cuts you a deal.

Yet Mephistopheles never took to ginks.
Elohim? Tough customer, living or dead.
Recall Passover's old Egyptian jinx?
He smote all firstborns fed the wrong bread.

Stick around; wait for a deal to go down.
These world-class enemies weigh your true worth—
But neither's able to muster more than a frown,
Or lessen the final truth of your bloody birth.

The Rites of Lucifer vs. the High Lama,
NOW PLAYING in any domicile on earth
As realism's antique diorama,
Gives every mother's child a narrow berth.

The Splendor of Truth an encyclical is called
The Pope published in 1993.
Once your teeth are gone, your flesh appalled,
The gruesome truth of death waits under a tree.

Better to have issued a papal bull
Declaring you must die by its decree,
Exhausted by the gravitational pull
Downward into soil or glistening sea.

The rankest idiot, using a borrowed brain,
Knows half life's equation can't stand alone,
And doubting the math would drive a king insane.
The calculus crowds graveyards, cut in stone.

Theology plus geometry are keys
To it all, Ignatius Reilly's mind insists.
Triangle trinity, clear as the ABC's,
Keeps the mad scholar from slitting his wrists.

Identities can't be changed in pure math.
Wasn't Pythagoras first to prove that?
And fingerprints survive an acid bath.
Go incognito, buy a Panama hat.

Past the chance of rescue once you're born,
Midway you get lost in a darkling wood.
Stark as an avalanche on the Matterhorn,
Time bereaves both maiden- and motherhood.

You're watching too many Westerns, Quick Draw.
Miss Kitty kiss your cancer and make it well?
Aged like the dickens, her skin dry as straw,
She haunts the lobby of HEARTBREAK HOTEL.

Her leading man in *Gunsmoke*, James Arness,
Made his debut as *The Thing from Outer Space*,
Playing the monster in Frankenstein dress
He shed to partner Kitty's style and grace.

Agreed that a dying dog was young once,
She still looks ancient as the Dead Sea scrolls.
Reputed for astounding erotic stunts,
Her best trick now is peeping through keyholes.

Had your head examined, Pistol Pete?
It might be prudent at this point in time.
Miss Kitty dwells at the end of Lonely Street—
But could she ever send them in her prime!

Ages since she lounged in HAPPY HEARTS PARK,
Her former firmness cries for an airbrush.
Will she ever get laid again on a lark?
Sure. The next time she draws a royal flush.

Her hair once shone with the luster of spun gold.
Today it resembles vacuum-cleaner lint,
Or a matted, dull gray mass of bread mold:
The color, without the spark, of RONSON flint.

Her house sits at the corner of Lonely and Gone.
A lush who couldn't hit the ground with her hat,
The Death of Hope and Despair she names the dawn;
Calls life "just womb and doom, simple as that."

LXII *Vanity Fair*

"The roses in my cheeks faded," she grieves.
"But who had the stomach to watch them die?
No bandit from Ali Baba's forty thieves
Would rob the beauty I was known by.

"Each fond memory now a blow to my heart—
Me who loved with the breath of all creation—
Increasingly I believe beauty is art.
How else can I endure its degradation?

" 'A cold and lonely, lovely work of art?'
That may still play for *Mona Lisa*, but
The first without the second is why I start
My days with a rusty wrench inside my gut.

"Heaven grants no recompense for my tears
As a woman once certain to drive men mad,
Thrown from pleasure's whirligig by the years,
And ignored by every tinhorn Galahad.

"Pictured in my soul as my steadfast love,
Matt Dillon didn't smear my lip gloss
With the force of passion I was worthy of,
Yet I wasn't about to settle for big Hoss

"Cartwright and his PONDEROSA spread.
For peaks of delight in wild, unceasing joy,
I frankly couldn't imagine him in bed.
He was never quite the complete cowboy.

"Marshal Dillon's strong and silent type
Maintained reserve keeping his heart in check.
My love was free, my body good and ripe,
But he wouldn't wear my lipstick on his neck.

"The heart that loves is always young? How sweet.
Lonesome for a living's the way I feel.
I guess I ought to move to Bleaker Street,
And cultivate a stainless heart of steel.

"Tired of running a cow-town HEARTS FOR HIRE,
I scrapped the fetching, enigmatic look,
And finished peddling ready-made desire.
Thought I'd retire; maybe write a book.

"These days the bumper crop of studs I see
Pass me up like an alligator hide,
Leaves me wondering why I guard my key
To the grave, and don't just die to soothe my pride.

"Peering through the window of lost time,
I know the grass is trampled, the flowers fade.
But nothing less than a pint of vodka and lime
Prevents my ending this with a razor blade.

"The years go by as shadows over the heart,
While death follows its calm, insidious way.
Will welcome trumpets sound for a new start,
Once I take my eternal holiday?

"From fallen arches to gout to gallstones,
Beauty is time's preferred flesh to debase.
Oh, let me sink in the weight of these old bones,
And roll off the edge of the earth into space.

"Age has burnt through me as a dread disease.
Love is blind when all the glamour's gone.
My daylight reflection makes my heart freeze:
A rigid stare, facing myself head-on.

"The disaffection fills my breast with scorn,
And makes the wind sound lonely blowing through.
As a captured sparrow in a cage, I mourn,
Feeling more like the sole of a worn-out shoe.

"The dolor coldly clutching my fruitless heart
Is time over time, age and more age upon age.
It seems like every year the hardest part
Is a birthday that's a bloody outrage.

"A melting birthday cake of fury is
The Daliesque accent the date deserves.
I need a point of view as weird as his
To withstand the shock of my own ruined curves.

"Time stamped its signet on my heedless brow,
I observed, the day the mirror stole my youth.
Yet that was nothing compared to the sorry sow
I now resemble. Can I tell you the truth?

"The very hour I'm sent to my account,
I plan to give God hell for this bad joke;
Quote some stuff from the *Sermon on the Mount*;
And hit him for a divine snort of coke

"To ease my entry into Beulah Land.
Because I quit the path of scarlet sin,
I fell from scratching love notes in the sand
To a rock pile that pocks my splotchy skin.

"For cleaning up my act, my reward has been
A stop at every Station of the Cross!
Does Vanity Fair pity my chagrin
At such a spirit-paralyzing loss?

"A world absorbed in a giddy dream of life,
Its wheels on fire flying down the road:
What does it care for a former alewife
With smoker's throat soft as a barking toad?

"It hasn't even noticed I'm not there,
Much less where my shriveled body is.
That's why I bear a burden the Lord must share:
I figure the blame for this mess is all his."

LXIII *Lone Ranger*

The only way to elude growing old
Is to die young and prove the obvious truth.
Repeat this commonplace a thousandfold,
Still billions cling like clowns to lost youth.

"He whom the gods favor dies in youth"
(—Plautus), recall as senility draws near,
And doc's ready to yank your last tooth:
Longevity was never unvarnished cheer.

Sadder is mourning too long the dead and gone.
Unwept, youth drops its petals one by one.
Does age erase this from the heart at dawn,
And mar it again with each fallen sun?

You can't revive the thrills of yesteryear.
Instead a stranger riding a pale horse
Pulls up beside you and leans over to sneer:
"I'm none you know, your guide back to the source."

Inspector Remorse, in a voice clear as a bell,
Could offer you no better guarantee,
Tolled again by every tongue in hell,
As wind prepares the limbs of a hanging tree.

This isn't the Lone Ranger or Clint Eastwood.
No steely stare, no "Hi-yo, Silver, away!"
He speaks from within a cape's floating hood:
Bright teeth, black sockets, lit like an X-ray.

Your headless horseman is real, Ichabod Crane.
No *Legend of Sleepy Hollow* sings his praise.
A pumpkin? No, he'll toss you a ball and chain
To wear in the halls of hell on warm days.

James Stewart doesn't gallop to set things straight.
Your star on a stallion wears a hood, not a hat.
Why spare you? He wouldn't spare Sharon Tate.
He merely asked her, "What's new, pussycat?"

Is this world, then the fireworks, all there is?
The Lord God gave thee breath, but the end is hell.
From bundle of joy to hell's angel, that's show biz.
Satan's too nice to mind if you stay a spell.

The world's on fire, down in Egypt's land?
The dungeons of damned on old mud-ball Earth,
From Hudson's Bay to Tierra del Fuego and
From Okinawa to the Forth of Firth—

Or rather Firth of Forth—have labyrinths
Joining nations by fiber-optic cable.
Beneath the surface of cemetery plinths
Lies a chaos worse than the Tower of Babel.

The last you hear en route below is your heart
Pound like an angry fist at a murder trial.
"Defense objects!" it shouts at the upstart
Who books you in Pandemonium's mug-shot file.

ID'd first, before they beam you down,
Make sure they match your kisser to your crime.
Smile for the folks or crease an infernal frown.
It's all the same to your ancient host this time.

No hawk-billed U.S. Marshal reads your rights.
Hell's functionaries ignore federal law.
Once their employer gets you in his sights,
He leaves your life an empty man of straw.

Do your damnedest, Luke. It's not enough
To quench the blaze on your final birthday cake.
First you spend ages nailed by a handcuff
To an apple tree beside hell's burning lake.

The second death? You're thrown in the lake of fire.
Practice your backstroke, before they pitch you in.
No stagecraft helps you float by hidden wire,
Swimming in flames that churn, whip, and spin.

Don't scream for aid, weeping in sore distress.
Sheriff Do-Right won't go near those parts.
The local law? His scepter stirs Loch Ness:
The Prince of Darkness, dressed as King of Hearts.

Hell's not on your map? Then make a wish:
"Pilgrim homeward bound has a small request:
That the hands of time fan out like a starfish,
So life's illusions never lose their zest."

Time has no less than absolute control,
Through the motion of every molecule,
Over every single living soul.
You should've been taught this in grade school.

Time is the worst that happens, nowhere man.
The shekels you squirrel away won't help much
To buy stock in eternity's savings plan,
Your time-share just right to leave you in Dutch.

You have to be stationed someplace in time.
Otherwise your bathos wouldn't exist.
Then cloaked in sable or soaked in organic slime,
You vanish as if your mom were never kissed.

It's appointed unto man at last to die,
And after that the judgement, ready or not.
Rocking the cradle of death, what lullaby
Deludes you with glad horizons, hotshot?

In essence you've been a doubly marked man
Since the doctor cut your umbilical cord,
Presenting you a limited lifespan
Enforced by time's omnipotent landlord.

LXIV *Epoxy Lips*

That's hash on your plate. Dig in, cowpunch.
The chuck wagon won't serve you chili chow mein.
It cooks grits for breakfast and grease for lunch,
Dinner a heart attack on the gravy train.

You're better off to skip a BLT.
Why not try leaf of lettuce on toast?
Reduce your bloodstream's gummy sludge debris,
To delay the end whose claim is uppermost.

"Howdy there, maverick, what'll it be—
A gob of spaghetti and a quart of cow?
This time tomorrow, you could reach home-free,
Since today you're almost dead, so take a bow."

Cholesterol has squandered plenty of chips,
Sending fat crapshooters forever home.
"The circle is perfect," say death's epoxy lips,
"From teething to toothless, birth to the bed of loam."

Those lips' lamprey kiss clamps down to drain
Your being dry as epidermal dust—
With Junior silenced, the youth in your voice slain—
And leave your likeness cold as a bronze bust.

To be sure, a bronze bust will never be made
To mark a passage meaningless as yours.
This poem's the only place you'll be portrayed—
But not kept in stock at decent bookstores.

And here's a puzzle Sherlock Holmes can't solve:
Wherefore someone cares to read about you.
Why the grit to persist doesn't dissolve
Long before now is strange as Xanadu.

Chronology saps your nerve endings numb.
No Mountie spots you freezing and stops his sled;
No St. Bernard saves you with demon rum.
Wandering trackless waste will equal DEAD.

It's life's great letdown's killer psychic quake,
On a scale from SCARED to WHOLLY TERRIFIED.
You can thank progress that you're spared the stake,
Yet half a chance exists you do get fried,

So cross your fingers. Pity Mom's disgrace,
Her baby's picture splashed on the front page,
And the tragic tears which thrust her last embrace
Trembling through the bars of your prison cage.

It's high time you got the hell out of Dodge,
Before your odor draws the hounds to your trail.
And don't hole up at the old MASONIC LODGE:
It's now the EBENEZER COUNTY JAIL.

Run, black sheep. Wash in the blood of the Lamb
At rescue shelters, so Mom dies in peace.
Trust your instinct, grab your knapsack and scram,
If a nightmare wakes you sweating cold grease.

Take the back stairs and drift into the wind:
Disappear while dew is still on the roses,
Dogged by the fateful crime you can't defend.
A fugitive's best escape route soon closes.

"Seabiscuit raced with fire, slash, and zam,"
One sportswriter vowed in 1938.
If apprehended crossing a TVA dam,
You took too long to beat it out of state.

Seabiscuit's speed, "kissing the boys good-bye,"
Is nothing you can attain, yet try your best.
You'll never be known for doing anything sly,
But move heaven and earth avoiding arrest.

With age carving a road map down your face,
Your vicious crime's more obvious week by week.
Leastwise you can give the law a good chase,
So don't choke on that chaw stuck in your cheek.

LXV *Morning Dew*

The telegraph gave electric life to his name
When Billy the Kid shot his way out of jail.
Of course, this set up the famous endgame:
Pat Garrett would hammer his coffin's final nail.

A broadcast flash can finger you as well,
Blanketing your range of getaway space.
A manhunt will land on you with a rebel yell,
And close a world of freedom you won't replace.

The FBI will blast an APB:
"Inbred boob on criminal death trip.
Likely origin eastern Tennessee.
Cold-blooded killer. Can't let him slip.

"Not sought for mutilating cats, 10-4?
Nor for giving his wife a cliffside shove.
The rap's not knocking over a liquor store:
He's charged with slaying the self he did not love.

"Issue him a cease-to-exist order,
And once it's done, let us in on the fun.
Use any handy video recorder,
So we can view how you give him the gun."

LONE ODDBALL CUTS DOWN DOUBLE POINT-BLANK,
A *Nashville Banner* headline screams in red.
So what if they show you masked, robbing a bank?
The story doctored, your double is still dead.

WANTED DEAD OR ALIVE, posters will say,
And your photo prints like Bigfoot in overalls.
A fat reward the Feds are ready to pay
The jasper who clamps a bear trap to your balls.

HAVE GUN, WILL TRAVEL, bounty hunters think,
Spying your puss on a courthouse bulletin board:
"This hombre's dingbat kingpin of BONEHEADS, INC.
He won't outrun our souped-up '60 FORD."

They search the land through hailstorm and fire,
Stalk your monster footprints in muskeg and mud.
Their tank's doors emblazoned HELL FOR HIRE,
To the four winds they follow you like a flood.

Or moving silent as the morning dew,
They ferret you out way back behind the sun.
Down desert dirt roads, their tracks pursue
Whatever jobs Dick Tracy leaves undone.

Exhaling tongues of flame, they seethe and swarm
Like ants whose mass idea is seeing you dead,
As thousands of lightning strikes in DESERT STORM
Bombed Iraq till the clouds billowed red.

BAD NIGHT IN BAGHDAD, read one wry headline:
"Iraqi fireworks filled the sky overnight,
Unable to touch the hated U.S. swine,
Whose smart missiles rained as letters of light."

A burning shroud of laser-guided fire
Dropped upon the Mesopotamian plain.
Enemy guns, foiled by the Yankee flyer,
Missed the direct dispatches to thousands slain:

Overnight letters, cyber-controlled,
Though none could reach the beast Saddam Hussein.
The sly dictator kept on wearing his gold,
And switching the circuits of his brutal brain.

The fury of airborne bombardment pounds
Like godless thunder bursting from the earth,
While anti-aircraft artillery rounds
Scatter as seeds of war's infernal birth.

Saddam always retained at least three doubles,
Through plastic surgery doomed to bear this curse,
Who spent their idle hours blowing bubbles—
And riding in a chauffeur-driven hearse.

Late or soon, the dead undo the Saddams
Blackening history down to the present day.
Who scorns to tread upon the fronds of palms
In a dance of life brushing the worst away?

Pilots weave thru Baghdad's scorching skies,
One daily phrased it in 2003,
When Saddam's regime of plunder, rape, lies,
And regular mass murder ceased to be.

Still no earnest conclusion neatly comes,
No grand victory speeches served by the slice.
Death tolls persist in yielding larger sums,
Sticking to the flag like beggar's-lice.

No wizard can foresee the final price.
It's not the easy invasion but the end
Which ought to steady the hand tossing the dice,
As the showboat rounds another river bend.

Tyrants prefer their power absolute,
Yet time erodes all things and does not fail.
The mocker mocked, a despot gets the boot
Pursuers plan, once they pick up your trail.

LXVI *Headless Snake*

"Calling Eumenides," command will bark.
"The suspect wears blue boots, a pink beret,
Purple jeans whose rivets glow in the dark,
And a vest embroidered, KILLER'S HERE TO STAY.

"He's driving an old DODGE with antique plates,
Approximate model 1956.
His sin's a shame to these United States,
His tongue as forked and foul as Vegas Vic's.

"He radios, throwing posses off the scent:
'Break—I'm *The Unnameable*—over and out.'
So far he's kept the cash reward unspent,
Wearing a cloak of insouciance, no doubt.

"From Choo-Choo Town he fled to Muscle Shoals,
Was spotted in Wichita, then San Antone.
All forty-eight have tripled their STATE PATROLS:
Now run like the sun covers a time zone.

"Bring home the bacon, you vultures, cooked or raw.
We'll bake him black and grind his bones to ashes.
Once he was sighted south of Saginaw,
But kill with care: a headless snake still thrashes.

"Next seen in Opryland on the super slab,
Then showed up bangin' a U-ey, downtown Big D.
One tip said, 'Shovelling coal past a cab
In the bullet lane for Watergate, D.C.'

"Texas Rangers are banned south of the border,
So onward into battle: shoot to kill.
'Destroy with extreme prejudice.' That's the order.
The prize a bushel of greens, send us a bill.

"Last lead was Cigar City, Bikini State:
Ran like a dog for the Everglades, looks like.
Radar's blank, but Smokey smells bear bait.
Now copy the mail, and keep an open mike."

Ernst Barlach's bronze *Avenger* can't top them,
His flying wedge and sword a wicked slice.
And all the cows in Texas couldn't stem
The mad momentum to put your soul on ice.

NO STONE UNTURNED: their creed for dealing death
To slime and scum they chase for daily bread.
Don't think of stopping long to catch your breath:
Run yourself ragged, better than slow down dead.

Dubbing their operation SONS OF THUNDER,
They name their F-CAR *Backfire Bomber*, Slim.
Studs on its tires like tank treads pull you under
To chew you to shreds, ripping life from limb.

If hell on wheels runs you off the road,
It's all but over, *la dolce vita* mute.
They mine your veins like silver's Comstock Lode:
You cross your Great Divide, they claim the loot.

"That's one less KO'd killer more to go,"
The bullnecked bounty hunters text the Feds.
"Remit our fresh blood money, now you know,
And next time sick us after some dirty Reds."

Their grinning pursuit hotter than blue flame,
They rumble in a tightening dragnet.
Like an old mule, you're glue if you turn up lame.
You're meathead stew before you wipe your sweat.

A goner, numbskull, into a world of dirt.
Is your double downfall jive? Time kids you not.
You're roadkill soup if you don't stay alert:
They'll cook your corpse in the devil's dinner pot.

LXVII   *Catholic Shrine*

Destiny turns the radio on and *bam!*
Empty words to fill the empty air?
Some chance informant uses INSTAGRAM
To catapult you to the electric chair.

Your spastic colon gauges your alarm?
Intestinal strength won't defeat this foe.
Squirm like a worm from the law's limber arm:
Try disappearing deep in Mexico.

Pickled in tequila, go bananas.
DT's will change a drunk with vertigo
To Davy Crockett. But don't knock Santana's
Daughter up, or mention THE ALAMO.

Yep, Davy Crockett, king of the wild frontier.
While wondering who what why when and where,
Fantasize that your scalp is in the clear
If Davy bags a big enough bear.

And watch for *federales*. Do you suppose
They can't smell rats pass gas like rotten eggs?
Belching whiskey fumes under their nose,
Head to a lost haven for outlaw dregs.

Mr. 666 in Stockholm, Sweden,
Counts you as his disciple when he disputes
What really happened that last day in Eden.
He claims Eve was eating peyote roots.

Hiding in Mexico, living in bad dreams,
TECATE chasing tequila through your brain,
Concoct a batch of screwy stick-up schemes,
And avoid Pancho Villa's new campaign.

Cover your ears, should Pancho appear perchance.
His men would cut one off to keep you in line.
Be cautious asking señoritas to dance:
CANTINA MARÍA's a strange Catholic shrine—

And a good cause to hurry home to the States.
Confusing the cops' offense is full-time work.
Uncertain how extradition translates,
Sneak back and lie low as a grocery clerk.

Next, prepare to resume life on the run:
Nowhere's safe in the world of videocam.
A shoplifter can kill you without a gun,
If the scene's background shows you stocking SPAM.

To flee, smudge your cheeks, wear combat fatigues.
When the wind barks bloodhounds, bear down and vamoose.
Fear the hardball played by the law's big leagues.
You're captured and tried? Payback yanks your noose.

The Gang of Twenty-One Faces in Japan
Taunts the police in notes designed to enrage.
Your two-faced front is a far simpler plan,
Your wit too weak to lessen the force of age.

To count past ten, you have to remove your shoes.
Ten toes later you're completely stumped:
Fresh out of numbers and fresher out of clues,
As twenty-one leaves your reckoning trumped.

I Was a Fugitive from a Brain Gang,
The book your depraved career of crime has wrought,
Foretells the defense on which your hopes will hang:
No presence of mind; total absence of thought.

LXVIII *Twilight Zone*

Cornered by G-men, grab your only chance:
Pry off your mask and pray they hold their fire.
Your future under arrest? No tap-dance:
You stand alone on justice's high wire.

They haul you in for a fat sergeant to ask
What kind of butcher the dicks dumped in his lap.
The precinct captain, raising a pocket flask
To toast your visit, declares your case a wrap.

"Who's the creep, with a far-off cross in his eyes:
The weird hex, the spear-like, wounded gleam?"
"He's king of the news: FADED STAR IN DISGUISE:
FLED FROM ROLE IN FATAL COMEBACK SCHEME;

"SOUGHT FOR KILLING SELF OR EVIL TWIN.
A court must now decide the bizarre truth.
Both ways his double fault, shedding his skin,
Proved him a figure worse than John Wilkes Booth.

"There's no jail in the country bad enough
To house the author of such ignoble acts.
He's real cocky tonight, but that's a bluff.
Wait till a jury gets its hands on the facts."

A product of poor breeding you may be.
Should you indeed ever have been born?
What you're in for here is the third degree,
Where yonder breaks no new and glorious morn.

It's after eighteen years of drunken hell
That a bare cell in a cold police station
Makes you breathe your overpowering smell,
And defend your crime's unpremeditation.

In stir detectives swarm around like sharks.
Their insults and blinding lights turn you green.
Ignore how the chinless, chief bulldog barks,
And use the *Miranda* rule: don't come clean.

Wheels will grind to send you up the river
Posthaste, so take the fifth, clam up, and hope
That ill fortune's arrows emptied their quiver,
While God forgets a low-brow misanthrope.

No, better still, launch a preemptive strike,
Plunging disorder into the whole scene.
Once in custody, swing for the bleachers, Spike:
Jabber like a human jumping bean.

"I wish to file a missing person report:
My misspent youth is lost on an endless binge.
If he doesn't surface soon, I'll go to court
And get him declared dead without a twinge

"Of conscience and without a whiff of guilt.
I regret, however, the wastrel has no name.
He used to live in the house that Jack built,
Long before he began this fool's game.

"Truth is found at the bottom of a well.
Justice must be done, though the sky falls.
I'd tell you more yet never learned to spell,
And anyway, I'm afraid nature calls.

"There's nothing I can do about it now.
I wash my hands of the reprobate for good.
And on that point I give my solemn vow,
If only because I believe I should.

"The fact may be he's gone to his reward.
Indeed his life was hardly without spot.
I trust I'll find you in complete accord,
And further this deponent sayeth not."

Think fast talk will cheat the law, cheapskate?
Your neck's in a noose for blood you can't disown.
No help in hell cuts rope and cleans your slate,
As you dwell in time's dimming twilight zone.

Despite crystal cathedrals believers build,
You'll never drive your demon out the door.
What if you fail to recall the man you killed?
Well, what do you think birth records are for?

Get smart and swear your twin couldn't relate?
No wisecrack stirs this judge: she won't postpone
Your trial, abruptly setting an early date
To hear the evidence, since your cover's blown.

LXIX *Cowboy Complex*

How about your special aggressor genes?
DNA analysis proves that twins
Share them, so don't try to invoke caffeine's
Harmful effects, as the wheel of fortune spins.

Find a good lawyer quick for your crazy case.
You're done for, lacking a savvy mouthpiece.
He'll help you seem less beastly, Baby Face,
Dressing his lamb in disinfected fleece.

Your alibi? You like to impersonate.
With NOVOCAINE nerves, look innocent, relax.
Fake appearing benign as a milk crate,
No motive known why Brother got the ax.

The ugly bumpkin rubbed you the wrong way?
One varmint less to crowd your sawdust pile?
His baggage made your tree house creak and sway?
Your only answer's one more stupid smile.

"The accused suffers severe absence of taste"—
You benighted, mealy-mouthed, dead-end kid.
Pretend your childhood left you a moral waste?
They throw the book like a buzz saw at what you did.

To escape the chair, play your big scene straight.
Dispute the facts; say the mirror lied.
In case a frame-up proves the time and date,
Style yourself a junkie Jekyll and Hyde:

"Plagued by poltergeist, gnawed by thoughts of knives,
I fear an impostor seized my heart and soul.
If it please the court to credit a cat nine lives,
I'll reincarnate myself and come back whole.

"Railroading me like Sacco and Vanzetti,
Ever wonder why the heathen rage?
Because they know I'd never be so petty
As to kill an obvious phony half my age."

Won't play in Peoria, stooge. Seek a change
Of venue, then quickly switch to a new tack:
That AMERICA—LOVE OR LEAVE IT! sounds strange,
Since Washington was born in a two-room shack.

Like Richard Nixon, you don't have a dog's chance
To dodge the charge unless you lie through your teeth.
Deny the likeness, vowing the goofy trance
Of your fool's features conceals a clown beneath.

"I've seen the name; unable to place the face.
Down in Dalton, I heard him mentioned once.
Sorry, but I can't help you solve this case:
My sole crime is being a hopeless dunce."

Show them you're cracked: mirrors confound your mind.
You took the deceased for Alfred E. Neuman,
A moron masking a mutant Freud defined
As an ape with a cowboy complex, half human.

Billy Joe Bludgeon and J.C. Hatchett got off:
Tossed in CESSPOOL ASYLUM to unwind;
Wallow in crap, swill slop at a trough;
And curse the killing, cannibal ties that bind.

Sammy "The Bull" Gravano got a new face
From the Feds, once he caved and spilled his guts,
But you command no gangster power base.
Better convince them you're completely nuts—

A prize whacko, a mind demolished by booze:
"I sped through Bonkers Bend on blind impulse."
The shrewd D.A.'s bent on exposing your ruse?
Throw him a curve—a spitball! Drool, convulse

When cross-examined. Scream, "This slander's hurled
At God's own servant, disguised as Bugs Moran
To stage Judgement Day at DISNEY WORLD!"
Spread your arms and cry, "Behold the man!"

LXX *Good Neighbors*

Don't stop when shock and surprise sweep the room.
Stick to your guns, not giving a good goddamn.
Rant in the witness box, a prophet of doom:
"Repent and write me a check! I AM WHO I AM!

"A ticket to a criminal crapshoot
Brought you to savor my defense destroyed.
You assumed I'd simply watch and sit here mute,
Yet I'm pleased to see you, truly overjoyed.

"Before a dark and disbelieving world,
I hold myself aloof from the mass of men.
Raising the blood-stained banner of Christ unfurled,
I've found myself innocent time and again.

"To save a fool like me, he kindly died,
Washed my sins away in his cleansing blood.
None but our maker knows how hard I've tried
To reach you sheep swimming in Noah's flood.

"Explain your daily stance toward Jesus Christ.
The gates of heaven have only the one key.
Regardless the way your soul food is sliced,
You can't refute a witness real as me.

"Prepare to follow the hallelujah trail!
O ye the lost, this is what breaks the heart:
Your life is merely a liquidation sale,
Where Satan enjoys a major head start.

"Held so hard by the dark part of your soul,
Drop your net on the other side of the boat.
Discover the portal of time's through-hole,
And sever the hands locked around your throat.

"We must let justice roll on like a river,
Righteousness like a never-failing stream.
I nominate myself first to deliver
Upon the promise of this mighty theme.

"More than once, I've stood on the stairs to hell,
And turned my frightened face to glory's light.
Maybe I stumbled, some might say I fell,
Yet I'm here now to put this planet right!

"Are you ready for the Rapture? Say amen!
Ready to lift your soul to the blood throne
And go to Zion tonight? Amen again!
Ready to pull the sword from the blarney stone?

"Have you made news in heaven today, my friends?
The love of God's the best of all good things.
DEATH IS CERTAIN—LIFE IS NOT commends
Its meaning to your expectant heartstrings.

"Cyclone Mack and Billy Sunday raved
At a doomed and dying world that paid no heed.
Thousands were lost, yes, thousands more were saved,
And still the earth's perpetual wounds bleed.

"Can't you see you're all the stuff of sin?
It's slipping through your hands like fine sand:
Your chance to change forever what you've been.
You think I'm crazy? Judge, strike up the band!

"Your sins will creep as a flame in short grass,
Until you stand within a bonfire blaze,
Persuaded that you deserve a free pass:
ADMIT ONE TO THE DOUBLE DEVILS MAZE.

"Stop the music! All the credit's his!
I know my soul was never lily white.
I'm not worthy, but serve the one who is.
Because he lives, I'm ready to die tonight!

"Jesus was the founder of rock-and-roll,
Rolling back the stone that sealed his crypt
By activating God's remote control.
Don't try to tell me the big rock just slipped.

"Through death to everlasting life he passed,
And there he drinks the milk of paradise.
The universe began as a bomb blast:
Now heaven includes the whole for ONE LOW PRICE.

"Yessir, Jesus was always a Rolling Stone.
'Have you seen your mother stand in the shadow?'
Jagger and Richards mastered his baritone
At a BURGER KING in Boulder, Colorado.

"Because I live, my deeds are led astray,
Yet yours top all the devil's ever seen.
If you resist this truth and cling to clay,
That's between you and God. My hands are clean.

"Trade your JACK DANIEL'S for Calvary's wine,
And a shaft of golden gospel sunlight.
The hosts of evil around you are serpentine:
You have to chop their heads off every night.

"I sure can't shove salvation down your throats.
Too old to cut the mustard anymore?
O sinners, some shit sinks and some shit floats.
To smelt gold, good neighbors, you must have ore!

"Sin's black rippling water is spreading out,
As age keeps track of your remaining days.
To help repel the dark despair of doubt,
Stay well clear of culture's latest craze.

"I won't repeat myself, so write it down.
And while you're at it, visualize this:
Jehovah's anger blazing fierce, his crown
Ringed by wrath as bands of angels hiss."

LXXI *Simple Sentence*

"Looking forward to the end of time,
Let us wait for Resurrection morn—
Although our flesh by then is dirt and grime—
To judge the first-hand evidence I have sworn.

"Meantime I want an audience with the Pope.
I figure he and I might get along.
He alone will comprehend the scope
Of how you folks done treated me all wrong.

"The FULL GOSPEL SOLID ROCK TEMPLE OF
SALVATION has its own special take
On steps to reach the golden throne above:
Stomping their feet to make the temple shake.

"At the FACE OF GOD DIVINE DELIVERANCE CHURCH,
They told me the Pope is God's classiest guy.
Why would he leave a prize like me in the lurch,
Who offers splendid witness to glorify?

"The RUNNING RIVER OF LIFE TABERNACLE
Declares the vilest dregs can get redeemed,
Hooked by the Holy Scripture's bait and tackle—
Or is this some empty nonsense I dreamed?

"From AMAZING GRACE ACRES TRAILER PARK,
Blown to bits by cyclone in thirty seconds,
I learned the Lord's bite is worse than his bark,
And no one owns the chart by which he reckons.

"The UNITED MINISTRY OF OPEN ARMS
Sees all things joined through invisible bonds:
Serial killings linked by magic charms,
And ice cream tied to disemboweled blondes.

"THE MOUNT SINAI HOLINESS CHURCH OF
DELIVERANCE claims lineage back to Moses.
Now as I conclude my lesson of love,
Where are your thanks, my dozen white roses?"

Your sermon boosts the insanity defense,
Yet no place wants your kind around at all.
They wish your simple sentence would commence:
An alternating current thunder ball.

So change strategy: stare like a zombie; swear
You never favored the corpse in your born days.
A courtroom trick, you renounce the whole affair,
As amnesia spreads an alcoholic haze.

Deny the charges and stand there empty-eyed,
Your dark, duplicitous mind striking you dumb.
Or term it justifiable homicide,
A fine public service to murder the bum.

Throw yourself on the mercy of the court,
If all your impudent, wild tactics fail.
"I wish to draw a card of last resort,
Having been belched from the mouth of a whale.

"I should've killed myself," you want to say,
"And not my image many years ago!
But I was a younger then, and so today
I stand before you and sing, *alive, alive-o!*"

This long shot quotes worse odds than euros to yen.
What back-room bookie beats Jimmy the Greek?
The press will write you off with underspin:
"We find no defense logical to critique,

"Bombastic madness his best hope in the case.
To soften the guilty verdict's outcome,
Here's one positive factor he could embrace:
They can't execute you for being dumb."

The game plan flops? Now your joints are jammed
In a tense, judicial struggle to stay alive.
Your door to tomorrow has been firmly slammed:
Legal tradition since 2005.

A bitter result, the Lord's ways are queer.
Count your blessings the trial won't rouse a mob:
Vigilantes consider you small beer.
Now drink your milk. No hemlock ends this job.

They'd eagerly string you up, otherwise;
Hang you high on the road to Mansonville;
And damn your defense as a howling pack of lies,
While vultures patiently watch from Peckham Hill.

"That's all, folks!" the hangman would gladly shout.
"What hit him?" "A complete state of death."
"There's really nothing left to jaw about."
"All his tomorrows departed with his breath."

He'd say, the night your lights went out in Georgia,
"Zero's the chance we hanged an innocent man:
Not merely suspect like Lucrezia Borgia,
But guilty as sin, savage as Caliban."

You swinging there all alone and dead,
The buzzards would start at your head and work down.
While meat remained, they'd be happily fed,
The sun beginning to bleach your bone crown.

LXXII *Jailhouse Rock*

Keep hope alive by sparking some legal sport.
Your double jeopardy signals a fascist plot.
And bank on a base of underdog support:
Appeal to four high priests of flesh and pot.

Their folk tribunal pulls no moral weight:
Tim Leary, Hefner, Madonna, and Gorgeous George.
Yet counsel can paint *Screwball vs. State*
As the vilest threat to freedom since Valley Forge.

The ACLU leaps to lead your cause,
Your wagon hitched to a star-studded plea.
They deem their client immune to unjust laws
Of nature: the nitwit wouldn't hurt a flea.

Your imbecilic stature feeding their zeal,
They ride to the rescue on procedure's back,
To spring you from imprisonment's ordeal
In the land of the free, home of the BIG MAC.

The brave campaign your white knights will mount,
Pro bono paladins picking a paper fight,
Is an iffy venture. Ask tomfool to count:
Your fate belongs to four kooks' mental blight.

Blindfolded Madonna moons you, thumbs down.
Doc Leary abstains, as his nirvana soars
With Hefner's addled by a cocksman's crown.
But George roars like a lion, on all fours.

The verdict hung, the tally's one to one,
Stranding your last-ditch rally high and dry.
Your faith in the courts is wholly undone?
Then logic's course is clear: curse God and die.

The landmark judgement buries you in jail.
You face the music, the law ties up loose ends:
Shuts your Pandora's box with a penny nail,
The hammer echoing for your death-row friends.

They call it justice, punk, so climb the walls.
While networks film you slumped in prison stripes,
And anchors quiz you if time flies or crawls,
Rest from your monkey act on the ceiling pipes.

No ELVIS ALIVE IN LIMBO!'s *Jailhouse Rock*—
Instead a wailing ballad by Lorna Doome—
Weaves through the hand-held bars of the whole cell block,
Each man locked like a rat in a shrinking room.

Your appeal dismissed, time's EXIT light
Foretells your leaving God's superstore,
The penitentiary branch. Fainting in fright,
Condemned colleagues groan and twitch on the floor.

The eleemosynary ORDER OF ELKS
Wants your dead head perched on a flagpole.
The WORLD COUNCIL OF CHURCHES' Joan Jelks
Prays the devil's dog devours your soul.

The JUNIOR LEAGUE would cover you with ants,
The UNITED WAY bury you alive.
The SIERRA CLUB would feed you poison plants,
The RED CROSS drain your veins in a blood drive.

How do you reckon, judging from afar,
News you're about to die will make you feel?
However brave and dumb you think you are,
It melts your mind as a blowtorch burns steel.

And neither mind nor blowtorch aids escape
From a cell secure as a vault at FORT KNOX.
Bang on the bars till your bedpan changes shape.
The only progress your plaint brings is the clock's.

The next take is your chance for earthly pardon,
But your end of the STATEHOUSE hotline won't ring.
Ever since Adam and Eve left the garden,
The Governor saves execution's sting

For partners in crime with Cain and AUSCHWITZ.
So plan your last meal: sausage and sauerkraut,
Brains and eggs, or tea and cake from the RITZ?
They grant your wish, then blow your candles out.

KILLER'S CONDITION GRAVE, the *Post* will report:
GOVERNOR GLOOM REJECTS LOCO APPEAL.
MAD DOG SHOT DOWN—NO MORE DAYS IN COURT,
The *Globe* proclaims, and the *Tribune* gloats, NO DEAL!

ONE MORE LAST CHANCE!? Not what the headlines shout.
Once they're printed, you barely have time to blink.
Praise God if the jailers let you read about
Your last hope lost, yet don't even try to think.

Then taste your own medicine, renegade,
The smack sour as rancid Tuscan red.
You'll wish it was wine, not American-made
Voltage rolling your eyes back in your head.

The shock of your life stops your oxygen, slug:
It's no sea cruise that takes you out of this world.
The singing switchman toasts you, turns up his jug,
Then pours on juice till your pubic hair's uncurled.

LXXIII *Mighty Thor*

If the ending finds you in a sullen mood,
That's easily understood, given the facts.
But keep your composure, facing certitude:
Positive jolts, while negative counteracts.

The padre gone, your last words close the book.
"Blame this matter on O. Reginald Scinn.
God is my witness: I never liked the crook,
Who robbed my cradle and claimed me next of kin.

"First cheating in school and sports, I quickly moved
To breaking the speed limit, then cocaine.
I woke to my life half over. Time proved
I'd killed what I loved, born without a brain.

"To those who make the same mistake, I say:
It's getting late; you too become plant food.
You nailed the wrong guy, so cross your hearts and pray.
Father, forgive them, they know not whom they screwed.

"O, fill me with fire, where I singe in shame,
To teach these slimy bastards some respect,
Who act like deciding guilt's a card game,
Leaving my hereafter completely wrecked.

"The error done this day shall soon return
To deal you blood-sport junkies justice denied.
Closely observe my hair and toenails burn,
And learn my lesson from death's other side.

"One parting thought for all you spotless souls:
Whether as billionaire or street sweeper,
Your days a bed of roses or burning coals,
Each of you will dance with the Grim Reaper.

"So long to life. I start eternity now.
My name was Everybody-and-His-Brother.
Yet don't fixate on this, or crease your brow:
After my present death, there is no other.

"I heard tell of the streets of gold beyond
The crystal sea and figured I'd take a look,
But all I found was a scum-covered pond,
Which ended my dalliance with the Good Book.

"Well, that's enough of my high-minded talk.
Your pleasure today would see this fish fry.
With one more river to cross, watch me walk—
And to celebrate, I'll drink the town dry."

Suppose death row hosted your twin instead.
Harper's reports that doctors in Ecuador
Save some from fatal snakebite, raising the dead
By power surges worthy of mighty Thor.

Jump-start your victim back from death's brink?
Cured of your venom by 50,000 volts,
He'd cheat Old Sparky, slyly smile and wink.
Outdone, the warden frees your shackle bolts.

"Hey, tell 'em Killer's back," you'd razz the press.
"He ran God's gauntlet riding the third rail.
Electrocution failed, so now I confess
Committing untold crime on a vast scale,

"You tabloid hacks. The blood in my heart as black
As a syphilitic ape's, go try to find
A soul as rotten, moral fiber as slack
As mine, or fellow feeling half as blind.

"I'd bring my murdered man back from the grave,
And kill him again to see him feeding flies,
Watching his horror while once more I gave
Eternal nightmare form before his eyes.

"Going free, I hurl my sin in your face.
The tribe's weak will to vengeance just ran out.
Mark twain: I play both halves of the human race.
Think fast, as you swim with sharks in seas of doubt.

"I rode the lightning's chariot of fire,
And made it through to start a whole new life.
You fruitcakes look like nerds in a church choir.
Want my advice? SUPPORT DOMESTIC STRIFE."

You'd love that, huh, waste-product? Lots of luck.
Caught and convicted, justice cooks your goose,
Your future flat as if hit by a MACK truck.
The lesson here? Bypass the calaboose.

LXXIV *Jolly Roger*

Are you prepared to grind through a crow's guts?
Democrat or Republican, fish or fowl,
There's no escape by the window your crime shuts.
Wherever you turn, the Ripper's on the prowl,

Waiting for the moment your guard drops:
A dogged, surly assassin, evil-eyed;
The equalizer, roaming until he stops
The Weasel cold when your two worlds divide.

Hold it—he's the Weasel?—the Ripper's you?
Incarnate confusion, sorting which is which.
No matter. The rat unravels who's who,
Crumpling his shifty partner dead in a ditch.

Here's the deal, jughead. *Mano a mano,*
You and your shadow clash to halve your life:
Before you can clear your fat head of guano;
Before light reveals the flash of a knife.

Compose your face and let the showdown start,
That tells which simpleton snuffs his sidekick first,
Throwing a quick glance like a poison dart
To prove your works and days innately cursed.

The format sudden death and no stalemate,
Aim for the heart, Lefty, winner take all:
Like conjoined twins purging a birthright of hate,
Self-loathing shadowboxing on love's blank wall.

That's quite a trick, to kill with a dirty look,
And this mortal coil can't sustain you both.
Find nature's rules in science's black book:
Peel your scales, or your season sees no growth.

Two birds perched on a wire and you want to bet
Which will fly away first? You ought to tie
One of them down. If you and your brother Chet
Politely wager who'll be first to die,

You lose your life both ways. What's there to save?
Take him out as a cow's tail swats a fly.
You look like wild dogs just walked over your grave.
A reckoning shall come soon, so stand by.

Together you're real felones-de-se.
Is this the will of God? Everything is.
Bumping each other off is dumb, but hey,
It's justice. You get yours, and he gets his.

The obscure will of God grinds slow but sure.
When Greek meets Greek, then comes the tug of war.
Because no flesh of yours is meant to endure,
Loss is not a question of either/or.

A likely duo, you princely pair of thugs,
With a monster-toothed snarl in your toxic grin:
The Shadow's solution would spray you with slugs,
But skip the suspense, silence the violin.

Cruise on now to your sinister rendezvous.
Eyes on the road, and heed those dangling dice,
A symbol like your JOLLY ROGER tattoo.
Bracing for blast-off, hear Cassandra's advice:

"Turn right on Haight Street, left on Rambler's Row.
Downtown has radar on Twain Avenue.
On Luchenbach Freeway, feed the western flow,
And avoid passing anywhere near the zoo.

"Speed is your foe when time's in hot pursuit.
The faster you travel, the closer he rides your tail.
The faster you fall, the bigger the hole in your chute.
The faster you drive, the sooner your engine will fail.

"Beware of shortcuts. Seek the slowest route:
NO EXIT, unmarked CROSSROAD, queer DEAD END.
The speed no object, the timing absolute,
Your trip can't miss that roadblock round the bend.

"DO NOT MERGE onto Screaming Eagle Road,
Where taillights march like red ants into the night.
The traffic signs aren't framed in secret code,
So LIVE TO RIDE and you'll arrive outright.

"No detour dodges a highway tollbooth.
You can't try every tankard on the shelf.
The one thing you won't outsmart is the truth:
There's nowhere you can get away from yourself.

"Somewhere, somehow, sometime, records will show,
You stop and never leave your last red light.
If not now, when? If not here, where? Forego
The queries and confront the ocean of night."

That covers it, Butch: brief and matter-of-fact.
Reality crowding time's gambling hall,
Don't frown at your cards and swear the deck is stacked.
So what, sourpuss? Just scratch your head and stall.

It's blackjack or five-card stud, not tiddlywinks.
Take the long view: double or nothing, see?
You're living proof a recycled scumbag stinks,
What you are becoming all you'll be.

Now cut the cards. The tables of fortune wait,
Your chance as good as the next's, but don't claim kin,
With five ways to lose on an ace-high straight.
Make that six, for the joker inside your skin.

Soldiers in Nam would leave an ace of spades
In a corpse's lips: the GI calling card.
I WANT *YOU*, it threatened of future raids.
You draw the big black shovel? Swallow hard.

Your personal drama plays deuces wild.
House rules allow no blameless state of grace.
No double indemnity here: mere child
Or blackbeard pirate equal in time's embrace.

The "dead man's hand" is two pair, aces and eights,
What Wild Bill Hickok held when Jack McCall
Shot him once and opened his blood's floodgates.
Some days in South Dakota, ripeness is all.

Back-shooters Jack McCall and Robert Ford;
The cowards Robert Ford and Jack McCall;
Should have drunk a poison cocktail poured
Right then and there, a cyanide highball.

If McCall had warned, "Hickok, grab some sky,"
And given Wild Bill half a dead man's glance,
His name wouldn't be black as a badger's eye,
Nor his grave a spot where outlaw bikers dance.

Gunned down in Deadwood, killed at SALOON 13,
Hickok re-imagined on TV
Earned a great deal more of the long green
Than Jack McCall ever figured to see.

LXXV *American Gore*

Hands on the table, sneak. Don't damn the odds,
Should hazard cut your capital to the bone.
Henchmen patrolling the floor are hit squads
Enforcing time's interest against your own.

The ante's all the hours left to your name.
Everything here's a risk, wrong or right.
Bluff or fold, the jackpot stays the same:
Your bridges burn once they're out of sight.

And yet your worst result will break even.
Also your best? It's the only game in town.
Psychics call it cosmic seven-eleven:
Win or lose, you jump in the river and drown.

Good night, Irene? Good night, Elihu.
Roulette or craps, your odds won't decrease.
Double zero? Same as double-u:
As double dead as gods of ancient Greece.

MONOPOLY's a numbers game as well.
The wealthy kingdom of death is Park Place.
Although your lot's air rights never gel,
Reflect on stardom's *Nike of Samothrace*:

Demoted to a pool at CAESARS PALACE,
A world away from her proud promontory.
The Strip's wonderland needs a real Alice
To punctuate the imitation glory.

Seven lands you at Appomattox Place;
Eleven leads to Amelia Earhart Lane;
Throw double six for Little Bighorn Trace;
Roll snake-eyes, you've cast the eyes of Cain.

Read your fortune in a twisted biscuit,
Your future told at a Szechuan restaurant?
Advice for growing grass. And why risk it?
Go sail Cape Fear, or swim the Hellespont.

The preacher Ecclesiastes says that there's
Room for every purpose beneath the clouds.
But when it comes to your fortune, who cares
How you fare amid the jostling crowds?

Learn your future from the stars in the sky?
Are they the order of the universe?
They'd only tell you, "Good luck and good-bye."
The future's not a play you can rehearse.

Each car you pass could have a bomb in it.
Each soul you meet could stick a knife in your heart.
You bet your life, a hundred times a minute,
No crashing airplane tears your limbs apart.

They'd strain your minced remains for fingerprints
To identify the ground beef you'll be.
No cousin would claim your smithereens, since
Confusion infests your cracked family tree.

Pearlfish crawl up a sea cucumber's anus
To find protection from underwater foes.
This globe's a giant, bleeding rectum, Janus.
Where do you hide if a wind of vengeance blows?

A gecko lizard hides in animal dung.
Look for a mound of steaming cow manure
Deep enough to muffle your loose tongue,
And save you like a serpent in a sewer.

The winds of vengeance burn, blind, and blast
Across the continents, all down the ages,
The future launched and lashed by the present past,
While man's soul recalls, renews, and rages.

Germany bombed England, Scotland, and Wales,
Yet still the stoic British wouldn't break.
As Churchill lived on cigars and cocktails,
His nation felt the bowels of hell quake.

BIG BEN told perfect time throughout the Blitz,
Dodging bombs by merely standing still.
Even resisting a few direct hits,
It daily declared Britain's valiant will.

On D-Day, June 6, 1944,
The landing was death's dominion on the beach.
What date yields more graphic American gore,
Washed up for college history profs to teach?

"High tide red with the blood of hometown boys
As buoyed helmets emptily bob and float,
Pink foam on the waves intensifies the noise
Of fury," one war correspondent wrote.

The smell of death's tumult was everywhere,
The beach shielded by sheets of German fire:
A myriad wounded, dying, beyond care,
Or shredded like bull's-eyes, caught in barbwire.

14,000 died in two or three hours
As the battle's course turned against the Huns,
Bequeathing corpses soon bewept by flowers
Drooping over graves that followed the guns.

There soldiers slain, with crosses above their heads,
Never returned to their own from foreign fields,
Lie keeping the peace every family dreads.
Complete is the power death's majesty wields.

In time's eternal bivouac are spread
Their tent rows pitched invisibly on the grass:
This ordered arrangement of the random dead
Saluting silent pilgrims as they pass.

Obedient slaughter soaked the ground red,
Survivors spared—why?—by tumbling dice.
Those killed were an experiment history fed
To use them up as laboratory mice.

Bodies rolling side to side in the surf
With a lazy, slow-motion time advance,
Enough blood to drench the cemetery turf
Now guarding the cliffs, bathed the coast of France.

LXXVI *Wolf Man*

5,000 GI's sank beneath the flood
Of killing done by terrified men at war:
Incarnadined the sea with American blood.
Can Germans today say what they fought for?

"We must have been demented," many think.
"Madness gripped our raging, martial race,
To guzzle the maniac Führer's spiked drink,
And wear history's genocidal face.

"The Nazis traveled back 12,000 years
From 1933 to '45,
Keenly shifting their heartless cruelty's gears,
Soon gunning *übermensch* in overdrive.

"The butchery's numbers gained a scale unknown
To humankind in its whole bloodthirsty past:
10 million victims most efficiently thrown
Down the pit where even babies were gassed—

"Plus countless millions more on the battlefield
Of city, town, and countryside alike.
The harvest of death reached a stupendous yield
By Germany's decade-long thunder strike.

"60 million's a figure accountants give,
Resulting altogether from our deeds.
Hearing that, the soul must struggle to live
In a garden choking neck-deep in weeds.

"How do we atone for the sins of man,
Whose depth of evil we mastered beyond doubt?
We shoulder the worst blame and guilt we can,
As vengeance calls us the cold-blooded Kraut.

"In Normandy 9,000 American graves
Overlook the endless living sea,
Where men in boats beached in exploding waves
To set a score of captive countries free.

"Another, nearby cemetery is German,
Whose markers bear a thousand dates of shame.
What force of deformed, disease-breathing vermin
Would toss such beardless boys into war's flame

"To feed insane savagery's last hours?
The great creator's ways of wisdom: could
Even they foresee the depraved powers
Loosed in the pride of Prussian nationhood?

"Perhaps we never suppressed barbaric genes,
Convinced our culture was highly civilized,
But mistaking what that status truly means.
When a wolf man welcomes night, is he surprised?

"Take the executions at Malmédy
Of captured Americans by the SS,
With Belgian families shot trying to flee.
Nothing can make our lethal numbers less.

"Choosing the chance to free the worst in us,
We seized it glad as junkies shooting dope,
Never pausing a minute to discuss
What happened to our moral gyroscope.

"And 'gyroscope' just lets 'holocaust' sound
Like a technical glitch of little worth
For prehistoric hearts no longer bound
To respect any goodness left on earth.

"When murder by medical trials became known
At Mauthausen, which our mentality wrought,
'No repentance could possibly atone
For the crimes unveiled,' one British colonel thought.

"'These glacier-veined, Neo-neanderthal
Egos playing a pseudo super race
Pushed their Teutonic civic honor's fall
To the bottom of human nature's staircase—

"'With a hubris hatched in Munich beer halls.
To halt any further *Fräuleins'* childbirth,
Make all the beaten jerrys cut off their balls,
And hasten their nation's absence from the earth.'

"The black water of evil had rippled out
To bathe the land in waves that consumed its mind,
Pursuing conquest devoid of self-doubt,
Confident claiming the zenith of mankind.

"Can you conceive it? A people sees its place
As superior to all others everywhere,
With license to purge the lesser human race,
Confirming the will to wickedness foursquare.

"They meant to leave nothing on the table,
No action forbidden by their hell-born heart:
'Yes, Cain was right to slay the weakling Abel,'
As though he were an alien upstart.

"The Nazis failed to give inbreeding a thought—
For their offspring. Was this an Achilles heel?
A thousand-year Reich could come to naught,
If morons wrecked its genetic megadeal.

"But no, they'd simply annul 'the unfit,'
Unable to implicate THALIDOMIDE.
Still birth defects could boom and never quit,
Raising the prospect of species suicide.

"Excuse this detour into science fiction,
Mindful of H.G. Wells and Dr. Moreau.
Yet scion after scion's gross affliction
Might will descendants a terminating blow.

"The Nazis, far baser than Dr. Moreau,
Designed no monsters, being born that way.
Their figures in uniform were just for show,
Cloaking their serpent selves in battleship gray.

"The senior Nazis acted with entire
Indifference at their Nuremberg trials.
Their prosecutors never made them perspire:
A shadow lineup of torpid reptiles.

"And the she-wolf of Buchenwald, Ilse Koch,
The commandant's randy wife who flayed tattoos
To fashion lamps for German gentlefolk?
Hanged in her cell, a case of butcher blues.

"The oldest remaining survivor of AUSCHWITZ
Died in 2012 at a hundred and eight,
Known for calling the camp 'worse than the pits
Of Dante's hell'—the fiery furnace of hate."

LXXVII *Amazing Waste*

"A century's suns would scarcely cleanse the stain
Of innocent millions dead on German hands.
The ocean of blood we shed as children of Cain
Convicted us then of heeding Satan's commands.

"Yet evil constantly seeks its next home,
Some eager despot always glad to rise:
From Bonaparte looting treasures of Rome,
To Africa's chronic ulcers feeding flies.

"Rebooting the new millennium's smooth start,
September 11, 2001,
Attacked civilization's hopeful heart
In deeds all decent peoples on earth shun.

"Enacting terror's most televised event,
Which plunged the gentlest into vengeful grief,
A snarling pack of germ-fed jackals sent
As devout killers unleashed their brute belief.

"A phalanx of rabid hellhounds tried to snuff
Liberty's torch with a stone sphinx's breath.
Counting their massacre mission the right stuff
Came devils dealing thousands instant death.

"Infernal guidance schooled their conceit and fed
Its violent undertow a fiercer flood.
This flight crew of alien demons shed
On silent screens explosive clouds of blood.

"That hour the Trojan horse was myth no more,
But a bowel of foul curs in a winged beast:
Envoys of Lucifer's diplomatic corps
Nursed on hatred's theological feast.

"A savage nature led their creed to find
In mass slaughter a passport to paradise,
Leaving the path of peace a dream gone blind
In the pure fury of blazing sacrifice—

"Upon the fascist altar built anew:
Brainsick fever to pull freedom apart,
Thrusting their nightshade into crystal view
Beyond the reach of reason, right, or art.

"Pluto's werewolves plotted amazing waste.
Their colossal crime blotted out the sun,
Betraying a wounded world too often faced
With another round of ruin to be won.

"You think 'germ-fed jackals' a bit extreme?
Then call them 'jack-off Jekylls'—will that do?
Or manic wankers draining a daydream,
Psychopaths from a new barbarian zoo.

"Some of these visited Vegas strip clubs
To screw their courage to the sticking place
As madly masturbating Beelzebubs,
Crazed by the vision of undergarment lace.

"Out for a preview of their heavenly prize,
Their eyes grew wide in throbbing sockets like
A craps player alcohol fortifies—
Or a hermit grasping gold in the Klondike.

"Virginal angels blessed the bestial scheme,
Eager to donate sacred maidenheads.
Killing to hear celestial sex scream
Makes hatred pine for harems on featherbeds.

"And the girls, who waited a mighty long time
To surrender their vaginas' last defense,
Cheered the wild success of the heroes' crime:
Their desire for penetration was immense.

"Seventy-two houri were promised each
Hijacker. Surely that's a challenging task,
Since every virgin's ripe as a Georgia peach,
Gushing for anything the killers ask.

"Orgasm's at the heart of martyrs' heaven,
With plenty of ease to finish ROUND ONE.
Grant each martyr seventy times seven:
Keeping count's a crucial duty done.

"The angels would all be scrambling for a turn,
Embroiled in truly fabulous cat fights,
Proving how hot their starved libidos burn,
Asserting instant defloration rights.

"It's a drastic way to get laid, that's a fact.
Yet the guys missed something huge, did they not?
Why seek the hereafter's carnal glory act,
When Vegas provides it all as CAMELOT?

"The empty, onanistic loser boys,
Prepping for their orgy's reward on high,
Agreed to play the puppet who destroys
A thousand lives for screwing in the sky.

"Both genders in this plot were trampled under
An atavistic culture's feet of clay.
Birth beneath totalitarian thunder
Dooms the subject mind to TRUST AND OBEY.

"Don't try to tell a German that's not true.
Martial regimentation was never worse,
Meeting little dissidence to undo,
Than Nazi freak-show domination's curse.

"And 'freak show' once again is what you heard.
Hitler the goofball artist breathing evil,
Himmler the weasel four-eyed grade-school nerd:
Ogres bred in the Black Forest primeval.

"Fascists everywhere share a basic goal,
Whether by idea, treasure, or war:
Control and power, power and control.
It's this the hijack monsters murdered for.

"So what happens once no more virgins remain?
Their number's bound to run out after a while.
The harems, tired of hearing the gang complain,
Try to recruit young nymphs by grace and guile.

"The heroes enjoy encores up to a point,
But finally they present a stern demand:
'We're not sure we want to stay in this joint,
Unless you restock the original brand.'

"And fresh recruitment proceeds none too well,
Since virgins have to die first to get in.
The killers announce they'll check out sex in hell,
Then bang!—it's *Paradise Lost* all over again."

LXXVIII *Medical Madness*

"There's never any shortage of human deeds
To horrify the heart of an angry God.
The earth's giant agony still bleeds.
If it stopped, the peace would seem too odd.

"More victims of joint cruelty and creed:
2 of 7 million Cambodians dead
From a blaze of intellectual locoweed,
Murdered where Marx's hothouse logic led.

"Or did his vain disciples read him wrong?
Well then, how many Soviets died for that?
One tyrant's thought was another's theme song,
Both devils adjusting hell's thermostat.

"What horror worse than the rape of Nanking,
In deaths-per-minute, racked up one by one?
Not even mayhem Mao hatched in Beijing.
How would that connect to your hated Hun?

"35 million starved to death in Mao's
GREAT LEAP FORWARD, probably as many
On Stalin's collective farms, where milk cows
Were valued above a child's life's half-penny.

"Mao's Great Famine from 1958
Through '62 has received a new look
At its cause and consequences' empty plate,
All bleakly analyzed in a recent book

"Which bears the merciful title *Tombstone*,
By elder Chinese journalist Yang Jisheng.
It seems Mao placed his faith in a wishbone
To help a truly reckless purpose take wing.

"Idi Amin's half-million killed in Uganda?
The royal Saudis gave this beast haven.
800,000 Tutsis in Rwanda?
When was U.N. righteousness more craven?

"Another million corpses are Sudan's—
Plus a domain of newly shackled slaves?
Unlucky members of the conquered clans,
Whose labors produce their own early graves.

"Pizarro's Incas, Cortez's Aztecs?
Vandals, Vikings, Vlads, and Visigoths?
French Huguenots massacred, Cherokee treks,
Christians extinguishing men in loincloths?

"Leaving a Paris conclave, the Protestant prey,
Doomed by the dead Catholic king's wife,
Were all slaughtered on St. Bartholomew's Day,
Inflaming religious war's ungodly strife.

"12,000 Polish officers shot by the Reds?
A Beria/Stalin perfect moral text.
Japanese whacking off captured pilots' heads?
A colorful cast. Who'll volunteer next?

"Stalin blamed his Polish purge on Germans,
Who discovered the mass graves in '43
In Katyn Forest. What judgement determines
A cauldron of evil's poison recipe?

"The graves were filled in '40 and '41.
Each side ad-libbed a propaganda campaign.
Both piled up corpses by the kiloton,
So when was finger-pointing more insane?

"And now this little matter of Japan,
Which loved to practice modern mutilation.
Their killing fever on the march from Bataan
Revealed a savagely degraded nation.

"Most unpleasant to reminisce about.
Immaculate swords decorating their dreams,
In war they achieved a massive flameout,
Blinded by how their antique armor gleams.

"A host of Allied troops were sorry to see
Atomic bombs suddenly bring war's end.
They wanted the warriors of the bonsai tree
Butchered as livestock for a beheaded friend.

"Bound by honor not to be taken alive,
Empire soldiers would gladly have complied,
So that their sacred emperor did survive
To glorify how proudly they all died.

"Their doctors yet more inhumane than ours,
At secret UNIT 731,
Each of the two soulless AXIS POWERS
Adopted Dr. Frankenstein's stepson.

"Both fancied they now wielded an arm of God:
Absolute rule's crazed corruption indeed.
Medical madness behind the old façade
Imposed a whole new Hippocratic creed.

"Remember, it's from Germans you're hearing this.
Atonement isn't granted, it must be earned,
Not by implied apology hit or miss.
Shame must long be suffered to be learned.

"Allied bombing of cities killed around
600,000 German civilians, most
Women and kids, men gone to the battleground.
How's that for burning pumpernickel toast?

"Firebombing Tokyo charred sixteen square miles
Of structures built with bamboo, paper, and pine:
A hundred thousand dead among the piles
Of rubble, ash, and ruined Shinto shrine.

"Here's a question all mankind should ask.
You've seen the veneers of culture rot to hell.
Is stopping this ever a feasible task?
Oh, yeah? From what clairvoyant citadel?

"Not the neutered UNITED NATIONS, nor
The WORLD COURT's slow motion in The Hague.
The goal is one never attained before.
What hand can halt humanity's worst plague?

"Noble it is to labor for world peace,
Delayed gratification showing the way.
Yet the odds stubbornly fail to decrease,
And violence never misses a birthday."

LXXIX *Mourning Dove*

All war is tragic, whoever defeats whom:
Internecine or death's baby machine.
Regardless how fervently peacemakers fume,
On earth no people's record is wholly clean.

Acres of pasture lie silent in the sun.
A thousand troops lie dead on the same field
Barely an hour later, killed by the one
Evil against which none has adequate shield:

Humanity. Death retains the last laugh.
In blood and smoke and flames, one loses heart.
Armies take orders from hell's general staff,
Academies where carnage is fine art.

"Only the dead have seen the end of war,"
Plato observed 2,000 years ago.
From Marathon to the fall of Corregidor,
The tides of time suck blood from a rainbow.

"Wars will come as long as this world's here,"
Concludes a crusty veteran, Ed Haines.
Wouldn't Lincoln and Churchill think it queer
If history happened without labor pains?

In Lincoln's *Second Inaugural Address*,
Delivered March 4, 1865,
He was concerned with claiming victory less
Than helping his sundered nation somehow strive

To find peace in itself, so its fractured world
Could bind its wounds and grow together again.
To absorb the shock of the TWIN TOWERS hurled
To dust, one poet gripped his stricken pen:

"Let this devastation bequeath a shrine
Where broadcast, blazing terror shattered through:
For every faith from Perth to Palestine;
For every faith the hounds of hell pursue.

"Upon the ground that cradled so many slain,
May a simple, soaring monument rise,
From ashes, dust, and continental pain
To greet all future suns' uncertain skies.

"Let it be made the tallest spire on earth,
Its height projecting the hope it stands for,
Where new depths of horror were given birth
By fiends who lit the flaming pyre of war.

"May it say to tyranny's treacherous will
Mocking a better world in an ape's face,
That liberty wields force no fire can kill,
Represented by this undying place.

"Let it be crowned with the red, white, and blue
Homage of 3,000 lasers of light
Concentrated into a virtual view
Of stripes and stars emblazoning the night.

"And may it be a tower never broken;
Its meaning, on the wings of a mourning dove,
Circle the earth in every language spoken
As freedom, justice, mercy, goodness, and love."

When cumulus clouds pile their turrets above
Far mountains, and larks sweeten the air in song,
At twilight a diving skyhawk kills a dove,
Stressing the sense of a world laid out wrong.

Lie on your back and fight off wolves with a stick
To help discern how your planet proceeds.
Half the earth behaves like a gorging tick;
The other half gasps and cries and bleeds.

War talks around a kettle of dog meat;
Pirates pouring out of Chinese junks;
Miners saved by a dying parakeet;
Foraging grub from dens of badgers and skunks;

Carnage igniting along the Cimarron;
Sunup to sundown baking in dust or mud;
Jumping a sourdough's claim in the Yukon:
Nothing's born but wears a label of blood.

The rain of napalm torching Tokyo;
Hunger that boils over in seething slums;
The thunder of stampeding buffalo:
Younger braves dreamed of the wind and the drums.

Severed heads on stakes in the Holy Land;
Buddhist monks cremated by gasoline;
Guidons popping in gales of blowing sand;
Nomad warriors howling down a ravine;

A lethal blast of methane gas from a lake;
Terror networks nursing a red rage;
Fury fed like a seven-headed snake:
Violent forces are death's living wage.

A dark torrent of arrows fills the sky?
Great fear can make your body sweat blood.
What sense of beauty guided a samurai
Sword to open the heart like a rosebud?

When a deep freeze forges steel in prairie sod
Where spotted cattle grazed on grama grass,
Even to hack out a grave is cursed by God.
Thus cannibalism claimed Donner Pass.

LXXX *Small Spark*

The halls of state are built from blocks of stone,
With polished granite floors where tyrants meet.
Down marble walls the ash of protest blown
Plagues a stubborn reign that scorns retreat.

Supreme command disdains the echoes' tone
Of anguish coiled in language crowds repeat.
Response lands hard when riots rock the throne
And rattle chandeliers in the royal suite.

From malice to madness, sick regimes have shown
They'll wreck their whole domains to death's drumbeat.
Earth's a cavern of skeletons overgrown
With lies, if murder holds the judgement seat.

The strongman's closely guarded undertone
Fuels the killer cars of his dragnet fleet.
Scripts by keepers of secret graves disown
What cracks unseal in a floor of concrete.

Yet the world turns to see czars overthrown—
And Stalin dread a poison trick or treat.
Fiends like the Stasi, usurpers like Perón
Leave deeds in archives, testament who can cheat?

Corrosive as concentrated ozone,
Treachery's pall and neighborhood spies compete.
But rule by fear bares blades its foes will hone
Against attacks by terror's trained elite.

What answers threats barked from a microphone
By masters blaming citizens' blind deceit?
No curfew curbs the marrow, no slaughter's groan
Harrowing night with news day pales to greet.

If life is spilled, will force wound flesh alone?
Wrong gnaws at hearts, unrest engulfs the street.
Marchers brace for a combat chopper's drone
To whip their clothes like a butcher pounding meat.

Diving in doorways when gunfire pins them prone,
Who ponders what revolution's orphans eat?
Blood circulates where tyranny's flag is flown,
To trample the black banner with dancing feet.

Where is the despot desiring to atone
To souls he finds a duty to browbeat?
Dissent is a field of weeds he wants mown,
With ciphers slain his civics can delete.

Yet if *Winged Victory* were a sculpted crone,
Or no lost palace buried in ancient Crete,
Would annals issue a chronic monotone,
Artistry range from mannered to effete?

What forge tests a people with no Saint Joan,
No church's false inquisitors to entreat?
When the fascist wolf preys on the wild roan,
Her colt sleeps cold and feeds on thorned mesquite.

Top staff insist a crisis is overblown,
Accustomed to driving from the backseat,
But the fabric tearing apart can't be sewn
Up again like a rip in a bed sheet.

The rest is diversion strategy alone:
Appoint a smoother PR exegete.
Style the chief's hair to look a bit windblown;
Extol his youth as a talented athlete.

Perhaps his wife could enlist silicone
To project a public image more upbeat.
Yet a small spark can ignite a war zone,
As grievance and oppression overheat.

The Alamo endures in San Antone,
Texan tenacity never obsolete.
Lone Star boots aren't stitched to be outshone,
And oil can rouse the blackest sheep to bleat.

Spawn of a cutthroat father's testosterone,
The oligarch's a malignant deadbeat.
As host Hitler muzzled the megaphone,
His Olympics Jesse Owens' magic feat.

Then bombing spared the cathedral of Cologne:
Thank Eisenhower, war's surprise aesthete.
But the Nazi nation's hatred was homegrown:
A zest for evil impassioned its heartbeat.

Control unbound means demons to condone,
Means crushing voices with a sharpened cleat.
Popular will grants no guaranteed loan,
And brute power signs no legal receipt.

But gathering rage can roar like a cyclone
Thrashing plains of Patagonian wheat.
Dismiss the presidential chaperone,
His pennants waving yesterday's conceit.

Does vengeance relieve prolonged suffering's moan—
Gestapo snuffed like a strutting parakeet?
Badges of shame where generals' medals shone,
Shackles declare the warlords' guilt complete.

Flash mobs will mock a Mussolini clone,
His lawless stranglehold stung by a tweet.
Blood's flux erodes the strictest danger zone:
No checkpoints halt its steady, simmering heat.

Troops can't quell an earthquake, quench or postpone
Fury that chokes like soot as it chills like sleet.
Once freedom's magma explodes its fuming cone,
Is the thrill of prisons burning bittersweet?

A whirlwind strips the crop Caesar has sown,
And wraps the hanged dictator's winding-sheet.
Blood's buried flow has undertows unknown:
Riptides return to drown an age of defeat.

LXXXI *Morse Code*

Once you've been everywhere and tried everything—
And learned how every pleasure has its price—
Ready to hang up your gloves and quit the ring,
Don't forget the domain of cards and dice.

This mystifying stop bemuses all:
The desert metropolis Las Vegas beckons.
Join the bedazzled who accept the call—
And feel your wallet shrink in sixty seconds.

But don't fumble it how the hijackers did.
Treat it like a different universe:
Explore each marvel agog as a schoolkid,
Until you figure out the joint's a curse.

The place will make you puzzle, stammer, and cuss.
Arrive first-class in a flashy sports car,
Then leave in the last seat on the cheapest bus—
After a starving gaze at the MEGABAR.

It's early still to give yourself up for dead.
Your magic numbers don't tally so far.
Take a vacation, much as DISNEY said:
Dye your hair and wish upon a star.

Everywhere, Osaka to Aberdeen,
Las Vegas entices the wide world to play.
For super excess, Vegas is siren queen,
From Vladivostok to Guanabara Bay.

Squander your life savings on dice and cards?
The darker stirrings of liquor, sex, and luck
Cover the light bill for the boulevards'
Marquees offering all an easy buck.

PLAY POKER WITH US AND LOSE YOUR PAYCHECK,
Is terms the million watts never disclose:
"Hang out here till your life's a total wreck—
Yet please depart before you decompose.

"If you come across a flash of coarse gold
In a sprinkling of dirt panned from a salt flat,
We'll multiply it for you sevenfold!
Now show us an honest broker who tops that!"

How soon begins their fancy fabric of lies,
Weaving the byword ANY NUMBER CAN WIN.
What's their sendoff once your credit dies?
"You only needed a little backspin."

WHAT HAPPENS IN VEGAS STAYS IN VEGAS—right?
It implies behavior, but it means your money.
Implies vice is no worse than flying a kite,
Yet the rate of lives ruined is not funny.

At the GOLD SPIKE, you still see penny slots.
NO LIMIT, says the HORSESHOE, Fremont Street.
A handful take home MEGABUCKS jackpots;
Plenty leave beneath a clean white sheet.

A gold spike finished the coast-to-coast railroad
Joined in Utah in 1869:
The word DONE flashed nationwide in Morse code.
Born as a water stop on a new rail line

In 1905, Vegas would stake its claim:
Gambling made legal in 1931.
Thus opened its steady rise to global fame.
They flatter and fleece you, all as harmless fun.

Games of chance and pleasures of the flesh
Are greed and folly, sandwiched by glitz and lust.
From CHEETAH'S to ELVIS–O–RAMA to John Tesh,
They'll find a hook to win your empty trust.

They'll find a hook to turn your dreams to dust.
The press is silent when the STRATOSPHERE
Launches a dying jumper whose luck went bust:
Complicit not to shed a crocodile tear.

Two hundred grand on one spin of the wheel,
Some blow-in bet and won, as fortune smiled.
Doubled his wager, boasting nerves of steel:
Disguising a death wish in greed gone wild.

A kid from Tampa won a ton and a half:
Went home rich, then three years later returned
And blew his entire bankroll. His epitaph?
DOLLARS CAN'T BUY WHAT DUMBO NEVER LEARNED.

At the cross of Christ, soldiers threw dice to see
Who'd get his cloak—a dubious jackpot.
In Vegas you're after a flashier grand prix,
And resurrection's not the counterplot.

The slots players in rows like church pews—
As focused as parishioners on their knees
For earthly absolution, win or lose—
Worship the shade of casino money trees

With faces waxing more evenly dull,
Held in line as sheep prepared to be shorn.
Not a single head would their masters cull,
Where moral character's never to be born.

Some chump will stake the whole shooting match
On a tempting hand of cards. Challenging chance,
He lures opponents into a briar patch,
Invited by a calculating glance.

"You've lost your little nest egg and complain?"—
The pit boss asks, amazed at what he heard.
"Did sense forget to occupy your brain?
A man can lose his life without a word!"

LXXXII *Ghost Ranch*

The first casinos were run by Chicago mob
Figures. Known inside as The Outfit,
Management performed its essential job
Of skimming the daily take for the house split.

The showgirls, magicians, and animal acts
Make Vegas headquarters of razzmatazz,
Backing up the plain financial facts.
The VOODOO LOUNGE atop the RIO has

A view at night of arriving airplanes'
Lights aligned in the sky like a string of pearls:
A constant stream of suckers which maintains
The profits, UFO's from distant worlds.

In Vegas phones arouse and money talks:
Dial your flavor of playmate à la mode.
Topless barmaids eye your glass like hawks:
Keep it half full, bub, or hit the road.

God Almighty and John Three Sixteen,
Two candidates for Las Vegas mayor,
Took those names to keep their images clean,
But neither became even a bit player.

Sin City's not a place where men of the cloth
Can have an impact at the ballot box.
Preaching just comes across as caustic froth
To polish the settings of high-rollers' rocks.

Winnings water Vegas's staying power
That draws the human jetsam tempest-tossed.
One mogul built the West's tallest tower
To advertise his play and damn the cost.

The global center for irrationalism
Exploits the crucial role of simple chance
In beating the odds, as through fortune's prism,
The neon rainbow's bands of color dance.

The nocturnal, 24-hours-a-day
Party machine and shameless fantasy themes'
Happy-go-lucky, jingling sound of play,
Give every fool an open field of dreams.

Tobacco, booze, and blackjack set the tone.
Abandon your cares and become most anyone.
They make a king of misery's lowest drone:
For three whole days, don't let him see the sun.

Three days and a cloud of dust is the right way
To try Las Vegas. Staying much longer
In search of a land of plenty doesn't pay.
It merely renders the scent of sin stronger.

See Liberace's gift. The prince of kitsch,
His capes and fur-lined cars endowed a shrine.
Schmaltz had left him so baroquely rich,
He willed his city a mink valentine.

Surreal? No doubt even Dalí would laugh,
And grant this fop an undisputed crown.
Ask any Elvis you please for an autograph,
Spotting his copycats all over town.

Now Liberace's renown begins to fade.
The latest generation's never heard
His name. The museum staff, underpaid,
May close its doors—fame's dismal afterword.

Las Vegas's cityscape swiftly evolves.
When profits fall, the property falls, too.
There's no place quite as stark where money solves
All questions, from art museum to the zoo.

The GUGGENHEIM MUSEUM's western branch,
Which opened to giddy highbrow fanfare,
Was flattened like a barn on a ghost ranch:
Vanished in Vegas culture's thin air.

From blueprints by architect Rem Koolhas,
It sprang up beside THE VENETIAN's carpark.
Low earnings proved it too much gravitas
For a scene more suited to a loan shark.

The new LAS VEGAS ART MUSEUM died
Of hubris, of its self-approving dreams.
A frank band of pragmatists vainly tried
To wean it off its diet of moonbeams.

But a silk purse can't be sewn from a sow's ear:
The dense population of Philistines.
Directors high on expectation's cheer
Couldn't imagine living on rice and beans.

The supreme Vegas value dollars and cents,
Nothing is sacred where everything is fake.
Whatever stands will vacate present tense:
The moolah monster levels all in its wake.

Implosions are an ordinary fate
For casino designs quickly obsolete—
Sacrificed to a look more up-to-date—
Wrecking even the Presidential suite.

Don't miss a ride on the roller coaster to hell,
Whose steepest drops plunge to reach 4 g's;
Whose double loopers make your brain swell
Twice around 360 degrees.

The dogs of war at AREA 51
Wear uniforms adorned by winged skulls.
If proving-ground aggression's overdone,
How about angels sprayed on bombers' hulls?

LXXXIII *Shadow War*

Each night the LUXOR pyramid beams a ray
So high it's visible for a hundred miles.
Groove to the Vegas gestalt and find Cathay:
Just one among dozens of make-believe styles.

Virtual vision crystallizes in Vegas,
Where any place could turn up reproduced.
Can pseudo obscure all the ills that plague us?
It gives the devil's designs a big boost.

"This copy reminds me of Paris, even though
I've never been there," some zany tourist told
The local paper. "Now I don't care to go.
This PARIS makes the real one sound too old."

In Vegas only the numbers need be true.
Her tempting tentacles feed an empty land.
It's been that way since 1932:
The phantom fortune blows the desert sand.

With Robert Venturi's book, the Vegas Strip
Foretold some architecture's play façades.
Yet nothing rivals the total showmanship,
Vegas's Neo-neon feast of the gods.

Look on the city as pure *Dalivision*—
But skip the daily double at WHISKEY PETE'S.
If the cultured believe abject derision
Is apt, Vegas will comp them front-row seats.

Thrill-seekers haunt Las Vegas, USA,
To pay respects to Mammon and take a run
At turning the cube of luck every which way,
In a wild place determined, dared, and done.

Vegas is built so lights suppress the night,
While darkness hides behind the neon sheen.
Its long black veil of secrecy and sleight
Masquerades in a caring, cordial mien.

The town's illuminated interludes
In the constellations' huge night display,
Easily overcome the multitude's
Daylight dependence and make darkness pay.

The city disguises a non-public face
That speaks in whispers with a guarded tongue.
Its magic-makers set a measured pace,
Counting each video poker bell rung.

Slow enslavement by vice will capture those
Hardheads who idolize the goddess of chance.
Cracking an addled smile, loudmouth knows
How bankrupt gladness feeds a gambler's trance.

Because a killer whale must kill to swim,
Las Vegas masks its night of the living dead.
Cashiers, sentries who tend the crypt, condemn
Any hunch not running your numbers red.

The OFFICE OF LOST DREAMS BY WAYS AND MEANS
Is a shape-shifter that spirits you away
Quickly, should you beat their best machines,
With whores to lead your sucker's luck astray.

The INN OF THE SIXTH HAPPINESS well may be
The name given your priceless villa suite,
Yet a shadow war for your soul you can't see
Is why you're served by girls on feline feet.

Fractured Fairy Tales and *Daffy Duck*
Are what the harlots watch on their days off,
Laughing at gals who earn an honest buck,
Scratching their sculpted buttocks as they scoff.

LXXXIV *Shell Game*

In Vegas the angel of the backstreet bar
Couldn't stand the fumes and went on strike;
Then quit her job as a "future film star"
In search of surroundings truly lifelike.

Soon you slap yourself: "Have I gone blind,
Or is this a stool in the LAST CHANCE SALOON?
I must take better care of my fragile mind,
Or wake up on a Mexican honeymoon."

It's teardrops, jukebox, and the whiskey's free,
But caution: trouble spurs a fast horse.
The house will lend you chips at half past three,
Then seize your car at four with no remorse.

Or else you start a permanent vacation.
Found in the desert, skulls all look alike.
This isn't inside dope or speculation:
You could disappear from a nature hike.

On back the contract reads, CROSS ME AND CROAK.
Its fine print can stop you still as stone.
With many worse ways to end up than broke,
There's no way worse than one to call a loan.

A game stipulates jacks and jokers wild?
An incandescent journey to the brink
Of death turns a player meek as a child,
Rueing his luck, watching his future shrink.

The news A STAR IS BORN or KID FLAMES OUT,
Is two sides of the same counterfeit coin.
The first reports on a rigged heavyweight bout;
The other sends the fallen home to Des Moines.

That's if he doesn't become a pillar of salt
For staring back at the scene he leaves behind.
Whatever occurs, his fate's his own fault,
For seeking fortune none can expect to find.

AREA 51 is called DREAMLAND
By joyless patsies lounging around broke.
They exchange their empty hopes second-hand
Where mirror-makers specialize in smoke.

Most buses quit the Unreal City full
Of losers down to their very last dime,
Looking withdrawn and glumly gathering wool,
Or contemplating redemption through crime,

While exiting ruin via GREYHOUND.
Airline passengers? Many get drunk and loud
On any Vegas excursion inward bound,
But steal home silent and completely cowed.

After you clear the danger of wind sheer,
Then engines push and power pulls you high
Into a thinner reach of the atmosphere,
Only two ways exist: you fall or fly.

Scattered clouds and their shadows upon the earth
Slide like the shifting husks of a shell game.
And whether flight is to Dallas or Fort Worth,
The landing apparatus is the same.

Back on the ground, you're now the poker hand,
Constantly figuring odds simply to live.
Playing for peanuts or a hundred grand,
There are debts no plain dealer will forgive.

LXXXV *Stolen Fame*

All casinos greet you with open arms:
TROPICANA, MIRAGE, or CACTUS KATE'S.
As sidewalk hustlers hawk lucky charms,
Jerry Lee Lewis's keyboard rocks four states.

Called the Killer since school days, he's the king
Of rock-and-roll's beat like a battering ram.
Born to do nothing but play piano and sing,
He flings the world defiance. "*I Am What I Am,*

"Not what they want me to be," he proudly hurls
The dynamite igniting his rebel fans.
"The Killer's here to show you his secret, girls"—
If any can find the key in his magic hands.

Piano perched in the back of a pickup truck,
His mobile launch pad could roll and rock
In a Memphis flash, to songs so hot they'd suck
Oxygen from the air by spinal shock.

For *High School Confidential*, he did just that:
A sizzling strip of historic celluloid.
Combing his hair, he was the craziest cat,
Decorum by his act completely destroyed.

With three quick minutes of music, overnight
He leapt from total unknown to household word.
Soon fortune decided his star shone too bright,
While trouble left his spirit undeterred.

His first hits put Elvis's numbers to shame,
Yet how does a hillbilly rocker win for long?
Scandal spread as tabloids trashed his name,
But stolen fame returned on the wings of song.

His records tell the rest. From *Another Place,
Another Time* to *Great Balls of Fire*, he'll make
The sun go down to tones of amazing grace—
Then shake the rafters all night till bra straps break.

Has Lady Luck been kind to Jerry Lee,
The wildest performer since 1955?
No justice yet, but when was justice free?
Genius finds its own way to survive.

High time the gods were good to rock-and-roll:
The IRS is finally off his case.
If winter comes, can't spring unchain the soul,
When Killer songs can rattle aerospace?

His tour of 1964 they called
Rockin' the World has never been topped,
Leaving dance halls wrecked as it cannonballed
Across the land. The songs have never stopped.

Better to fill a pine box on a train back
Home than miss the Killer's fortissimo.
Even if Elvis drove up in a CADILLAC,
Whoever else plays, the Killer owns the show.

Ready to hear a living legend play,
And prove what the devil's music's all about?
Meet true delight before you fade away.
The roulette wheel waits to clean you out.

Step right up and roll 'em, lumberjack:
Strike it rich or lose your flannel shirt.
Stay calm while staking all on red or black,
And dig your own grave, spade in prime pay dirt.

Seven-come-eleven's the bet to make.
Ignoring that you ain't got a lick of sense,
Keep on seeking the ultimate lucky break,
Until your bedtime story changes tense.

In the grave, a whole lot of nothing goes on.
Life wild as a wolf dwindles to dust at last.
Live like there's no tomorrow, you sullen pawn
Of time, the quiet killer. Have a blast.

Round and round she goes and doesn't stop,
Till time's big lotto jackpot pays you off.
Then all the earth's gold won't help you swap
Your corpse for another shift at life's feed trough.

LXXXVI *Salted Mine*

If time is money, try to buy some more.
Sphere-music only costs a dime a dance.
Yet time still moves to its own cadent score,
Though store-bought love blossoms in TRUE ROMANCE.

No winding the clock that doubles as doorbell chime,
Once your body loses the strength to live.
The COURT OF INFERNAL AFFAIRS condones your crime,
But the end of your life is firm: it's got no give.

The power of positive thinking won't help much:
In the hardest hour, will thought see you through?
The mind can't fashion a big enough crutch
To cripple death, from Cracow to Kalamazoo.

Unchanging, immutable, the same always,
Death will slay you, with or without a gun.
No bribe suffices to buy a few more days,
Despite how many poker games you've won.

Round and round she goes and when she stops,
None but the roulette genie knows for sure.
Forget where fortune's ivory ball drops:
An endless winning streak is horse manure.

Vegas to Arizona is thirty miles.
One more last hand, before the state line?
Bad luck makes you hungry? Good luck beguiles,
Like finding silver in a salted mine.

Thirty pieces of silver wasn't a lot
Judas charged the pharisees to forsake
His trusting savior and help complete their plot
Committing history's single biggest mistake.

The realm of facts and figures is no joke.
Money to burn is useless in hell, *capeesh?*
In moral terms, you'd just as well die broke
As have the devil call you nouveau riche.

How do you spell STUPID? That a boy.
Show the skeptics you can add and subtract.
Your pocket calculator's not a toy:
It's the only way your brain can transact.

Learn how history works. Your life's outcome
Derives from all you do, the years you spend.
Focus on fate, on why your head feels numb,
And how your double's death ensures your end.

False, misleading statements leave you unclean,
Yet truth won't make you free in Santa Fe.
Observe the sundial's shadow: what does it mean?
You're vapor vanishing. Nothing more to say.

Your road become a dark, descending one,
Don't be a quitter. Drink yourself blind
Every day of the world. Under the gun,
Don't let your date with death unhinge your mind.

After many a summer dies the swan?
After many a bender dies the drunk.
Quick, before you cross the Rubicon,
Reverse and try to block time's slam dunk.

Sadness flies on the wings of morning, and
Out of the heart of darkness comes the light?
The angel of death arrives on wings fanned
By hellish zephyrs smelling of VULCANITE.

LXXXVII *Transcontinental Trek*

Now buckle up, funny face, and head west.
The maze of highways that crawls over the plains
In baffling vastness guides your hapless quest.
Daily the standby tow-truck tailing you gains:

An inch or two, a foot, a yard, a mile?
No dial on your dash shows what time remains.
A wildfire's scarred sod recalls meanwhile
The civil war raging like wolves in your veins.

Up every road's another one-horse town,
Where longitude is simply a dateline
You can't predict, so roll your windows down
And charge the wind in pursuit of sunshine.

Merging onto the nearest interstate,
You sense the winds of life have turned your way.
But let your automobile assume your fate,
You'll become a repair bill you can't pay.

Odds are better in the left-hand lane, sometimes.
At others the hand of chance favors the right.
Check your brakes and give to the MARCH OF DIMES:
Assure your safety on the edge of night.

Always there's the sound of distant drums,
About as audible as your heartbeat,
Which you may faintly feel throb in your gums,
Regular as the thump of concrete

Pounded by a loose flap on a tire,
While your transcontinental trek unfolds,
And the deadly mileage slowly creeps higher,
Marking what each breaking minute holds.

If roadside crosses demand, GET RIGHT WITH GOD,
Ignore them and proceed westbound hell-bent.
Defy life's storms as a human lightning rod.
There's little chance blackguards like you repent.

A NASCAR race matches the stress you fight,
Till giving up, you smash the retaining wall.
Yet being engulfed as metal and bricks ignite
Sure beats getting shot in a barroom brawl,

And racing's thrill provides bodies to burn.
Charlotte, Darlington, Talladega, Daytona:
Follow your star till it falls, when you turn
Your keys in and retire to Arizona.

Of course you prefer stock cars to rock stars.
There's no disputing taste, even in this.
It must derive from your driving bump cars
At the County Fair in a boy's total bliss.

Wouldn't you rather freeze *in transitu*?
First chill, then stupor, then the letting go?
A fitting end to foolish derring-do—
Or tragedy for a yodeler's tremolo.

Such death befell a rock climber from Reno,
But what includes that in your plodding saga?
It presents a new paradox for Zeno:
Your feckless brain can't tell goo-goo from gaga.

This clunker's not your limo in Hollywood,
That flicker of fame only history now.
The tabloid background checks misunderstood?
Your claim to art was hopelessly lowbrow.

The limo had windows black as midnight,
To hold you in vampire mode all evening long.
If boulevard neon kept the darkness bright,
The tinted glass kept your character strong.

Now tank up with EXTRA, put this wreck in gear.
The Rapture may seize you out in Idaho.
A long drive for nothing? Be of good cheer:
It's steady work to settle the bill you owe.

Even the all-time greats of rock-and-roll
Say life on the road's a hard row to hoe.
But how else could you manage to pay the toll,
Since you promise zilch as a gigolo?

LXXXVIII *Rolling Stone*

You're always on the road and on the run?
If the living's twice as tough, what the heck.
None's instructed that living will be fun,
And toil's reward can be a rubber check.

Do you suspect you're driving your life away?
Leave it to you to cop an attitude.
"Now, why was I given this?" you dare say?
Maybe your thought process is just too crude.

You spot graffiti declaring JONES WANKS CATS?
Defamation must not derail your trip.
Dismiss the revolting filth as HAZMATS
Holding your manhood in their poison's grip.

A billboard says, 1–800–GOT–LAND,
While silent signals of fading contrails
Trace a message you'll never understand,
And the sun beats you down like a bag of nails.

Although your simple mind-set lies inert,
You stand full ready to block a body slam.
Wearing a chartreuse suit and a fuschia shirt,
You think you squeeze more juice than HOOVER DAM.

A little time off before your big jump?
No, but life's real calm, soon as it's over.
You sleep till shocked awake for the last trump,
Your chance to win a brand new LAND ROVER.

Stay dead till you hear trumpets from up above
Summoning all the redeemed to cash it in.
Then you learn the grace of celestial love
Sentences you to Lucifer's looney bin.

An orchestra seat for fire and brimstone
Is your reward for a lifetime of service.
You thought you had to be bad to the bone?
Ponder the suicide of Melvin Purvis.

Meanwhile, your meager soul will have no rest.
Body defiled and spirit quite profane,
Do your time as the earth's dishonored guest.
Drive on with the wind whistling through your brain.

Cleave to the bucking bronc as long as you can.
Cling to his mane till your rump is black and blue.
They hang a horse thief, the Hatfield clan,
Who can't say why he's lost in their purlieu.

In U–HAUL hell, a weight you can't lay down,
Ride 'em cowboy, lunge from pillar to post,
Banging your head so hard you crush your crown.
OD on sunsets, then give up the ghost.

Whether by fits and starts or on cruise-control;
At a stop sign in the middle of nowhere; or
Creeping through the turmoil of your soul;
You won't survive your flesh's state of war.

But thank your stars you own a set of wheels.
Roll out of Georgia bound for the Bering Strait.
Mobility, one of life's sweeter deals,
Says hit the road, sharecropper. Why wait?

The windshield sign was lettered DIRT CHEAP
When you bought your heap in downtown Roanoke,
Telling the salesman the price was still too steep.
Now a tank of gas can leave you broke.

As soldier of fortune, look for loot full-time.
Wanderlust feeds your unrest bred in the bone.
Your limit westers somewhere ahead, with crime
A prime source of income, rolling stone.

Refresh yourself at the HALFWAY HOME CAFE:
Symbolize your deadly instant of shame.
The gasbag deep inside your breast will say:
"All I expect from life's a decent dame:

"A bang-up broad with a pair of flashing lights.
She won't need a double serving of brains,
As long as she helps me scale passion's heights,
And doesn't mind my spreading sweat stains."

"You impudent, ignorant pig!" the waitress yells.
"Go jump in a lake, you gooey pond scum;
You thick-necked tree trunk; you swineherd for hell's
Half-acre; you four-flushing, beady-eyed bum!"

LXXXIX *Opaque Eyes*

You've never been subjected to worse scorn?
Perhaps road rage would boost your self-respect.
If it makes you feel important, blow your horn,
And reach your destination really wrecked.

Destination Arizona, that is:
The place where true retirees wind down.
To arrive there, drink plenty of gin fizz,
Keep cruising, and stop in every shantytown.

When the Lord made you, he made a rambling man.
Coast down hills, sleep on the seat of your car.
Fit right into mortality's basic plan:
A double agent of death is what you are.

In a stroke autonomic as a knee jerk,
You betray your young features and cross them out;
Exchange their mien for wrinkles, so age's work
Crosshatching your skin steadily comes about.

The stage all set, the script is up to you.
Hit the trail till it peters out, you churl.
After you flunk St. Peter's interview,
Step aside for a precious baby girl.

"You live in pilgrimage," noted John Donne.
No spirit riddle fools a preacher poet.
Deceased, you mingle with dunghills, wayward one:
Once you turn to dust, the four winds blow it.

Your dust mixes with more akin to your own,
Sifting the sightless midnight of your eyes,
Drifting in tiny specks of flesh and bone,
And filtering sunsets red in winter skies.

While you pursue a ragpicker's repose,
Imagine that what you breathe is death dust:
Trapped among the cilia in your nose,
The finest flakes of the earth's changing crust.

Didn't you ever wonder, Hopalong,
Why they close the eyelids of the dead?
To thwart your fresh corpse's taking the wrong
Turn to eternity, seeing what's ahead.

Time's the greatest power, a wasting disease
Which visits all living things with ill intent.
Don't drain your battery praying on bruised knees,
Pressing a grievance the earth can't prevent.

The sibyl Cassandra's counsel was guidelines
To even up your journey's crooked chart.
The terrain is full of pitfalls and land mines,
Hence further caution, on your double's part:

"Don't see the bet if the dealer palms an ace.
Don't plunk your chips on mystic thirty-three.
Stay home nights if fur transfigures your face.
Don't break your mirror to kill a chimpanzee."

His mug so empty he must be a shill,
The vacant eyes are vents of a hollow shell.
His string of evil warnings breaks your will?
Peeling your mask, he parts the jaws of hell.

Besides, he's yourself in sheer disguise,
Your doppelganger working CAESARS PALACE.
Focus upon his pair of opaque eyes:
Can such blankness hold absence of malice?

Suppose each eyeball were a silver mirror
Reflecting your twinned image and that alone.
Could total human emptiness get nearer
To showing the face of the human unknown?

XC *Pyramid Lake*

A few last notes and then you're on your own.
Make a U-turn midway on Ozark Pike,
If a hitchhiker matching your phantom clone
Flashes this sign: NO TWO CURVES ALIKE.

Your cheap, crisscross retread comes unglued?
FOGGY MOUNTAIN BREAKDOWN STOPS JOYRIDE:
NO SPARE IN TRUNK; DIED IN FAMILY FEUD.
Scripture says only the earth will abide.

Fly like a bat out of hell? You'll throw a rod
And stall on a high plateau with one lone tree
For facing a frontier justice firing squad.
Forget the pass lane: the right road's the key.

CHILLY IN CHESTER, COLD IN COWPENS:
That's the typical weather forecast.
Peer forward through a telescope's wrong lens,
To help prevent your traveling too fast.

You hear it said, none but the strong survive?
Popular wisdom isn't the whole story.
Putting your life in Georgia overdrive
Won't see you become an angel in glory.

Not on a real tight schedule, take your time.
Stop when a stranded motorist flags you down.
Like you he moves to the sun's unfathomed chime;
Like you he's glad to make the next hick town.

Drive like the wind? What, make the sun stand still?
Time Bandits was a movie's teenage dream.
Once time's stalking grizzly claws its kill,
You count years like a stone in a glacial stream.

Ninety miles an hour on a dead-end road
Is time's seductive ruse to kill you quick.
Why use up rubber on neural overload
To reach the bottom of time's waning wick?

Follow the cowboys' slow-moving dreams.
Take detours by any roundabout route,
Thus indicating to four-eyed academe's
Footnote phenoms their path to the absolute.

Randomness rules out here. The *Yukon Express*
Is speeding freight that yields no right of way.
The onrush of time attempts no finesse,
Riding a juggernaut or a one-horse shay.

And time never responds to a jake brake
Noisily gearing down eighteen wheels:
Whether the haul is salt from Pyramid Lake,
Or counterfeit cash a load of hay conceals.

Recall the staggered signboards of BURMA SHAVE:
ASPHALT ANGELS—WHO GUARD YOU—WHEN YOU DRIVE,
Saying how close you hug the edge of the grave,
ARE MOSTLY THOUGHT—TO RETIRE—AT 65.

You carry firmly every jot you possess,
Till life and death break even at the end.
You're headed for checkmate in crossroads chess,
Not stalemate in North Cascades or South Bend.

Life and death break even? Sorry, that's wrong.
You live a little while and then you die
Forever, but forever is very long,
Deeper than space, and wider than the sky.

XCI *Cold Harbor*

Shove off, sweet prince. Go find a rainbow to chase.
Prove to what depth your destiny's double-dyed,
And play the cards you're dealt, accepted with grace—
No paranoid claims you're being crucified.

Godhead and Golgotha? Your scraggly bean
Would awe like a coconut crowned by cactus thorns.
And your bizarre car is no time machine.
Your wounds won't come from nails, but the devil's horns.

Did Pilate try you in kangaroo court, outcast?
Then explain your persecution complex.
Can you walk on water, calm the stormy blast?
The only cross you earn is a final X.

Compare this bad scene to a snapshot of hell:
Golgotha signifies the place of skulls,
Its ether heavy with death's pungent smell,
Its carrion dive-bombed by flocking gulls.

Its odor sharper than a serpent's tooth,
Decomposition aided by the winds,
It killed Immanuel in the prime of youth,
And still untold is how that story ends.

Your Stations of the Cross come to but three.
The gutter first, then prison, and the grave.
This plan provides no GET OUT OF JAIL FREE:
A process leaving no part Pilate could waive.

If the clock is crucifixion, you qualify.
Otherwise you're merely Mother's son.
Don't get a swelled head. It's nothing to die,
And being bad is the best bet to have fun.

All your cards clutched in your sweaty hands,
Fate confirms you have no ace in the hole.
Earth keeps no bed in all its quiet lands
Colder than satin sheets spread for your soul.

For cloud country, the trades blow west and south.
Carry a new corkscrew and a swizzle stick.
A boozer can't stay drunk on wind in his mouth,
And COKE is cold comfort alone: add some kick.

Not quite moronic, just a little slow,
Ride as happy as if you had good sense.
Visit the Elvis birthplace in Tupelo,
And hunt him everywhere you find footprints.

Your backseat driver now in the pilot's seat,
The *Index of Social Indicators* proves
You'll squeeze a pint of blood from a pickled beet
Before you can copy Presley's pelvic moves.

Elvis's stillborn twin in limbo might
Present a promising karma to pursue.
The shadow effect of paranormal sight
Could spur a seeker to try some voodoo.

Replay that sixties shuffle, the limbo rock,
To ease the mass anguish of purgatory.
Around the world, from Brussels to Bangkok,
Prescribe its posture to cure the vainglory

Of waiting for a pop apocalypse
To transport all to heaven's tableland.
The dance bends you backward from the hips:
Humility even kings understand.

Farther on a cross cries, JESUS SAVES,
Between Cold Harbor and the Slough of Despond.
Born to an earth of creature-comfort slaves,
Why worry now about a world beyond?

Get top yield from your DODGE's *Superglide.*
Pop caffeine pills to boost your driving force,
And match Apollo's chargers stride for stride.
No magic bullet revives a broken horse.

XCII *Graveyard School*

All systems are go, hot rod. The winding road
Bids you zero in on ultimate truth.
Alas, it costs your life to crack the code,
So don't expect to pay with a wisdom tooth.

What if your gravestone announced, HOME AT LAST,
The first housing you've had in a coon's age?
You'd blanch at hearing your lifestyle outclassed
By an epitaph you term an outrage.

Leave the road at ninety, either years
Or miles-an-hour. Both share a guarantee:
You never take your DIE–HARD back to SEARS,
And forfeit the choice to be or not to be.

6,000 stories in Rock City, but yours
Is a travelogue. It's time to make your bail.
ADDRESS UNKNOWN you'll paint on a hundred doors,
Before you're hauled feet first from your bone jail.

No need to worry then where to go next.
Eternity's blind chaos makes that moot.
So many years of nothing, you're perplexed?
According to *Hoyle*, time holds the trump suit.

Your goals invested in four spinning wheels,
The glow of an angry sunset slows you down.
Yet this does beat a pair of worn-out heels
To stand on facing a sheriff's cold frown:

"There's no hitchhiking allowed, don't you know.
We only let you walk and walk some more.
From here you take the path of the buffalo,
Which disappeared in 1884.

"And that was before the first administration
Of Grover Cleveland, so I can't really show
You the way. Ask at the first ranger station
You reach, if you get past New Mexico."

You turn by mistake on Transwestern Road,
Which leads over the Arizona Divide,
And pass a dirty hermit writing an ode?
Please give the ragged, crazy bastard a ride.

He could just have the answer to everything.
Ezra Pound looked nearly half that bad,
Locked in ST. ELIZABETH'S to sing
For supper and prove he truly was mad.

His *Cantos* remain elusive on the point
Of laying out his theory of mankind.
Some heretics are tempted to anoint
Him laureate of liver mush refined.

His imagination wandered everywhere,
Trying to cover five places at once
And capture his strange music from the air,
Poorly mixed with metaphysical grunts.

Whether he tapped the wisdom of the ages,
Borne on breezes across the pregnant sea,
And scattered genius upon a thousand pages,
Is still a puzzle hunting its lost key.

He often freed his mind on a test-drive,
In spite of being a fascist firebrand:
"Man reading should be man intensely alive.
The book should be a ball of light in your hand."

So here you are, alive and reading a book,
This one more like a burning coal in the hand,
Because of its snide, unsavory outlook.
Still you can label it anything but bland.

The graveyard school of poets had its day.
The subject may yet attempt a comeback.
While everyone knows that rhyme doesn't pay,
The assassin death prepares his next attack.

Advances and perspective reinforce
Each other, both in practice and in art.
None would compose like Milton again, of course,
But he gave Satan a fabulous new start.

Life is short, art is long, and all that.
Yet what if a work of verse just wears you down?
Browbeats you like a thug with a brickbat?
Can cold time knock off poetry's golden crown?

XCIII *Ocean Spray*

"Throw fear to the wind," wrote Aristophanes
In *The Wasps*. Why not take his bold advice?
A direct challenge or a comic tease:
Entirely enigmatic, crisp and concise.

Granted, it's out of context, and life's no play.
"Throw fate to the random winds," you've been told
Already, and how the counsel fires your clay
Determines how much fruit your vessel will hold.

Over 2,000 years divide these cues,
Each advocating the same heedless urge.
The matter still remains: what course ensues,
Once the words and a questing heart converge?

Embark upon your underfunded journey,
And always travel on Arizona time.
Your launch vehicle could be a surgeon's gurney
In a bit part as a corpse in *Tombstone Crime*.

You're headed where the prairie meets the blue,
And whether you're escaping, searching for gold,
Or simply captivated by the view,
The trail is blazing, and the dice are rolled.

Chase your fondest dreams down rural state
Back roads, living lean off the fat of the land,
Your pedals' pulse set for the pavement's great
Traffic system west of the Grand Strand:

The Grand Strand on the Carolina coast,
With outlet malls and golf courses strewn;
With wide beaches where sun-worshippers toast,
Absorbing the lethal rays of high noon.

HO FOR KANSAS!? Kansas isn't half
The places your awkward elbows are to go.
Don't hold your battle flag at half-staff,
Your marching music in pianissimo.

Conceive of yourself as such a crude force,
It pounds every minor bump in the road.
That way you won't outstrip your energy source,
Or buckle under an unfamiliar load.

The country's all before you, coast to coast,
From the Outer Banks to Hurricane Ridge,
With a ticking bomb at every milepost
To Frisco Bay from the foot of BROOKLYN BRIDGE.

St. Louis's GATEWAY ARCH bestrides your path.
Its great parabola mocks your rise and fall.
Home on the range or knee-deep in grapes of wrath,
You're blocking the path of time's thunderball.

The Show-Me State might spell your waterloo.
There *Easy Riders* see shotguns go boom,
Who spurn BUDWEISER or choke on mountain dew,
While Kansas City slaughterhouses fume.

DEDICATED TO ART AND FREE TO ALL,
The ST. LOUIS ART MUSEUM proclaims
Above its entrance, and though your sense is small,
Try some of the modern masters' mind games.

The key to much of their work is what's left out,
Then how each manipulates what remains.
Pollock's as tangled up as sauerkraut,
And Dalí's accused of causing migraines.

Rothko dispensed with line altogether,
While Morris Louis suppressed the human hand.
Calder hung steel to look light as a feather,
And Warhol sold his soap to beat the band.

The Mississippi's black, boot-sucking mud
Can bring your westward progress to a halt,
And hold you stuck until the next flood,
Begging God for an EXIT of asphalt.

Dug 50,000 years before your birth,
A void in the desert east of Flagstaff,
Meteor Crater's circle of blasted earth—
Old enough to make a prophet laugh

At *Revelation*'s golden candlesticks—
Can outlive you by a million years at least.
Will man survive his sloppy politics,
Whose churning billions furnish time's blood feast?

At Burgess Quarry in Yoho National Park,
Visit your first ancestors sandwiched in shale.
For light-years these trilobites lay in the dark,
Till Burgess cracked their geological braille.

You can spend the rest of your life shoveling shale,
Digging for an equal treasure of science,
And sooner receive a jackpot prize in the mail
Than lose your spot in time's Luddite alliance.

Spend the rest of your days shoveling shale—
Sure a nicer pastime than shoveling shit—
Yet still no luck turns up as you drink your ale.
You'll find your fortune ignored in holy writ.

Crater Lake's cobalt blue is one mile deep,
The wild blue yonder watered down and pale
Compared to this caldera's serene sleep,
Whose azure saturates death's trembling veil.

Aeons ago lava reached Puget Sound
From Mt. Rainier, a flow of ninety miles.
Catch an eruption? Your body's never found,
Like thousands lost with their dogs and dental files.

What hole do you run to when the sky's falling?
How do you inhale when the air's on fire?
You sink to a mere dumb animal crawling
To curl yourself in a ball, choke, and expire.

As an ice field crumbles into Glacier Bay,
Forcing the load of stone its push has ground
Down to round rocks, through the ocean spray
To float and then melt out, bottom-bound,

Your movement overland will also break
Off and disintegrate at being's end.
Remember this with every breath you take:
Your dust will blow in every gust of wind.

XCIV   *Polar Extremes*

See San Francisco, try the GRAY LINE tour.
View the scope of the coming killer quake:
All the homes PRUDENTIAL won't insure;
All the aging ribs to buckle and break.

Police have cadaver dogs to find the dead,
After a building collapse crushes them.
Either the feet appear first or the head—
Yet who recovers a finger's precious gem?

Unsafe as a soldier on Missionary Ridge,
Risking their necks to tempt Beelzebub,
Workers constructing the GOLDEN GATE BRIDGE
Labeled their crew the Halfway to Hell Club.

Detour wide of Truth or Consequences.
You'd get busted there for something obscene
Sure as shootin', when the sheriff senses
This maggot drilled his daughter in Abilene.

At Carlsbad Caverns, more than a million bats
Fly from the earth's mouth at dusk to feed
On a billion bugs that bite the desert rats.
So eat all creatures, measured to their need.

Yosemite Canyon rises straight and sheer.
Up top at the falls, one couple's last whim
Launched them as skinny-dippers of the year.
They jumped nude in the smooth black stream to swim.

Swept over, they dived into thought, hers to blame
Doofus who wrought this slapstick death in the raw.
Before they hit, she dropped him and his name,
The quickest split in the book of common law.

Its flower-studded meadows and the sublime
Grandeur of Yosemite's granite walls,
Are the canyon's two, polar extremes of time,
Between which all life's prior existence falls.

Nearby, sequoia trees live thousands of years,
With two named for Generals Sherman and Grant.
"Old soldiers never die" deserves no cheers,
Confusing men and trees in macho cant.

But Grant's *Memoirs* surpass those of his peers.
He writes of saddling up one night alone
To inspect his lines. Close in the dark he hears
The echo of his own troops' voices thrown

Back from Rebels right across a creek:
"Platoon salute commanding General Grant!"
What code governs a scene of hope so bleak?
With primal cause to aim his way, they can't.

What duty did they find to hold their fire?
The sacrifice in their deed bows your head.
A foe's regard can hardly rise higher,
Since come sunup, ample would be their dead.

Few commanders live to record such acts,
And few of these will admit to close scrapes.
Their daring overrides the danger's facts,
Their safety helped along by freak escapes.

Grant wanted a look, while a new moon shone,
Unmediated by paper, scouts, or staff:
Oblivious to a looming gravestone,
Barely dodging an early epitaph.

Half those men in the darkness probably died
When the slaughterhouse reopened the next day.
Your brain crashes on rocks in the blood tide,
The SUPER–COLLIDER clash of blue and gray.

XCV *Distant Thunder*

On Sherman's army's fiery march to the sea,
It came upon the SCHOOL FOR THE DEAF AND BLIND
At Cedar Spring, which made a quiet plea:
The children of both conditions filed in kind,

Each deaf child guiding a blind one by the hand,
To sit at picnic tables under the trees.
Troops all smeared with ash from scorching the land
Stopped dead still; a few sank to their knees.

They left without a word; no word sufficed
To relieve their faces chastened by the scene.
The school thanked the mercy of Jesus Christ.
Did the parting soldiers wipe their weapons clean?

Weren't such deaf children the privileged ones?
None ever heard the murderous thunder's noise
Of fighting fury, a hundred thousand guns
Resounding through the ranks of childhood toys.

New estimates of the dead from the conflict
Reach 850,000: ten percent
Of the male population, whom fortune picked
Not to come home when war's treasure was spent.

Thus "decimation" found its perfect match,
Its mathematic definition exact,
With every dead soldier's corps shoulder patch
To show he met his enlistment contract.

This total widely exceeds the lives lost
In all other United States wars combined.
And numbers don't assess the absolute cost:
A shattered nation the numbers left behind.

Visit Gettysburg or Chancellorsville,
Key turns in the country's long parade of death:
Land gone from placid field and wooded hill
To battleground for multitudes' final breath.

So much agony for so many souls,
A mind can delve too deep in sorrow's truth:
The endless, sounding bells of death tolls;
The boundless, bloody terrain of slain youth.

So many mothers lost so many sons,
Families blown apart by distant thunder.
Perhaps the dead turned out the blessèd ones,
Blind to their years of harvest ploughed under.

John Brown, hanged from a sour apple tree,
Couldn't conceive the scale of the fratricide.
A mere eighteen raiders were all that he
Thought it required to reverse history's tide.

Lincoln proposed enlistment for ninety days
At first, as enough to quickly quell a war,
Unseeing past Fort Sumter shelling's haze
The full measure rebellion held in store.

So many missing fathers, husbands, brothers,
Never returned to renew a last embrace;
So many fallen—plus how many others
Maimed, a fate wretchedly commonplace.

Nothing but time could dim this blazing night.
Self-inflicted ruin won't fight again.
Slaughter makes it hard to find the light
Shining through bullet holes in dead men.

What heart will bear to call up so much grief,
The butchered waste of internecine harm?
Pain so enormous shelters in disbelief,
Desiring the ranks of hatred to disarm.

The maimed in body and mind lick the dregs
Always left on warfare's dirty plate.
One-fifth was spent on artificial legs
In Georgia's budget of 1868.

The war-disabled have priority seats
Nearest the doors on the Paris MÉTRO.
Imagine how an amputee browbeats
A punk for his seat at DENFERT–ROCHEREAU.

The same seats are there for the very old,
And pregnant women tending a bloodline:
Three frank confines of frailty spelled in cold
Clarity by a simply lettered sign.

XCVI *Rainbow Bridge*

When Brigham Young declared, "This is the place,"
He ordered all his eager beavers to work,
Their harems to multiply a handsome race.
These pumped out kids like Bunnies gone berserk.

The Church of Jesus Christ of Latter-Day Saints
The outfit is titled by some gospel quirk.
Twelve elders neatly squelch the flock's complaints,
As Joseph Smith peers down with a sly smirk.

From Great Salt Lake to Zion Canyon south,
They fanned out far and wide with faith unfurled.
Still spreading their system from the horse's mouth,
From TEMPLE SQUARE they aim to convert the world.

Stop off and pay them a visit, tenderfoot.
Their version of heaven will send you, guaranteed.
Wallow your way through a life black as soot:
One scion saves you, swearing their strange creed.

You must be dead awhile before it works.
They have to trace your genealogy, too.
But documents complete, you win the perks
Of patriarchal paradise come true.

You find the scheme appealing? Take a chance.
Let instinct loose like geysers at Yellowstone.
Worship Satan in bacchanalian trance,
And count on kin to wing you to Zion's throne.

"Don't mangle my body, boys. Center my heart,"
Said John D. Lee in 1877,
Shot to give murdering Mormons a fresh start,
A clean slate to draw their blueprint of heaven.

Utah's a must, the most astounding state.
If its canyons and ghost-ship buttes cast their pearls
Before swine in polygamist podunk hate,
Its capital has the West's prettiest girls.

Blame the polygamists now on Bangham Young,
Their schism founded by Brigham's rebel son.
The stud considered himself so well hung,
A passle of paramours could share the fun.

In Mormon Dixie, St. George is the place
Where radiation blew from the bombing range
In the Cold War. The town was a hardship case
Of cancer eating folks like atomic mange.

Dr. Strangelove offered his treatment free
To fallout victims sunk in the flow of time.
"Pretty woman, what can the matter be?"
Maybe a mutant, mother's milk enzyme.

The quickening Grand and Green Rivers pour
Jointly into a thunderous gorge's spray,
Then simmer down along a canyon floor,
Cutting the buried past a passageway.

The Colorado River swallows the Green
Where mine-works mar the Cane Creek Anticline.
Death wears no veil more sea-deep ultramarine
Than oblivion blue, pooled as potash brine.

When water evaporates, so does the blue,
Leaving the potash salt as a white crust
Stuck in the middle of the sweeping view:
Fertilizer as foreign as moondust.

The river "too thick to drink, too thin to plow,"
Saw massive concrete tame the rage in its bed.
It scoured enough silt to brick up hell, but now
Its torrent carving wonders in rock is dead.

The Colorado's freedom ended in
February 1935.
Its harnessed rushing makes the turbines spin
In BOULDER DAM: wildness buried alive.

The force that through the green fuse drives the flower
Lies unacknowledged in the river's course,
Its noble current now transformed to power
Distant cities indifferent to the source.

The Double Arch near Moab's not some cheap
McDONALD'S, but is aeons older than sin.
In neon its real message would help you sleep:
WHO LIVES IN THE WORLD WALKS IN A LIONS' DEN.

The San Juan River's goosenecks cut their steep
Loop-the-loop into the planet's lost past.
Time that shaped these U-turns dug a deep
Death-trip total as Krakatoa's blast.

The Navajo's Nonnezoshi, Rainbow Bridge,
Great rock rib they worship as lord of the earth:
Long before Moses climbed Mt. Sinai's ridge,
This rainbow bridged epochs of death and birth.

The ARCHES OF TRIUMPH and OF CONSTANTINE
Adorn two dated capitals of power.
Unlike Rainbow Bridge, which formed unseen,
Their makers all would meet the fateful hour.

Dinosaur National Monument's rich find
Of fossils set the high for a single dig.
From one lode in sandstone, forty were mined,
Skeletons big as a Texas oil rig.

The dead or dying monsters, washed downstream,
Got stuck at a sandy, shallow river bend.
Buried, they turned to stone and became the dream
Treasure, the pickax professor's godsend:

A mass grave of lumbering beasts all curled
To sleep in a rock bed for the rest of time.
The ossuary mortals call the world
Is a rag-and-bone man's basement five-and-dime.

Science now says dinosaurs were smart.
Maybe they were, given their time and place.
Smart's a relative concept, much like art.
Who could know this better than you, huh, ace?

Perhaps the phrase "dumb as a dinosaur"
No longer describes your dullness, brainiac—
Although thinking is still a pesky chore,
A task for which you've never had a knack.

XCVII *Primeval Mud*

Every state has wonders, rube: go drink
It all in. Behold Montana's massive grace:
Climb Going-to-the-Sun Highway and think
How man stares neither sun nor death in the face.

Grand Canyon? Arizona's mighty slice
Of the past exposed, a billion years laid bare:
Rock history, whose bottom shelf of gneiss
Lacks fossils. Life and death were never there.

Before life and death was incipient slime.
Your problem's not that both pleasure and pain
Were absent on Earth once upon a time.
Your job is to die by degrees yet stay sane.

Correction: the lifeless layer of rock is schist,
The billionth year revealed to the naked eye
In the Southwest desert, rendering sun-kissed
The darkest nothing the past is defined by.

Zane Grey saw cougars leap off the canyon rim,
Evading the ropes of goons from a city zoo.
Your chance at noble death is hopelessly slim.
A live dog's better than a dead lion? You?

At Monument Valley, galloping John Wayne
Found fame as Western movies' biggest gun.
Two buttes there, Left and Right Mitten, hold off rain:
Desert's death-grip, hand in hand with the sun.

The globe's top sundial's giant gnomon looms
Skyward in Arizona at CAREFREE
RETIREMENT VILLAGE. Is this how desert blooms?
Should the old folks go dance in its shade, or flee?

RELAXED, SUNNY LIVING, states the brochure.
While Father Time is breathing down their necks?
His index expressing what the sun can't cure
Should nurse a dying burg of nervous wrecks.

Some mad builder's sick idea for a joke,
The joyless symbol stands, a sign for all.
Time's fell shadow wraps the world in its cloak.
Nothing alive eludes this velvet pall.

And why do people celebrate New Year's Eve?
Wherefore rejoice in the deadly march of time?
More apt would be to dress in black and grieve.
The stroke of midnight's not a happy chime.

To be sure, the same can be said of birthdays.
Miss Kitty's attitude is right about that.
Her archenemy ultraviolet rays,
Still worse is time itself, the dirty rat.

In Times Square, waiting for the ball to drop,
A million souls toast another year gone;
Another begun before the cheers stop,
Stealing in sly as a leprechaun.

Ghost towns litter Nevada's landscape,
Once busy mining camps where Mammon was king.
Only sagebrush stirs there: rustles like crepe
On planks where love's saloon girls would sing.

"Now nothin's left but the vultures and the snakes,"
Griped Mimi after climbing aboard the stage.
"It's finished when the madam pulls up stakes.
No sense in grievin', though, it shows your age."

Graveyards closed for business with the rest
Of a town's concerns, leaving weedy plots
And rusted fences being repossessed
By the soil: rows of iron forget-me-nots.

Revelry wanders the dark and lonely streets,
Searching for shelter where human warmth is gone.
Lost forever, the barmaids' sultry sheets
Resisting the light of rosy-fingered dawn.

Portales, New Mexico, is a place to miss,
A town of obscure openings galore.
Any or all might chute you down an abyss
That sucks you through a bare adobe floor.

Doors to nowhere, decide you must avoid,
So Two Guns, Arizona, is one of these,
The name too neat to keep you undestroyed.
Obliterate yourself quietly, please.

"Rainbow wood," formed in primeval mud,
Fills Petrified Forest with broken spars
On the Painted Desert. Growth rings red as blood
Are cross-sections of years distant as stars.

220 million years ago,
The rainbow wood was 200-foot trees.
Your own atoms meet chaos down below.
This timber makes eternity seem a breeze.

Araucarioxylon arizonicum names
Such petrified wood in scientific terms:
The fireproof substance hardened by hell's flames,
Forever sealed to both water and worms.

XCVIII *Atlantic Rollers*

DEATH VALLEY CLAIMS THE WORLD'S HOTTEST SPOT,
Boldly announces *USA Today*.
134 degrees is not
Matched by Sahara sand or badlands clay.

So far science can't determine the cause
That boulders slide across Death Valley's floor
While no one watches, confounding nature's laws:
A puzzle, and the earth has millions more.

If science isn't doping this question out,
Why not grant a lowly poet the chance?
Quantum physics, he knows nothing about,
But his noggin's blinking lights could try to dance.

You've seen a cold glass slide on a countertop,
Gliding upon its condensation alone,
No nudge impelling it to start or stop.
The same can't occur when night chills the stone?

The smoothness of the surfaces won't compare,
Yet the unseen rock-slide doesn't happen fast.
One yard per year requires no FRIGIDAIRE,
Each advance as little as the last.

Death Valley the lowest point in the U.S.,
The lowest point in your life comes anywhere.
From Pensacola to Portland, take a guess;
From Hudson's Bay to the Texas State Fair.

A national monument named Bandolier
In Texas marks the Apache's last stand.
The final phase of your bizarre career
Will falter in some uncharted borderland.

Barely scratching its surface, do your best
To scout the country that echoes, "Wagons ho!"
Since Columbus landed, the world looks west.
You find fool's gold? What matters most is to go.

Long before Columbus, Vikings set sail:
Five centuries ahead of the Genoese.
They foraged Vinland, heard their newborns wail,
But then departed this realm of endless trees.

Later they returned to Minnesota,
Clearing the trees to free 10,000 lakes.
If you conclude some lousy bastard wrote a
Book predicting your death, hit the brakes.

Alter your course yet keep your end in mind.
Find new angles to follow the risen sun.
Even if two-lane roads are much maligned,
They offer more ways to finish what's begun.

Clearing the land to open up the sky
Occupied Davy Crockett and Daniel Boone,
Who often met fresh dangers to defy.
Inspire yourself by humming a DISNEY tune

From sea to shining sea, Miami to Nome.
Carefully thread the needle of Flaming Gorge,
Or plod like a blindered mule where bison roam.
Time breaks you, strong as a vise in Vulcan's forge.

From Atlantic rollers crashing on granite rocks
To the northern sky's night display ablaze;
From the St. Lawrence Seaway's canal locks
To the isolated surf of Point Reyes;

From Savannah's twelve squares to Mt. Rushmore,
From Brighton Beach to Pacific Palisades;
See the country as time keeps fatal score,
Till life's peep show decides to drop the shades.

To Pasadena from the streets of Boston,
The San Juan Islands from St. Augustine;
From Duluth to the gentle hills of Austin,
To Craters of the Moon from Bowling Green;

From Ocean City's boardwalk to Carmel,
From Bedford Stuyvesant to Mission Hill;
To Mt. McKinley from the LIBERTY BELL,
From Plymouth Rock to downtown Oroville;

From the shores of West Palm Beach to Oshkosh,
From West Virginia coal mines to Boise;
From Tallahassee to the Vegas Wash,
From Sparta, Georgia, to Sparta, New Jersey;

From Jacksonville to Anchorage, Alaska,
From Natchez, Mississippi, to St. Paul;
At least as far as the wheat fields of Nebraska,
From Galveston to anywhere at all;

To Gulfport from Centralia, Illinois,
Azusa, California, from St. Pete;
From Camden to Albuquerque, Fargo to Troy,
There's any setting for you and death to meet.

From the Grand Tetons to the birthplace of jazz,
Kill Devil Hills to EDWARDS AIR FORCE BASE;
Key West to Big Sur, Cape Cod to Alcatraz,
There's ample room to vanish without a trace.

XCIX *Apocalyptic Fury*

Antlike searchers of wilderness today
Called mountain men journeyed into a great
Mystery, seeking to make their courage pay
In the face of time's eternal checkmate.

These early trappers were first to tame the West:
A hardy breed who harvested beaver pelts
While meeting the elements' most extreme test,
Between where the cold kills and the snow melts.

Beaver pelts for the eastern fashion trade,
And European taste of the era, too:
Fur collars, coats, and muffs on proud parade,
Supplied by men who stank like a whaling crew.

MANIFEST DESTINY drove them overland,
Mapping the future for pioneers' eyes.
Ill content to hear of it secondhand,
You're off to sample the same western skies.

Your gaze toward the horizon, even in sleep
Gliding across the prairies, skim the crest
Of faraway peaks; survey the boundless sweep
Of plains feeding the golden glow of the West.

The whole romantic fuzz on the frontier,
For better land thought beckoning yet beyond,
Gets in the blood like a stream of cold beer,
Even for a penniless vagabond.

Ever onward, doggedly on and on,
Probing the reach of the former unknown—
Where timberwolves circled and salmon spawn,
Past the Tetons' curtain of shining stone

Polished slick by aeons of ice and wind—
And drawn by Eldorado's empty grail
Urging you to endeavor to land's end,
Follow the western phantom's sunset trail.

Wandering always after the western gleam,
Against a constant backdrop of gray sage,
Perform your variation upon that theme,
Inspired to try composing its next page.

Roaring rapids which coil a river's course;
A hoarsely bellowing, misty waterfall;
The impact of sleet blown with shotgun force;
Thunderbolts lashing through a summer squall;

Are sounds to season a timid trail scout.
Chasms slashing across a torrid plain;
Impetuous tributaries pouring out
Of mountainsides, strong as a bullet train;

Scorching wastes around a dry lake bed;
A fog of volcanic ash from dragging feet:
Among the unhappy sights that lie ahead,
While time is toting up your balance sheet.

The crystal headwaters of the Red River;
The cactus-strewn barrens outside Tucson:
In an age or two, such opposites deliver
Weather enough to bury the PENTAGON.

Where a black cloud suddenly palls the sky,
Its blasts of hail can carve you a headstone.
On the lonely sweep of endless plains, a cry
Within that storm is a sigh in a cyclone.

The rolling uplifts athwart the South Platte
And Arkansas Rivers present a scene
Of shoulders bare as a lifeless salt flat,
Raised above the ranks of evergreen.

Cold to the marrowbone, or covered in sweat
And burning like a kerosene stove,
Contend with the four elements' death threat,
Caught in the web the great creator wove.

Should flash floods push torrents of mud between
Low banks, direct your path to higher ground.
If gales of sand or sleet are wailing, lean
Into the wind and continue westbound.

When huge cloud banks rapidly dissipate,
And a great wall of pinnacles rears ahead
With gem glitter flecking a glacier, wait
To watch the sunset flush the snowcaps red.

Crossing the front range of Rockies through
Thick forests of aspen and fir—where cold streams
Sluice in steep canyons, and caribou
Drank from the luminous waters, while sunbeams

As spears of light penetrating the cover
Of leaves and needles, perforate the shade—
Pause in the scented air like a windhover,
Pleased to have your plodding pace delayed.

Admire the clean bold lines of open land,
The free sweep of the wind in mountain valleys:
More bracing than drugs to help the mind expand,
Than powder from joy dealers in back alleys.

High on the ridges, greenwood showing yellow,
Past the difficult fords of Custer's Creek—
And a continent away from MONTICELLO—
Primes you for northers screaming from Pike's Peak.

The debris-fraught flux of the muddy Missouri,
Flooding out of the west across your path,
Would drown you in apocalyptic fury,
If the CORPS OF ENGINEERS botched its math.

C *Anthrax Terror*

When rivers freeze and night's a knife-edged glitter
Of winter starlight frosty overhead,
Let thoughts of springtime sun hold the bitter
Cold at bay that curtains dawn with dread.

If from splintering darkness, needle-pointed
Granules of sleet shriek on a fierce wind,
And reason begins to stumble disjointed,
Cling to stupidity as your closest friend.

Should gales blown with the blind rage of demons
Come howling out of the dark like lost souls,
Try to pretend you have delirium tremens,
And the sound erupts from hell's fumaroles.

Feel spring's new tenderness touch the low hills,
The retreating snow line on soaring peaks,
As March's thin sunshine slowly instills
The warmth that fills snake skins and bird beaks.

Along the thawing runoff beyond gaunt
Slopes of the Badlands toward the Bighorns, drive
Where spring-green meadows of wildflowers flaunt
Colors waking the land again alive.

On the Snake's huge arc through southern Idaho,
Cross the Divide through shimmering aspen groves,
Aware that whether in daylight or moonglow,
Dangers await you, singly and in droves.

In April as blue shows bright behind the clouds,
Followed by the rushing floods of spring,
Gone are the winter skies' leaden shrouds,
And birdsong stretches day like a bowstring.

When too soon after the gray light of dawn,
Updrafts on the wings of western morning
Return as if their currents had been drawn
From hell's fissures to issue a frank warning—

Descending upon you with sledge-hammer heat
Across the rolling vastness of the plains,
And peeling the parched fields of wilted wheat—
Before your last reserve of energy wanes,

Pray for the filtered sunlight and long grass
Cool under cottonwoods and locust trees;
For mountains rising huge and blue to mass
Quickly ahead and avalanche a breeze

Toward you braced with a life-renewing shower
Which drops the mercury as a dying flame.
Changing scenery can't exhaust its power
To expose a picture-perfect freeze-frame.

The spruce-freckled meadows of Union Pass;
A first, uplifting glimpse of zigzag peaks;
Or the drift rippling in water like blown glass;
Are restful visions a tired traveler seeks.

Stopped in the shade of a high basalt cliff—
Its columns upholding their jagged rock ledge
Feathered by stands of pine, from which a whiff
Comes wafting freshly down to the water's edge

Of a mild river flowing cool and blue,
As though the earth were new and the nation young—
Try taking a dip that's plenty overdue,
And dulls the sting of trail dust on your tongue.

But a bright green band of poplars at the far
Margin of a stream, and dim above
The treetops the shapes of distant ranges, are
Contrasts in time you must be wary of.

Where hogbacks, lone buttes, and long pine ridges
Separate meadows of deep grass dotted by
Willow thickets alive with vampire midges
Humming for blood beneath a broiling sky,

The remnants of gushing freshets start to choke,
Trickling around their rocks in mid-July
Through drab, boulder-studded canyons, and soak
Down into desert flats that drink them dry.

If out of nowhere, canopied by dust,
A galloping herd of wild horses streams
And pulverizes the desert's fragile crust,
Observe how the mica catches sunbeams.

As gaping you trek onward beneath the blue,
Blinding glare of a sky enormous past
All saying, the unchained roll of rivers through
The desert won't impede a thermal blast

Of dust abruptly rising angry out
Of the farthest dim reach of the red land.
So never ignore weather reports about
An ill wind that whispers across the sand.

Where the San Juans tumble crazily off
Into the desert, hide your face from a gale:
A dust devil might blow you a viral cough,
Like anthrax terror spread in poisoned mail.

The dry, crystal air destroys perspective.
Mirages hedge the horizon with spectral shapes.
Before you suspect your vision is defective,
Look for your face in a mirror and find an ape's.

But in chasing faded rainbows renewed at dawn,
Arcing over the cloud caps in the west,
The eternal glint of hope will lure you on.
Impossible fancies fizz through your dream quest.

CI *Roadhouse Rendezvous*

Beyond Tulsa the time comes to slow down.
West of the Pecos, the law ignores appeals.
You dance from ten feet of rope, amuse the town,
And the judge's MUSTANG drags you off by the heels.

BIGGEST SCOFFLAW EVER IN NORTH TEXAS!
CAUGHT WITH TRUNKFUL OF BOOTLEG OUTTA-STATE BOOZE
LABELED BY CRUDELY LETTERED TRIPLE XXX's!
NOW WALKS IN DAZE, COVERED BY MAZE OF TATTOOS!

Those salient points highlight the wild report
The scandal sheets saddle your image with.
Details open to question, be a good sport:
Claim your special niche in American myth.

Meantime soak up some Panhandle culture, Jake.
Buy COWTOWN boots, then try your local luck:
A honky-tonk hostess's moonlit earthquake
Rocking the ready bed of her pickup truck.

If heaven awaits out in the parking lot,
Hurry and kick the sawdust from your heels.
A roadhouse rendezvous's quick, so take your shot:
Go test her chassis, see how her frame feels.

Start off with a close dance: Calamity Jane
Will grind your groin with buckskin-tasseled hips,
Then spin your spurs fast as a hurricane
With kisses of flame licking from dewdrop lips.

Her satin TRU-WEST blouse is lovely filled
By live ammo: .38-caliber breasts
That act weightless. Erect as if self-willed,
Their buoyancy's tensile strength never rests.

They bounce tighter than heavy-duty shocks
On her DODGE RAM, whose trim says KNOCK 'EM DEAD.
No poem is praise enough when the jukebox
Engages her tender loins Texas-bred.

Her emerald eyes like forest-shrouded suns
Flashing through wind-tossed leaves in laser bolts,
Countless the ranch hands her bronco-bustin' buns
Have straddled and soon calmed into nursing colts.

She's eager, pure western, and all wild.
What more could a dude ask from mother earth?
The cosmos brightened the first time she smiled
Eighteen years after her miracle birth.

As straight-shootin' fun with a gun trick, she
Reveals her hidden treasure to boost your morale.
"My ripeness needs tasting," she beckons. "Come see
How juicy the fruit grows on a green-eyed gal.

"Looking for the moon in someone's eyes?
In thirty minutes I can change your life.
No man exists my flesh can't mesmerize,
And conquer any sort of gender strife.

"What grabs me as moonlight falls through the trees
Is the shadows' motion shifting here and there,
In rhythmic response to just the slightest breeze,
And urging me to strip my breasts bare.

"In Vegas they play the game DOLLARAMA.
For boy-meets-girl, my boots are filled with gold.
You'll never find a more uplifting drama
Than my undressing's wonder to behold.

"I look the best in my preferred attire,
Briefly summarized as without a stitch.
Your touch goes through me like electric wire,
And any spot on my skin is the ON switch.

"Nothing lasts forever," she says with a sigh.
"Some things don't last a warm Texas night.
Right now my lower burner is set on HIGH:
Give it some oxygen, help its oil burn bright.

"Fire raging at midnight is embers at dawn.
Pick a random page from *The Acts of Love*.
The queen desires to crown your captured pawn,
And squeeze him tight as an ISOTONER glove.

"While trees play a soft waltz of the wind,
The stars sparkling down into your eyes
Tell me this magic darkness ought never end.
Must I amplify a word to the wise?"

CII *Lucky Strike*

"As long as gents wear pants, I plan to please.
What could cheer me more than earning my fame?
I bare my thirty-eights to the night breeze
And aim them at what I want, a deadeye dame.

"*Best Chest in the West* is hardly half
The story of my bosom's bouncing balls.
Plot their marvelous motion on a graph.
Which is lovelier—when it rises, or falls?

"I prefer to call them my pleasure chest,
From a land flowing with milk and honey.
Don't just stand there, stranger, be my guest:
I'll keep my hands off nothing but your money.

"The best foundation for these is fresh air.
They require no assistance in pointing straight,
And no man's ever managed to merely stare,
Or needed less notice to motivate.

"None other offers so much bounce per ounce,
Once I choose my stud and open the gate.
Then as the climb to climax slowly mounts,
Ejaculation never comes too late.

"Jane Russell acted her own Calamity Jane,
In the hit movie *The Paleface* with Bob Hope.
Her breasts and mine make many gals complain
They can't compete with our assets' epic scope.

"Tough luck, I say in my normal, candid speech.
We both have the goods men seek, but *c'est la vie.*
And implants curve walleyed on a topless beach,
So bite your nails with envy: ours were free.

"Bob Hope called his co-star 'the two and only.'
Now mine wait for you on a silver platter.
So grab your chance and squeeze, they're getting lonely:
The finest grade of love's organic matter.

"To type Miss Russell's appeal in *The Outlaw*,
'BUST BECOMES BONANZA,' cried TIME magazine.
Nothing stopped its stupendous box-office draw,
Even though censors cut what they found 'obscene.'

"Call it whatever you want to, all you prudes.
You still like how mine flash in the bright sun.
Contrary to some women's varied moods,
My body and my breasts have simply one.

"While night air licks my nipples hard as rubber,
The ooze of my vital space bursts into flame:
A burning bush lit by my cowboy lover,
Who marvels how a tigress grows so tame.

"Doubled up in pleasure, I'm balanced right
For fire and flood our divine rite will unfold.
Doubled over, my treasure comes to light,
So shovel and soak me in a shower of gold.

"If Zeus loved that way, Miss You Know Who
Says no Greek nymph could beat the hand I'm dealt.
Show me what rhymes with Venus, and I'll show you
Vulcan's hammer so hot I make it melt.

"Remember that number, *Leda and the Swan?*
Quite a shifty character, big chief Zeus.
He only got laid using some kind of con,
But all I want is your hormones let loose.

"America's sweater girl, Lana Turner,
Helped bring large breasts into the present age.
Yet compared to me, she was a bra-burner
Acting out some weird, post-modern rage.

"I did belong to the Lubbock Bulldoguettes,
Cheerleaders for its high-school football team.
But they were butch as a band of suffragettes
Given one too many reasons to scream.

"I strive to achieve delight in equal shares
For both of us, regardless what Freud said.
Nothing tops the punch of my derrière's
Rebound from the sprung mass of a bed.

" 'Male and female created he them' is my
Favorite Bible verse, so stay awhile.
I'm well-disposed to your discerning eye,
One touch announcing my unrivaled style

"As passion's constant through all changing times:
Sex's radiant secret here today,
Whose cries of rapture replace wedding chimes,
No honeymoon needed for my best lay.

"Some women boast kisses sweeter than wine,
But my kiss penetrates both flesh and bone.
Whomever I choose to be my valentine
Has only to make his deepest desire known.

"Protocol doesn't matter; essence does.
Feel where all my living force is whorled.
Once your hot iron brushes my fiery fuzz,
Our genders join in flames that wind the world.

"Spontaneous combustion's what I like.
Come on, roper, let your reasoning go.
I light your maleness as my LUCKY STRIKE,
Entranced by your poker's urgent red glow.

"Ever wonder who wrote *The Book of Love*?
I bet I could've done a better job:
With Hester Prynne proud to be spoken of,
And Brigitte Bardot a bashful, frigid snob.

"I don't seek 'Love me tender, love me true,'
The first for cheap romance, the second for fools.
I'm not expecting Tom Mix or Lash LaRue:
Just cut on the juice, start your power tools.

"The mere thought of it quickly primes my pump.
One size fits all so hurry, hook us up.
Take turns astride the beast we buck and hump,
And feast on what fills a 38 C-cup.

"Plumbing my depth, don't spare an ounce of thrust.
I like to be ridden hard and put up wet.
Love is strange, yet here's advice to trust:
When I'm on fire, take all of me you can get."

CIII *Rhodes Scholar*

"A rotten brothelmeister, name of Dred,
Used to take a cut on my choice tricks.
He nearly died, the way his ulcer bled,
Once I ran off with the rocker Jimmy Dix.

"Independent now, out on my own,
I do things when, where, and for whom I please.
I live to ride with a lone rolling stone,
Who makes me hum like a queen of bumblebees.

"No half-passionate undergraduate, see,
Heating up curlers more than she does a man,
I reckon myself, at all of thirty-three,
A full erection's most emphatic fan.

"I need no bathing beauty frilly stuff.
What I offer's genuine Jane O'Shannon,
And a six-foot hunk of burnin' love's enough,
If he glows like coal and comes like a cannon.

"These arms of mine weren't made to be unmanned.
Lift this bar belle, see how her fanny flexes.
Work out like digging to the Holy Land,
Then turn me over, ride me back to Texas.

"I prize the moment when push comes to shove:
We meet halfway and drive your manhood home.
I won't trade fates then with an angel above,
As my bedroom beams soar like a pleasure dome.

"The birth of rock-and-roll's transcendent king,
The Killer, calls it *Lovin' up a Storm*.
Jerry Lee Lewis showed Elvis how to sing.
I'm happy to note you find me in top form.

"A stunt-man Casanova suits me fine—
Who doesn't drop his demoiselle on the floor.
Throw me for loops and call me Clementine,
Just so it leaves me indescribably sore.

"Or call me Wonder Woman if you prefer,
Who drives your staying power off the scale.
Let future mythos fondly say of her:
'She never disappointed a U.S. male.'

"Down in Dallas, they titled me LADY JANE,
A legal intoxicant produced by me.
No gentleman ever tried its taste in vain,
Yet tapping it requires no college degree.

"It enthralls whether a man is blue collar;
A range boss or a clerk in Lonesome Town;
A Bible-pounding preacher or Rhodes Scholar:
He never leaves my favors with a frown.

"Love's best elixir, ask for it by name,
Whenever I'm not around, ready to hand.
Strike a match and watch it nurse a flame,
After which you'll buy no other brand.

"I like my satisfaction guaranteed.
Performance level is my strongest suit,
Applied wherever I find a pressing need.
No money down, accept no substitute.

"I greet my party with lust aforethought,
So will you not, or will you be my man?
Pardon my forwardness: I know I ought
To let you make the advances. —What's the plan?

"I mount a wrangler like a Brahma bull:
Dig my hands in his beef and give him a fight.
Only the strongest haunches leave me full.
I love the jolt of sitting on dynamite.

"The manly image makes me glow inside:
That itch to get back in the saddle again,
Bounce on its pommel, and hit my horse's stride
Till stallion lather drenches my rosy skin.

"My crotch warmly gripping the saddle's horn,
I grab my stallion's mane for a long hard ride.
More woman you haven't known since you were born.
More woman never whipped a horse's hide.

"My legs spread like bellows, the fire they stoke
Blazes up at the mouth of my tunnel of love.
Hungry for lumber to fuel my stirrup stroke,
I scream like a siren, coo like a turtledove.

"Pump my engine with all the gas you've got.
Floor the pedal, work your way through the gears.
I run like twelve pistons and running hot,
My bliss erupts so loud it hurts your ears."

CIV *Ivory Tower*

"No need to wear your spurs when I lie down.
My pelvis packs all the oomph men can endure.
As my boiler blows, I yell enough to drown
A planet of grief. My ecstasy's that pure.

"Kindly oblige me. I'm ready to saddle up
And wail to my wild Irish rock and roll.
I'll milk you so hard you'd fill a DIXIE cup,
Then churn your sperm like butter to feed my soul.

"I ride sidesaddle too, in a modest mood:
More ladylike if refinement is desired.
Shifting my legs that way doesn't look rude:
I could stay mounted for days and not get tired.

"Fluttering in the chambers of your heart,
When was your last romantic interlude?
Don't be so shy. Step up and play the part
You were born for. My lips are angel food.

"The scarlet letter I want's an A-plus,
My merit badge as a graduate Girl Scout.
Why do Puritan squares all stammer and cuss
At impure thoughts sublimely acted out?

"Before the Lord, we're naked and we know it,
But what I crave is to be naked with you.
You needn't be an ivory tower poet,
Nor Romeo here on a job interview.

"The part some term 'the division of the legs'
Is the place I call 'where knock is open wide.'
My nipples sizzle my buns like powder kegs
Whose seismic shaking heaves as if God just died.

"I fancy no fiery master matador,
No rich wildcatter's sugar-daddy lies.
A midnight cowboy's what I'm longing for.
Ignite this starry darkness, mystic eyes.

"Birds of a feather come together. Let's
Live the proverb, partner: fire up the night
And race the moon to morning. I'll take bets
We hold an afterglow like a ball of light.

"Let's have us two a cosmic relationship,
Such as leaves us speechless under the stars.
It begins once my sweet spot gets a grip,
Then sends out shock waves halfway to Mars.

"There's a rush in my blood I can't control
As soon as my heart starts doing somersaults.
Give me the chance to let all my roundness roll,
While trying unprecedented pole vaults.

"Excuse my frank manner of pitching woo
Upon the sensitive tablets of men's hearts,
But I've got something wild for Y–O–U,
And rate my technique as one of the fine arts.

"Just now a brush fire kindles between my legs,
And I only know one way to put it out.
My breasts feel hot as two frying eggs.
Please lay them down, see what my love's about.

"Draw your love gun and cock it, cowboy:
Watch it be pulled like a divining rod
Pointing at the purest fountain of joy
You'll find anywhere this side of God.

"You have your own flesh and blood on your hands:
That's enough to convict you of primal lust.
My simple, non-negotiable demands
Are to couple and come, here in rancho dust.

"The battle of the sexes I engage
Always culminates in perfect peace:
A wrestling match of love at every stage,
Until the struggle's overwrought release.

"'Of marble men and maidens overwrought,'
Wrote John Keats in *Ode on a Grecian Urn.*
No consummation comes to maids uncaught,
Who miss what makes my bold libido burn."

CV *Prairie Fire*

The lady means to give you supreme friction.
No airhead nymph from PLAYBOY pages, she's
Naked proof that presence trumps depiction.
Her passion wows you, proud as Hercules.

Earthbound matter can't possibly replace
Her joy that wakes the world to ring your bell.
The female paragon of carnal grace,
She has no geographic parallel.

When a goddess speaks, how can you refuse
Mating's unsurpassable one-on-one?
There's no superior advent you could choose—
In Texas, or any spot under the sun.

Better accept her offer, Disco Tex.
This cowgirl jump-starts your cattle prod.
The way in's the way out: sheer savage sex.
Count her awesome skill your gift from God.

Say, "JAKE'S LUBE SERVICE at your disposal,
Miss 'Sure-Shot' O'Shannon. —Call me Rock.
I'm plumb seduced by your demure proposal,
Which opens my heart, oiling the rusty . . . lock.

"I claim no special flair as a sexsmith,
Yet already I feel my self-image rise.
Thanks to you my probe thickens its pith.
I've never seen it sport this heft and size."

The red-headed angel of honky-tonk,
Good for what ails a guy, whatever his job—
From cowpoke to corporate policy wonk—
Her starlit flesh makes all your longings throb.

She looks better than money in the bank,
Such a wealth of unspoilt beauty is hers.
Any place she appears is summit of swank:
She shows more riches nude than wrapped in furs.

No snub is intended other womenfolk
By calling this Lone Star lassie statuesque.
But the play of her complex curves' high baroque
Was never meant for sitting behind a desk.

The shape she fills could almost raise the dead.
Her fabulous form draws a man from the grave?
He won't come back with a halo on his head:
He'll want the best encore she ever gave.

Her touch is warm as a wild Texas wind,
Whose sultry gusts whip up dust and desire.
From I-40 to the Rio Grande's Big Bend,
Her shamrock brand smolders, prairie fire.

She talks like a songbird, walks like a sonic boom
In flame-stitched boots she calls her passion pumps.
You've heard the timeless usage *Va-va-voom!*?
When Lady Jane does Dallas, the asphalt jumps.

A red-tressed temptress, bright as the silver screen,
She's yours at the drop of a hat and throws her own
Hat down. Be polite to the rodeo queen:
Rock like mad in her royal velvet throne.

The all-out tug-of-war her limbs let fly,
Locking her partner in a scissors hold
To drill for a gusher big as the Texas sky,
Proves her libido perfectly uncontrolled.

Her skirt parachutes open and gently lands
In your lap? Dare you hint she somehow missed
Her target? Better trust her confident hands,
And sit back stunned by her Amarillo Twist.

Or head straight for the barn to roll in the hay.
Here's one cowgirl who never gets the blues.
She grabs your joystick and begs, "Bombs away!
Drop me a payload that pounds like a B-52's!"

CVI *Texas Twister*

Fight fire with fire, match her flame for flame.
The inviting blaze behind her brilliant eyes
Was Eve's in Eden, heedless of guile or shame.
Its cheer never fades; its ardor never dies.

All over Texas she can stop a storm,
Corral and whirl it backwards out to sea.
Her smile will turn December weather warm,
Or rhapsodize midsummer ennui.

Her nakedness unveils an angel of bliss.
The doorbell to heaven rings her telephone.
Thrills of glory imbue her luscious kiss,
And wonder rides the whip of her backbone.

Her hair glows like an eagle's wings on fire,
Her eyes green as the leaves of a laurel tree.
Her voice sweet as the strings of a golden lyre,
Her treasure hides beneath a scarlet V.

Her hourglass figure means time on your hands:
It streams from her breast to love's lower half,
So take advantage of fortune's shifting sands.
Failure to do this could carve your epitaph.

Tie your holsters tight and give her a twirl,
Measuring time by how her body sways.
The future fixes itself: you get the girl,
And dance to the metronome your heart obeys.

You get the girl; time arranges the rest.
Poisonous belladonna is nightshade.
Your beautiful lady, goddess of love out west,
Makes the bed wherein your grave is laid.

The opposite sex is being's master key.
Without true beauty, mankind would be lost.
Yet all its offspring finally cease to be,
And few die pleased by living's full cost.

Even Jesus protested against his fate,
Asking his father if maybe, just this time . . . ?
But Dad's crowded card had booked that date,
And crucifixion wasn't for petty crime.

"My God, why hast thou forsaken me?"
He cried. Calamity Jane takes what comes,
Converting it to billows of ecstasy:
Pure climax as the earth's rotation hums.

As hearts' teeming waters drive their tides,
Whose breakers breed life till the sun breaks down,
Death like a headless mermaid also rides,
Moiling the sea where all souls swim and drown.

Calamity Jane O'Shannon's brave id
Is beauty's assault on oblivion's sea-beast.
Answer her prayers till you rock the planet, kid.
Forget those horse-faced debutantes back east.

"It was beauty killed the beast." Thus ends *King Kong*.
And whether it's Fay Wray or Jessica Lange,
Her buxom blossoming doesn't last long.
Let Jane O'Shannon launch you with a bang.

That open ready boldness in her eyes
Can kindle your heart in the darkest dance hall.
Does her gaze beam through love's own tender lies?
The torque of her Texas twister conquers all.

CVII *Cosmic Course*

Are the stars holes of light in heaven's floor,
Composing night by divine punctuation?
Since Charon rows you straight to the other shore,
Heaven's a concept, not a destination.

The sun's a dying star that tolls like a bell,
In a wave rhythm's pulse like a living heart:
A cosmic clock whose starquakes' constant knell
Sounds where mortality's time limits start.

Over a million frequencies ring within
The sun's fireball. What is their waves' cause?
Explore the unknown and find a snake skin.
Science leaves much yet untouched by its laws.

To delve into time's depths, where now is never;
To thread a through-hole of the universe,
A funneling down which opens to forever;
Is a reeling ride in time's eternal hearse.

To tune in wavelengths of infinite space;
To glimpse by death's keyhole the hopeless void;
Brings recoil that bans the unbearable face
Of a future viewed with your own flesh destroyed.

To grasp the scope of death, to comprehend
What crushes all that stirs the human breast,
The mind must journey past where thoughts end
Annihilated. Sanity fails this test.

A vision flashed before you of time to come
Beyond your life, of geology's boundless blank,
Attacks like madness. Reason, relieved and numb,
Swiftly returns here from the opposite bank.

"Let's cross the river and rest under the trees,"
Was wounded Stonewall Jackson's last request.
The river you cross hums with birds and bees,
Its other side the shade of permanent rest.

Try to feature this rest as dreamless sleep.
It does no harm to want to reduce your terror.
You never rise again to laugh or weep,
But neither must you abide your secret sharer—

Your double who was dancing in the flames
To celebrate your fresh arrival in hell.
In dreamless sleep, no dancing master blames
Your blunders; simply leaves you where you fell.

Think how long your self shall cease to exist:
Till the end of time. When will time be done?
When asteroids blast this Earth back down to schist?
Or the planet freeze-dries to die with the sun?

The world will end in thermonuclear fire,
Many believe. Or does it drift away,
A cold and hollow shell, a sphere of wire,
The skeleton left behind by doomsday?

In new proof, the latter won't come to pass.
The sun will enlarge past Venus and explode,
Earth's long-dead globe by then a molten mass.
Or life could stop with a meteor's payload.

"RED GIANT" STAR EXPANDING IN OLD AGE,
Called BD+48 740,
Has entered its closing, planet-killer stage—
Just like the sun in 5 billion years or so.

It's pinball chaos, galactic marbles Earth
Plays for keeps and flies through swarming stones
In space. Where, from Reykjavik to Perth,
Does a fireball land and flatten four time zones?

Logic says the killer asteroid
Is out there somewhere now, headed this way
On a cosmic course the planet can't avoid.
Collision comes on mankind's final day.

CVIII *Primal Fault*

It's not whether but when the asteroid's due.
Blue Earth and red Mars will have a date to dance
Millions of miles closer, right on cue,
Yet the doomsday rock? It shows up by chance.

Some normal morning—how many years to go,
Astronomy can't just count, tick tock tick—
A mammoth space-ball's impact here could blow
Black clouds engulfing Earth and kill it quick.

Where would you be? Climbing Stratton Bald?
Tacking into the wind of Morehead Sound?
Hiking in Canyon de Chelly stone-walled?
Or riding the *Midnight Special* westbound?

You've smoked most of the oxygen you can use,
And death's a drawn-out oxygen overdose.
None cares to act as bearer of bad news,
But the end of time for you is getting close.

This planet appears to orbit on dumb luck,
Dodging debris from off in the universe.
How man's wee home survives as sitting duck
Is a puzzle which obscures the doomsday curse.

Everything in the universe entire
Is sparks still flying out from the Big Bang
Of 13 billion years ago, all fire
Exploding when creation's alarm clock rang.

The star-studded realms of deepest space
Are where the family of man one day must go,
In order to attain temporal grace
And orbit around another sun's glow.

This preconceives an orbit the only way
Earthly life is sustainable long-term.
Perhaps a novel course will come into play,
Improvised with a rogue computer worm.

Whose vision can predict a turn like that?
Neither the black-bound Bible nor Einstein do.
What line of descent *Genesis* begat
Is planning an extra-planetary zoo?

Would they board a spaceship like Noah's ark,
Blasting off for a new Earth two by two?
Or will the world gather in CENTRAL PARK,
To die at the sun's backyard barbecue?

From fundamental things like rocks and trees
Existing on a fairly human scale,
To the globe-spanning size of skies and seas—
Horizons that drew the ancients to set sail—

Earth is quite a hospitable habitat,
Compared to anywhere foreseen in space.
Survival always solved with a thermostat,
Who'd gladly abandon this brilliant home base?

The NASA astronauts who spent their lives—
Columbia, Challenger, and *Apollo*'s dead—
Represent the keen courage that drives
Mankind, suspended in space like a death's-head,

To ride a rocket past the welkin's blue,
Thundering out of the planet's atmosphere
And reaching towards an unknown rendezvous
Upon humanity's most foreign frontier.

Ramon, McCool, Anderson, Husband, Clark,
Chawla, and Brown, *Columbia*'s crew lost,
Who perished when an imperceptible spark
Grew to consume them, met the fiery cost

Of exploration the mind of man pursues.
Chawla observed Earth in its halo of sky—
And told her Houston engineers the news—
Mirrored back from the pupil of her eye.

Deep in the heart of Texas, tragedy struck
That snuffed their mission out, nearly complete.
Bankers, oil men, and cowboys tried to duck
As *Shuttle* wreckage landed at their feet.

The will to discovery springs from a brave heart,
And none but its force can save the human race.
These voyagers gone to glory made a start
To conquer the terminal danger, outer space.

The firmament maintains this globe within
The airlessness outside its azure vault,
Yet junk from beyond the planet's tight spin
May finally detonate its primal fault.

Who thinks this small world turns out all right
Believes in more than science can assure.
A holy war perhaps, a heavyweight fight,
But not the planet's fragile temperature.

Earth, like a yo-yo twirling around the sun,
Can't manufacture energy from the stars.
Somewhere way down the road in the long run,
Won't macho have to ditch its muscle cars?

CIX *Random Search*

What time remains, measured in layers of rock?
Does all life then reach the end of the line?
Face the blackness and tremble with aftershock,
Whose cure is a double shot of moonshine.

Recorded history's what—5,000 years?
A grain of sand on a vast blanket of time.
Humanity perched on that pinpoint, life's frontiers
Unfold as always in soil, sea, and slime.

Since astral bodies are eaten by black holes,
Your small demise won't carry a feather's weight.
Your stay in the stars is brief as a flaming coal's,
Compared to how long the coal took to create.

Ringed by radiance, gobbling dust and gas,
With burnt-out stars swirling in its grip
Bound for their doom, a black hole's supermass
Is nullity's answer to God's fingertip.

Think: you become nothing; nothing at all.
The past intrigues; eternity terrifies.
You emerged from copulation's cattle call
To a cosmos, all but whose mystery dies.

Yet even the bleakest reason can't plumb
The heart of total darkness's deepest black:
Utter nothingness, sense forever dumb
And breathless as a bronze memorial plaque.

With 10 quadrillion stars big as the sun,
The Great Attractor pulls galaxies toward it.
Imagine how much your mind could have done,
If it had sucked up knowledge thus and stored it.

All things mortal are futile is RULE ONE:
Defining trait and term of life on earth.
From vile cockroach to Yahweh's only son,
Time shows creatures how little breath is worth.

False assurance shields you round the clock
From facing facts so well you stay in bed.
Fear each minute might be your last? The shock
Would leave you useless, eyes lost in your head.

False assurance typifies your day.
Never more than steps away from death,
How could you live, worried every stray
Blood cell can stop your brain, then your breath?

If you think each time you pass a dark door
How crime's clawed hand can blow your heart away,
To empty your pockets and so run up the score
Of a murderous mind's random search for prey,

You won't enjoy the best of mental health,
Unable to shake a deep, enduring chill.
Pretend you're safe from wrong's deadly stealth,
And spend each moment blind to its urge to kill.

Reside cocooned in gold atop TRUMP TOWER:
There still is just one way to cross the street.
When wickedness steps forth to prove its power,
Poison kills, even in a penthouse suite.

The asteroid that killed the dinosaurs
Apparently dug the Gulf of Mexico.
A broken lift falling sixty floors
Can kill you at the end of the rainbow.

You're a killer too, in your own right.
Find the cost of your crime everywhere.
For evil's action, death's a daily flight,
A planeload of pawns blown up in midair.

A plane's tiny community of terror,
While it sinks from the sky to spiral and crash,
Has no time to blame the correct error
Before it becomes total human hash.

Atomization erupts with explosive force,
Once the silver plane and its shadow converge,
That grants body and spirit instant divorce,
And wrecks the noble work of the demiurge.

Dwell on the grief your world is built upon,
10,000 generations of human dead,
And end up hooked on dope with Kubla Khan.
Don't let horror's abyss implode your head.

When to death's dark swollen river, like
An old hobo you have finally come,
Try to stick your finger in the dike,
And don't let any Dutchman call you dumb.

CX *Apollo's Arms*

Earthlings shiver like San Diego's the norm.
The least cold snap, they heave coal in the stove.
With all the fossil fuel keeping them warm,
The greenhouse hybrids should wear peach and mauve.

Huddled Montanans wait for the next chinook,
Mastodons mere peat to toast their toes.
Grand Canyon's rock a lot to overlook,
No ancient extinction shakes their dainty pose.

Yet where is colder to lie than a stone vault,
Or stacked in catacombs, bones bundled dense
As Devils Tower's flutes of cracked basalt?
And crypts rarely come with heating vents.

The antique Greeks would sleep in tombs to get
Advice from the dead on almost anything:
On whether a horse race was a sure bet,
Or a love affair could blossom next spring.

Now monks who sleep in coffins clutching a rose
Practice repose to hold for a thousand years.
But turn the furnace down till their pinkies froze,
And cut these off as graphic souvenirs

Of a mausoleum's stratospheric chill,
The frigid cling of a fresh winding sheet?
They'd sooner roast like pigs on Satan's grill
Than pack a steel casket as frozen meat.

Antarctica's air, colder than parts of Mars,
Has gale-force winds at minus sixty degrees.
The grave, for Bowery bums or movie stars,
Is colder than a glacier's deepest freeze.

The feel of absolute zero is close enough,
Like being buried beneath a lunar dune.
It behooves many to shed their foolish bluff,
Facing forever cold as the man in the moon.

So cold the phone calls freeze from sun to sun.
Nothing but cold silence rings in the grave.
Its cast of thousand millions? Not a one
Conveys a single sound to a living slave.

From here to hereafter's a fearsome haul, duke,
Your trip to the end of night only a start.
Terror's face on the dying's not a fluke:
Each knows this life's no timeless work of art.

Light at a corridor's end, past death's door?
Some say it awaits the instant life is done.
Leave this hateful world a running sore,
And surrender to the death star called the sun.

Open the door, then throw away the key:
Step into ever after blazing bright.
They claim to have stood at this exit carefree,
Absorbed by a blinding burst of daylight.

Behind death's portal lies no real harm:
A place where crime and cruelty disappear;
Where snide, sardonic poets learn to charm
The proles with pure, non-alcoholic cheer.

Feel no fear, returnees all insist.
Bathe in a radiant, blissful sense of peace.
Nothing to fear? So why not make a fist
And bang on the door demanding quick release

From the bone prison, incarnation's curse?
What's wrong? Don't you buy their testimony?
Afraid to trade away life could bring worse?
You're right. The whole concept cries baloney.

It must be the small percent whose trips don't fit—
Whose near-death tale recalls torment like hell,
A sense they had stared down a gaping pit—
That makes you fear to fall in death's dark well.

You get to that point too soon anyways,
Cross that entrance into the great Perhaps:
If into Apollo's arms, the Ancient of Days',
Or Lucifer's, none can spark this last synapse.

Only one threshold short of what awaits,
You're not unlike a human cannon shot:
You pass through either hell's or heaven's gates,
Or—nothing, and you're blind as an ink blot.

On death's bed Aldous Huxley took LSD,
But it's dumb to marvel, "What a way to go!"
His death trip started in 1963,
And whether fair or foul, who's to know?

Not every acid trip's a nice surprise.
Not every OSCAR-winning film is bad.
At death's address, rejoicing is hardly wise,
To waken in hell and learn you've been had.

So onward, upward, outward, anywhere
Your restless, wrinkling flesh desires to roam.
Yet beware familiar words of common care
When the earth opens to claim you: "Welcome home."

A clouded, apprehensive look in your eyes,
Try chasing away your fears if you choose.
What now? what next? where to? beget replies
Ranging from Nova Scotia to Vera Cruz.

From mountains to prairie to oceans white with foam
And clouds that build you castles in the sky,
The stars will always guide you going home
To where you lay your body down and die.

May death grant you the strength to finish well:
Enter eternity holding your head high.
Let Satan and his minions manage hell,
And don't look down until you learn to fly.

CXI *Rough Justice*

The desert buttes have long shadows, schmuck.
As your sun descends in the west, drive with care.
The site of your endless sleep is potluck,
When your dull gray DODGE is pooped beyond repair.

Where lost cities of gold drew Coronado
To stew on the desert in steel battle dress,
Pass by Fort Defiance with crass bravado.
Lunge like a fresh run of the PONY EXPRESS.

A skull and crossbones adorns each signpost,
Sprayed on the back by a wise, unknown hand—
A vandal's sketch of how time turns you to toast—
As you log your trip's last leg to no-man's-land.

Touring through the country of common plight,
You know your steering's fine, then oops, you don't.
Still believe in sappy endings? Right.
All movie magic has one; your tale won't.

Ma Barker's real first name was Arizona.
A wild shoot-out killed her in Florida, though.
Time tracks you down half a day from Sedona:
Far from home and no place left to go.

Its tires worn bare, its license plate revoked,
And this heap collapsed in a soul-rending groan,
Your chronic unrest expires gasping and choked,
As your breath escapes into the ozone.

The paint peeled off, the body rusted through,
And the engine locked, you'll stand on asphalt,
Thankful recalling this pointed preview
Of the show-stopper: your flesh's final halt.

You're welcome, you absurdly worthless drudge.
It's not how you look, it's what's under your hood.
This script mars your prestige with an ugly smudge?
Hope no one notices. Then again, who would?—

You saddle tramp, soon dead in clothes you stole.
Stop pouting. You're due a brief burial rite,
Once hoboes boot you into a shallow hole
And kick in some dirt at dawn's early light.

Mumbling words for one they've never seen,
They rifle your pockets, take your last thin dime.
For highway nomads, it's roadside routine,
Yet be forewarned: they seldom wax sublime.

"He died completely broke," they underscore:
"Hereafter, never will his bunions thrive.
His age looks to be about 84,
A couple of months short of 85.

"Funerals are for mourners, not the dead,
So we don't owe this stiff a moment's thought.
It's possible his was only a hollow head,
And a DODGE jalopy's all his blood bought.

"We would have liked to adopt his car and cruise
Through DISNEYLAND to reach the west coast,
But the DODGE had fewer miles left than his shoes.
Now we'll pierce his ribs with a fence post,

"Just in case—the Lord will figure that out.
And dust to dust—something along those lines.
Questioning if his soul departed in doubt,
We must move on. It's back to the salt mines!

"We snatch both dimes off a dead man's eyes,
But he had only one in his watch pocket.
And when was there a dawn in eastern skies
To stop us hocking his poor mother's locket?

"We style ourselves the true salt of the earth:
Dried sweat coats our skin in a grainy crust
Which prompts the polite to yield us a wide berth,
Their faces frozen in wonderful disgust.

"None of our crew's an angel, nowhere near.
Might even make some good new stokers in hell.
Just so's John Law won't catch us loitering here,
Let's bid this sorry dirtball farewell."

This happens outside of old Tombstone, pal:
Where silver, whiskey, and six-guns would mix;
Where the Earps ambushed three at O.K. CORRAL,
A flagrant case of Tombstone politics.

Join the notable folks who died in their boots—
Or in satin slippers, if such was the case—
At the Cochise County seat. This venue suits
Your end, and proves it still a dangerous place.

The setting of your grave is Zzyzzyxx Road:
Far edge of town, bearing north-northwest.
There you find your being buffaloed,
As your worn-out body seeks its final rest.

What better place to perish than Tombstone?
Straightforward symbolism on the cheap,
To throw the literary dog a bone—
But here no woods are lovely, dark, and deep.

When "Buckskin Frank" Leslie gunned Kid Claiborne down
Outside the jail, the judge ruled self-defense.
It made Frank's name as fastest gun in town,
Who proudly posed for frontier monotints.

His plugging Mike Killeen concerned Mike's wife,
Yet shooting a lady brought his downfall.
Sent to YUMA PRISON to finish his life,
Frank bragged that he killed thirteen men in all.

But Molly the fourteenth left him half alive:
He served six years and lost his dashing looks.
Washing dishes, he died in a Frisco dive,
His record today buried in dusty books.

High rollers in Helldorado—Doc Holliday,
Bones Brannon, Charlie Storms—would deal until dawn:
Boom-town buzzards skimming the miners' pay.
As soon as boom turns bust, the gamblers are gone.

The tart Gold Dollar lived with Bill Milgreen.
One fine evening found a wasp in her honey.
BONNIE, STABBED BY GOLD DOLLAR, BARROOM QUEEN:
So reads the headstone bought with Bill's money.

It's rough justice, but what's a girl to do?
She had to guard her Tombstone territory.
If the law shoots horse thieves, whores have laws, too—
And Bonnie has Boot Hill to tell her story.

The standard scene which ends in silence and smoke
From a warm gun ill suited the tart's taste.
Yet if refined, her prim demeanor broke,
Planting a blade in the bitch's back posthaste.

CXII   *Parisian Pleasures*

Wyatt, Morgan, and Virgil Earp became
Wild West heroes, yet murdered in cold blood,
Proving the stubborn stamp of mistaken fame.
The name Earp should be dragged through the mud.

The brothers were killers, thieves, pimps, and cheats,
Whose crimes befouled their ORIENTAL SALOON.
To show up in books as swell characters beats
All odds, their blood like juice in a brass spittoon.

Tombstone had worse, sure. Take Jack Stilwell,
Whom Wyatt blasted in Tucson rail yard.
The paper called Jack NEW MAIN EVENT IN HELL,
Wishing some others would fill his undercard.

History just a giant crapshoot, why
The Earps are legend, not a breed of swine,
Made Nixon wish he'd told a bigger lie,
His dying reputation on the line.

B.B. Rebozo was Nixon's best friend.
Wait, maybe his name was Bobo Rebeze.
Scandal cost more than Nixon had to spend,
Leaving even Bobo kind of queasy.

In your case, scant hope to turn things around.
This lamentation's all the press you get.
You can't hire PR from a hole in the ground,
But your portrait wants some bad brushstrokes yet.

For public impression, your worst enemy's you:
Undisputed champ of the fashion gaffe.
And your handshake's like a film of contact glue,
Pumped with the grace of a newborn giraffe.

Far too late to enroll you in charm school,
This may have fixed the problem long ago.
Yet now you're so incurably uncool,
You command the social skills of a scarecrow.

Even a master flack can't help you, crumb.
Once ground to a halt, that ends life's escapade.
First school, then work like a fool, then die: ho hum.
It's over so fast, there's hardly time to get laid.

Grow from mischief's urchin like Huck Finn
To happy flimflam man or scary loner.
Moral questions are academic when
Your carcass calls it quits in Arizona.

Arizona skies are soaked in blue,
With now and then a sudden thunderstorm.
If God gets grounded, divine wrath comes true,
So step inside should lightning grow too warm.

The ground around you readies for a jolt,
As heaven's artillery rumbles down the skies.
Since there's no answer to a thunderbolt,
Don't tarry where pure electricity flies.

An anger of half a million volts appears
Upon the horizon deep in the afternoon.
Seek shelter till the random flashing clears—
That is, unless you're crazy as a loon.

What if you get struck by lightning and live?
This happens when God sets the voltage wrong.
He doesn't really determine to forgive
Your sins, but he can't abide your swan song.

At Tombstone's CANCAN, Lillian Russell played:
Parisian pleasures, Old West clapboard style.
When fire leveled the town for its building trade,
Like Troy it rose in brick on the cinder pile.

Aunt Allie Earp said one hotheaded mob
Almost lynched Johnny-Behind-the-Deuce.
He badly botched a stagecoach holdup job,
And shot the driver without the right excuse.

Some claim they've spotted Virgil Earp's ghost
Walking past the CRYSTAL PALACE SALOON:
Always manning his crucial listening post,
Under the Southern Cross or at high noon.

Nothing good will come of waking a ghost,
And Tombstone is no ghost town in the sky.
Never turn your back on a friendly host,
If you want to look your killer in the eye.

CXIII *Bad Medicine*

THE TOWN TOO TOUGH TO DIE outlived the mines,
The miners, madams, chefs, and French whores;
The Clantons, McLowerys, Earps, and concubines;
To mark your last half-mile by closing its doors.

The sheriff tows what's left of your ruined coupe.
If he found your grave, chaos could ensue.
The daily *Epitaph* would run the scoop,
DRIFTER BITES THE DUST, and hail the new

Eyesight half-blind madam mayor's received.
Unknown the Gorgon her graft from you instates.
Who'd guess the laser's launched a lamia peeved
By mirrors, crosses, bats, and SELL-BY dates?

Because of your death's severe frosty night,
Your eyes endure, a one-in-a-million chance
To save a fortunate mortal's fading light,
And leave its focus sharp as a surgeon's lance.

When in the strange course of human events,
The doctors let some miracle go wrong,
A corneal transplant counter common sense,
The upshot rates the crash of a Chinese gong.

Your fatal vision willed to other eyes,
Misdeeds of your wasted life would torment
The waking world with the sulfurous surprise
Of a horrid shrew's mouth like a sewage vent.

Your curse thus visits Tombstone's glory hole,
The mayor spewing indiscriminate spite.
She'd spit at children on her morning stroll:
Target practice, testing her reborn sight.

Sheriff Blaine is helpless to buck this threat.
Impeachment power doesn't back his badge.
His deputies? Well, just say they're all in debt,
And riding shotgun saddled with Mayor Madge.

BAD MEDICINE LOOSES MONSTER ON CITY,
The paper gripes mere days after the fact.
WHO EVER CALLED THIS WALLEYED WITCH PRETTY?
COUNCIL MEETS, REPEALS ELECTION ACT.

Protestors stage a hometown coup d'état.
A risky move: insurrection can spread.
The mayor wants exile in Panama,
And soon one group demands the mayor's head.

TRANSPLANT BRINGS UNCIVIL TURMOIL, most
East-coast dailies write with self-control.
SHE-WOLF SPREE SPARKS MELTDOWN! a *New York Post*
EXTRA roars to panic the nation's soul.

While jumpy columnists try to make sense
Of order's full collapse in a week and a half,
Editors analyze the odd events
Out west which undermined the mayor's staff.

The wildest rumors swirl and flash into print
As the town's future threatens to implode,
The scandal lacking only a gunflint
To ignite the public anger's payload.

DEATH OF ROLLING STONE, reports will leak,
BEGAN WEIRD CHAIN OF CITY HALL MISTAKES.
MAYOR BLAMES SHERIFF IN FIT OF PIQUE
FOR DIGGING UP BUM; SWEARS ALL MEN ARE SNAKES.

Hold it. Maybe Blaine won't search around
Your beat-up ride abandoned on Zzyzzyxx Road:
Just tows it in and tags it LOST AND FOUND.
He never seeks the driver whose car he towed?

And your mourners cover up their graveside tracks?
The terrorizing transplant can't transpire.
Her Honor remains a half-blind battle-ax,
Who minces as though her bra were barbwire.

Mayor Madge's massive mounds of flesh
Could be seductive only by coercion.
Her girdle must be made of steel mesh,
The sentence death for a deputy's desertion.

A worthy democrat, she'll cause no harm,
Tombstone saved from the curse of your baby blues.
If her leadership's a little short on charm,
It's her bodyguards, not the law she screws.

CXIV *Royal Tombs*

The dark Dragoon Mountains loom between
Your death and the next sunrise. Them thar hills:
Old haunts where gunshots echo down a ravine,
And mimic hearts whose faltering rhythm kills.

Northwest the specter of Phoenix seethes in smog,
Where Saguaro grew and golden eagles soared.
But myth won't help when you die like an old stray dog.
Rebirth from tobacco ash in your floorboard?

You must be kidding, you gin-soaked buffoon.
Try 20,000 leagues under the sea,
During total eclipse of a midnight moon,
To figure how complete your sundown will be.

And yet progress outmodes what's exhumed,
6,000 years old, from a cave in France.
Modern sentiment mostly had presumed
European cannibals mere romance.

But of late, refuse found in a single pit,
A rich, Paleolithic garbage dump,
Shows beasts' and human bones alike were split
Open to eat the marrow. Logic's jump

From matching bone fragments to judging the cave
As home to man-eaters, was easy to make.
And hash marks all the bones were hacked with gave
A clinching piece of proof to ice the cake.

Who's not a cannibal, grown hungry enough?
Some English settlers starving at Jamestown
Turned to the dead as their crucial foodstuff,
Grimly wolfing their comrades' corpses down.

Bony Christian knights of the Fourth Crusade,
Besieged in a city their force occupied,
For victuals gripped the battle-tempered blade
To butcher children, supping hollow-eyed.

Recall the doomed Donner Party's ordeal;
The frozen Andes' plane-crashed rugby team;
The shipwrecked *Medusa* rafters' basic meal:
All lurk in civilization's bloodstream.

Next, they've found Neanderthal cannibalism—
Now hardly surprising—in a cave in Spain.
Who knows what's in humanoids' abysm
To cause an academic hurricane?

Yet hoboes never need to eat each other.
They can always filch some LIBBY'S pork-and-beans.
"It's dog eat dog, but eat not thy brother,"
Their grumbling goes while cinching up their jeans.

Despite such etiquette, death won't be serene
If coyotes find you first at sunset.
The gaily gashed sky lighting the scene,
Your fresh blood on their fangs serves to whet

A feeding tussle which dismembers you.
Parting in plumes of dust at break of day,
They scatter with every scrap still left to chew.
You deserve the right of dignified decay?

Twelve centuries' royal tombs at SAINT-DENIS
Were sacked, all their skeletons tossed in a trench
For blind payback in 1793,
With teeth now kissing tailbones. Terribly French.

If kings and queens can fill a common grave,
The mass of humanity fares vastly worse.
A hundred billion have no bones to save,
Pulverized by laws of the universe.

No trace of them survives for those today
Who proudly walk upright and pass this trait
Along to future generations who say,
"It's us what keeps old human nature straight."

CXV *Wild Horses*

Should you fare better than saints' holy bones
Whose broken shards Roman clergy embrace
In gold-trimmed vessels, as grand organ tones
Proclaim their healing power? Such ghostly grace

Is why St. Teresa's kneecap, borne by train
To ATOCHA STATION, stoked the mystic heart
Of a crowd of Madrileños. Well, that's Spain.
Are your remains less mobile ripped apart?

The "fate worse than death" tore limb from limb,
Meant to deny all chance of resurrection.
Drawing and quartering felons fueled grim
Mob desire for killers' vivisection.

That was England, to be perfectly frank.
Holland made horror too, to be quite fair.
Hardly an acre of land comes up blank.
Talk of peace when murder's everywhere?

Your bleaching bones, from Phoenix to Santa Fe,
Could litter the red sand as desert décor,
Be splintered by wild horses, or find their way
As relics sold at a reservation store.

The Old West always needs more souvenirs.
So many movies, so few artifacts.
So little left of history's trail of tears;
So little trace of Zorro double acts.

Your bones would sure relieve a shortage of scrap
The thriving trinket trade struggles to fill.
So many megatons of plastic crap;
So many phony stories time can't kill.

LEGENDS OF THE WEST are twisting fiction
Too often to believe they aren't a plot
Of fantasy that makes the past's depiction
A clash of what is wished and what is not.

Bat Masterson died in Chicago selling shoes:
A comedown sad for a famed western hero.
Not the finish a fierce gunfighter might choose,
Yet who at the end amounts to more than zero?

Stripped and sunned to a bright, fleshless state,
Your bones can aggravate reality's claim,
Which fact and fiction both negotiate
To intensify the revenue game.

Your carcass picked clean and the clean bones gone,
Once the roadside tourist trap sells out,
Leave your naked soul to meet the dawn
With not one molecule of faith or doubt.

The white bone of a fact is very well.
The best poets relish plenty of these.
Through facts they imagine heaven and hell,
Happy as a rat with a pound of cheese.

It's better coyotes claim you than buzzards peck
And excavate your bowels with their beaks.
Coyotes soon devour your human dreck,
While buzzards can pick at carrion for weeks.

Losing your brains to a flock of ugly birds
Is a lousy way for any life to conclude.
Yet buzzard droppings or coyote turds
Are happier states than burning devil's food.

CXVI *Promised Land*

As inscribed on antique maps, HERE BE DRAGONS
Should have warned of perils unknown ahead,
Where greenhorn pioneers could mass their wagons,
Not risk the entire column strung out dead.

At Mountain Meadows, lying north-northwest,
Where blood lust slew a hard-luck wagon train,
Wolves dug dozens of dead from shallow rest.
One scout saw twenty feeding upon the slain.

"The wolves ate women and children first," he wrote.
So would your coyotes, given the choice:
Tender sinews to soothe a howling throat
And slake hunger's verdict of blood in its voice.

An air-raid siren sounds like a howling wolf,
Its wail heralding imminent megadeath.
Were women and kids spared in the Persian Gulf
By war's contemporary shibboleth?

The "highway to hell" leading out of Kuwait,
Once the invaders fled with tons of loot,
Provided occasion to incinerate
The looters: a flying bomb turkey shoot.

"Nothing can live unless something dies," said Clark
Gable (—*The Misfits*) to Marilyn Monroe.
And Marilyn too would soon be lost to the dark
Where starlets and Presidents, priests and assassins go.

When a hyena steals a cheetah's kill,
Nature's constitution makes it clear
How every creature bows to hunger's will,
With every affection built on primal fear.

There's no such thing as a cloud without water;
There's no such thing as living without blood.
Half of what lives is early sent to slaughter;
The other half wallows in dust and mud.

Dodge City's ethics knew but cash and killing,
Men shot down like dogs dead in the street,
Some broke and drunken drover always willing
To draw on the dealer none who live can cheat.

Then Dodge, business down when its killing feast,
Its lawless heyday of cattle drives was through,
Found that shipping bison bones back east
As fertilizer remained for revenue:

A comic end to the Great Plains buffalo trade.
When hides ran out, they still sold bones at least.
10 million animals skinned by the BOWIE blade,
Clearly the question for man is, Which was the beast?

When hides ran out, they still could harvest bones;
Still could harvest bones that littered the plains;
Could harvest bones that lay, common as stones,
On blood-soaked prairie washed by cleansing rains.

"King of the animals? No, king of the beasts!"
Leonardo addressed Ovid—meaning man,
Even all his plump, carnivorous priests.
Ponder the butchery paid for one lifespan.

A town by Montana's Bitterroot Range has
An arch of elk antlers over Main Street.
This hook for tourists gives the place pizzazz,
And gathering antlers does beat planting wheat.

Some motorists believe the elk were slain,
Instead of shedding antlers every year.
Before their outrage rises to complain,
They learn the custom over a glass of beer.

Beneath loose dirt in reach of coyote paws,
Perhaps they miss you as death's odor abates.
You lie safe in one piece as the world withdraws,
And leaves your corpse to whatever dirt dictates.

You sprout no wings, but bugs unplug your ears.
The snake in your bosom's babies teem and coil,
Shredding your skin once bathed with childhood tears,
And breaking down your body into soil.

"Since life pursues an unavoidable course
Towards death, we must enliven it by our own
Colors of love and hope, with art the source,"
Thought Marc Chagall. Give yours an earth tone.

When ants etcetera get you processed out
Of the house of flesh into the house of dust,
The red roof rarely leaks in desert drought,
Your bed dry as a crack in the moon's crust.

What's left but traffic buzzing your new home,
The grave-diggers off through bleeding drapes of dawn?
Unrevived by the blitz of flashing chrome
As cars speed east and west, you're just plain gone.

You won't fertilize amber waves of grain,
Nor a green churchyard under village elms.
When both your motor and mind can't stand the strain,
Science can't salvage what time overwhelms.

Displeased with nature? Machines share the blame.
Increase your mileage, prolong your forward thrust?
Adjust your hood's hawk bill to sharpen your aim,
And buy a bumper sticker: L.A. OR BUST.

Or try a touch of humor: EAT MY DUST.
If drivers behind you can't take a joke,
Complete the trilogy: add IN GOD WE TRUST,
And choke the bastards in clouds of exhaust smoke.

Your newfound goal is noble: the Golden State.
Chuck Berry pays it homage in *Promised Land*.
But you can't reach heaven pedaling this crate,
Can't pump its pistons cranking a rubber band.

Should you perceive you ride alone in the dark,
The cause will oddly dawn as plain as day:
Your odyssey offers no PALISADES PARK
For souls wending west of Far Rockaway.

Time's never on your side: it flies too fast.
Freedom Land's no place you arrive by road.
Your DODGE breaks down, your future becomes past:
Your matter returns to nature's mother lode.

The planet on its axis spins too much:
From birth to death is winkin', blinkin', and nod.
Whether you ride the brakes or double-clutch,
Your brief life is born of and buried in sod.

CXVII *Daily Mail*

Your shameful story could be said to possess
The spectrum: vice, religion, rock-and-roll.
Mama's Little Angel Makes a Mess—
The Musical, PLAYS NEXT AT HOLLYWOOD BOWL.

And leave Calamity Jane out of this.
The only mess she makes is water-based.
As John Donne says, she has *two* mouths to kiss,
Happy with either one you wish to taste.

Resurrection? Your chances look too sparse,
Last Judgement yet a few poles down the line.
And Halley's Comet fizzled, a stellar farce.
This happened back in—1989?

Folks are always searching for a sign
To tell them how to be and what to do.
Not only people born without a spine,
But prophets, poets—politicians, too:

Some magic number, bullet, potion, touch.
And madmen are forever looking out
For mathematic certitude's crutch:
The year to end all years, sing and shout!

The year of perfect vision, 2020?
Say, why not 2222?
Become one of doomsday's cognoscenti,
Wondering when the world plans to get through:

Expects, hopes, ignores, forgets, whatever.
The world and all its human retinue,
Most of which is neither wise nor clever.
Near end-times, what does mankind ballyhoo?

Crackpots' claims would fill the *Daily Mail*,
From Jeane Dixon to William Butler Yeats.
Each summer thunderstorm or blast of hail
Could spook the rabble to storm heaven's gates.

Suppose you live till history's next gyre.
What earthly proof suggests you'll make the list
Of those elect freed from Babylon's fire?
And yet your epic admits an odd twist.

If blown-up cities rain on their old digs,
As keepsakes of the Spirit of '76,
Then wash to sea like splintered toys and twigs,
You're spared the ruin. But first you cross the Styx.

A remote possibility will persist:
The plaster cast as employed at Pompeii.
They fill your bones' cavity lobos missed,
Retrieving your last pose for graphic display.

Some casts caught couples making love—no more.
That sparked these words by a wandering poet
To tease us out of thought: "Passion: before
We die, let's not hope for but truly know it."

How's your sex drive, killer? Showing some age?
Don't forget what fun your libido had.
Stud or not, you play on an empty stage,
Once cast like a dummy in a CLOROX ad.

An old man's mating call is far too faint
To get a rise from siren, mother, or maid.
Augustine met no trouble turning saint,
After his dues to Venus had been paid.

You're President of the United States of Love?
For your sake, would that one could credit that.
Perhaps your confidence needs a little shove.
Here's the ticket: a new ten-gallon hat.

CXVIII *Egyptian Hieroglyphs*

The last you fell in love was way back when?
And ditched your wretched squaw in New Orleans?
Calamity Jane? Same as she's always been.
If she offers don't delay: drop your jeans.

Her scarlet ringlets sparkling in the sun,
A seethe of excitement follows where she goes.
With amorous power not to be outdone,
Her mythic figure's furnace brightly glows.

Soft on your skin as shadows on the wall,
Her flesh can warm the world on the coldest night:
Kindling the instant day lets darkness fall;
Strong as the sun comes burning back to light.

Don't try to run, Cupid's got a gun,
His aim better than science can assess.
Her fabulous physique is second to none
In her maker's divine altogetherness.

Many say even her sweat smells clean:
That's a claim biology's yet to prove.
Her hair inflames a supernatural sheen;
Her rhythm quickly finds the perfect groove.

She's random roadhouse heaven made to order,
With an eveready, if-you-please smile.
Soon as you drive across the Texas border,
Her magnetism jams your radio dial.

The message isn't Egyptian hieroglyphs.
Nothing's inscrutable about her gaze.
Jane O'Shannon's beaux are lucky stiffs,
Her stare as frank as a four-alarm blaze.

Her golden calves have now inspired a cult
That worships at the shrine of her shapely legs.
An entire social movement may result
To fertilize her priceless golden eggs.

She's the subject of infinite male dreams,
Ambition of their gender's yearning heart:
Their love's Parnassus upon whose summit gleams
The truest perfection desire can impart.

This very hour melting in someone's hands,
She's hotter than a Houston 4th of July.
Forget how while the Rock of Gibraltar stands,
Mortal strength and beauty droop and die.

Hey, remember the HOUSE OF THE RISING SUN?
In Cajun country, that's as good as it gets.
All you need is ten bucks and a working gun,
To enter this house whose sun never sets.

But you can't light a fire without a spark:
Simply an elemental fact of life.
So maybe you're not blithe as a skylark.
At least you kill—no, dumped your awful wife.

When diamonds aren't forever, be civilized.
Why didn't you dial 1–800–DIVORCE,
Instead of stopping the laughter you once prized,
Transformed to braying scorn, by brute force?

"Ding-dong, the wicked witch is dead!" you crooned,
Expressing suspect, unrestrained joy.
Thrice her size the slattern had ballooned,
Until you junked her like a broken toy.

Your used-to-be became your nevermore.
Nothing appears too special about that.
Yet wasn't she just shy of 44?
Every woman puts on a little fat.

She had a right, the erstwhile skin-and-bones,
To add some definition to her shape.
You should've preferred an IPOD's headphones
To shutting her up with a roll of duct tape.

You never knew, her face in monster mode,
Whether it was hell or Halloween.
So you closed the whole gory episode
By leaving the law a screwy crime scene.

CXIX *Silver Spoon*

There's mayhem dwelling yet within your veins,
Which made you more than kin and less than kind
To your murdered twin, whose foul body's chains
Burden you still, dragging him behind.

It's most unpleasant living with a corpse?
Why didn't you think of this before the deed?
The killing glance you threw him really warps
Your outlook, doesn't it? Well, how do you plead?

The nag now adds a new notch on your gun.
Correction—you never shot them. All the same,
You've begun to sound like Attila the Hun.
Refuse to tell a GALLUP POLL your name.

So how's the romance, sans Calamity Jane?
Sans the desire of your late, lamented wife?
Once virility waxes it must wane,
For Arnold Schwarzenegger or Barney Fife.

Old hammerhead wizens, his pith turns to mush.
Strike with your iron still hot and red as a rose.
That rod's in your pants to give the girls a rush.
Wild oats aren't sown by graveyard garden hose.

The girls aren't shopping for a water gun.
The seeds of life are what they aim to grow,
Hardly averse to feats of healthy fun
They call their rocking bedroom rodeo.

You named your ding-a-ling the Big Bopper,
After the singer killed in a plane crash
With Buddy Holly? If it's such a whopper,
Be careful it doesn't cause you whiplash.

Priapus bronzes unearthed at Pompeii—
Legitimate phallic braggadocio—
Convince you the Vesuvian doomsday
Is the way you wish your afterlife to go?

You feel you want a plaster, posthumous role?
And shun the lucent hues of petrified wood,
Whose silicas glow in stone transmuted whole
From deadwood fibers? Pick the personhood

Of a chalk death-cast mere moisture dissolves,
Over the sparkle of cryptocrystalline quartz?
Despite the long delay the change involves,
Ponder its . . . immortality, of sorts.

Feature the dazzling disguises to choose among.
Take a rock alias good till Judgement Day.
Beauty fades, its jewels forever young,
So try this mineral Champs Élysées.

Zircon, onyx, jasper, moonstone spar,
Lace agate, opal, moss malachite,
Zebra garnet, amethyst, topaz, or star
Sapphire: each can brighten your endless night.

Since bones dissolve in Tombstone's acid soil,
Petrification is really your safest bet.
Mull it over while you sweat and toil:
Dust or diamond, rock or eternal regret.

To geology such fancy can't occur,
Yet imagine the money chase if it could.
Envision the treasure hunt if people were
Prized for their buried bones like rainbow wood:

No forebears' grave plot would have true peace.
Great-grandson's greed will dig them up too soon,
Only to find his ancestors' decease
Too fresh to finance baby's silver spoon.

CXX *Mummy's Curse*

Westerners, as the dead were frankly called
In ancient Egypt, followed the sun down,
The pharaonic cowboys' pride appalled
To wear a mummy's scented dressing gown.

A mummy says of CLEOPATRA perfume:
"Death with her essence of cat all in my clothes
Is whorehouse Hades, hell in a queen's costume."
Pure bliss to shed the flaking flesh he loathes.

Tutankhamen would quickly abdicate
His bandaged bulk and his gilded headdress
To end the flashy tours he's learned to hate:
His plundered tomb as worldwide success.

It's become a total nuisance for him now,
Causing him to gripe in the afterlife,
Sick of cities from Memphis to Moscow:
"Will no one hand me a hara-kiri knife?

"This swank Egyptian sideshow has to stop.
I've seen enough of today's world to know
I'm just an excuse for some museum shop
To sock away a ghoulish pile of dough.

"Egypt bewept its hero king sublime
When Ramses the Great ascended to his gods,
Yet overthrow killed me before my time:
My Prime Minister played and beat the odds.

"My murder sparks the myth of the mummy's curse,
Once Lord Carmarthen visits my crypt and croaks.
I honestly can't decide which fate is worse:
To subsidize art or personify that hoax.

"Able to lie in secret clothed or nude,
Normal folks buried in 20-gauge steel,
Sealed forever from life's brief interlude,
Don't savvy how us stolen mummies feel.

"Wait! It's been determined I wasn't killed,
But slowly succumbed to some innate defect!
Such drama serves to keep the gallery filled—
And leaves my regal reputation wrecked.

"Hold the phone! Cold science marches on:
A CT scan now proves I broke my thigh.
A chariot crash?—in sport or with sword drawn?
Infection finished me off: the bones don't lie.

"Yet what's the difference how I really died?
The Valley of the Kings was home to me.
My corpse, whether corrupted or mummified,
Still fed my glad successor's pedigree.

"I simply know I perished for good and all.
Then much was done to mask my death's aroma.
Please let me rest in peace beyond recall,
And never wake from time's eternal coma.

"I'd far prefer my tomb's old lullaby
Of passing camel hooves and quit this zoo.
If scarabs ate me for a karmic high,
I'd pardon archeology's vandal crew."

Is a pharaoh's grave a gateway to the stars?
Only if what that means is Hollywood
Celebrities disgorged by fancy cars,
Welcoming Tut to a new neighborhood.

No time off for King Tut, it's ghastly work:
Round-the-clock shifts from Rome to Tokyo,
While nosy throngs from Pope to grocery clerk
Inspect his gear. It's a death he'd fain forego.

MADAME TUSSAUD'S WAXWORKS, hopeless one?
It's crazy, the swagger some bipeds assume,
Tossing daydream touchdowns to Ron Raygun.
Cancel your vanity, champ: go push a broom.

Share her CHAMBER OF HORRORS' crowded cell?
Learning her past, you'd bolt for Brazil in a week.
In Jacobin Paris, once her friends' heads fell,
She made death masks of her old palace clique.

Las Vegas now provides her newest venue:
A funhouse of the phony funding the fake.
The statues are all surface and no sinew,
The casino all muscle splitting the take.

CXXI *Country Churchyard*

Back to your bones. If not strewn far and wide,
They're undiscovered. Call it beginner's luck.
Then some surveyor stops to park alongside
And finds your grave as he steps from a state truck

To set his tripod up and widen the road.
They pave you over with tons of tarmac,
Undisturbed, but honor is rightly owed:
On a boulder there, they bolt a standard plaque.

You've earned respect, you and your missing half.
After all, you sure can read and digest
The drift of this fable, maybe even laugh
To learn your death rids the earth of a pest.

Sir Philip Sidney spoke the gospel, no lie:
The pleasure of poetry stumps the riffraff.
Their proper reward, once these dumbos die?
"Their names die for want of an epitaph."

Inertia in hearing this oration out
Might post you points on a scoreboard in the sky
For sheer dogged endurance, you lazy lout.
Well, thanks for listening. Here's mud in your eye.

When burgeoning hordes trek this vale of tears
Without an ounce of interest in fine verse,
Bovinely sold short stock in worthy spheres
Of mortal work, then bow to the waiting hearse—

When Frenchy rhythm tamers' prissy wiles
Sap the force and stress of Saxon tongue,
And hidebound poets hawk insipid styles
Whose flimsy instruments are never strung,

Their animation lively as feet of lead,
Packing a wallop like puffs of styrofoam,
Limp as wet linen, fresh as month-old bread,
Crisp as raw clam, strong as plastic chrome—

When poems are soft as crumbling goat cheese,
Shoddy as squatter shacks, their figures fake
Or flat as flowers squashed in *OED*'s,
And sterile as the floor of Great Salt Lake—

When Helicon's font becomes a kitchen sink,
Parnassus Road is clogged with lemonade stands,
The muses talk too much, their feet stink,
And poetry journals' fiefs are wastelands—

Then you who read through death's vile refrains,
Accepting insults as if gagged and bound,
Who spend in effort what you lack in brains,
Merit a plaque for your grave's patch of ground.

Casual readers have more delicate need.
They look for reassurance, not abuse.
Snarl like a rabid mastiff, their frail breed
Will turn tail and run, but not you, Moose.

The prize? Your resting place is boldly X'ed
Where truckers running hot can blow off steam.
Bearing no quaint, country churchyard text,
Your marker presents a universal theme,

Since budgets don't distinguish vagabonds
By epitaphs tailored to differing times.
The tablet is cast in iron, not in bronze,
Yet no expense was spared to square its rhymes.

CXXII *Last Supper*

Poetry, by the way, is reason on fire:
Thus credit yourself a feeble flicker of flame.
You may not own a broken orphic lyre,
But some librarian's bound to know your name:

"Aren't you the one who kept a book three years,
Returned its pages stuck together with gum?"
To ease the bibliothecary's tears,
You called its author Aristotle dumb:

"I guess I got the wrong guy. What a switch.
Who married Jackie Kennedy? Some big sheik.
I thought he'd give me tips on getting rich.
How would I know his grandfather was Greek?

"So now I'll shy away from smart books:
Just read the sex and sports magazines.
The rich are really a bum band of crooks
Anyhow, with their shell-game routines."

HERE LIES ONE WHOSE NAME WAS WRIT IN WATER,
John Keats's simple tombstone says in Rome.
HERE LIES ONE LED AS A LAMB TO SLAUGHTER,
Vachel Lindsay would christen your last home.

A more upbeat plug will word your plaque:
Its dream-spun verses underwrite your debts.
Die you must, but dead you shall not lack
The testament a rootless drifter gets.

Its meaning takes a minute to unlock,
An appeal beyond logic by design:
To run off vagrants loafing around your rock,
Marring the site of your stark desert shrine.

The phrasing's hopeful angle is make-believe
For all who reckon they rise above your state;
Who figure their names won't sway a sexton's sleeve,
Nor a last supper fill their patient plate.

Regard the wording as futile epitaph:
The final written record of your fate,
No lengthier than a prose paragraph.
If only its message meant, HELL CAN WAIT!

Death's tough beneath a four-lane sheet of gloom,
Yet solves your crux of leaving no true heir.
No chain gang brings silk flowers for your tomb,
But paving crews provide PERPETUAL CARE.

TOMB OF THE UNKNOWN TOURIST the spot is called,
No mention why it's just a shallow grave.
A clean rest stop for those whose cars have stalled
On their way to the nursing home of the brave.

It's little more than a wide place in the road
Covered by highly developed blacktop,
Yet it never asks to be weeded or hoed,
And features no TIMELESS TREASURES gift shop.

You become part of a cross-country highway
Connecting Venice Beach and Bangor, Maine.
But you lose the chance to sail heaven's skyway
For drowning your wife in Lake Pontchartrain.

You should've sunk her corpse without the bag,
Yet wrapped her up for fishermen to find.
The law won't care if she was a bloated hag,
And doesn't give a rip if love is blind.

How many pounds was she packing anyway,
Rounded off in hundreds, more or less?
Whatever avoirdupois she had that day,
You can bet she soon began to effervesce.

CXXIII *Swell Surprise*

Now at the fork all earthly bonding finds,
This talkathon has been a preacher's treat.
Quite rare to land a sucker who barely minds
The length of a hard sermon in Dixie heat,

Besides the swelter soaking your shirt in sweat.
Summer here stifles. It's better to wander west
And ride where the wind blows free. Your doomed duet
Is washed up when your wheels are dispossessed.

This lecture's been a stem-winder, true.
Oftentimes the old ways are the best.
Apologies for thus depriving you
Of desperately needed beauty rest.

Shake hands with one who lives on bread and wine:
The grinning groom who sets your sparks in tune,
And pumps more life in your flaming '59.
What a chance to chew, cuss, spit, and commune.

Your red-hot DODGE is a 3-D cartoon,
A BATMOBILE for Gotham's skyline.
It should've been used in David Lynch's *Dune*
To stem that movie's blockbusting decline.

Your humble servant was always fond of fins,
Those angles of uplift a sight for sore eyes.
As long as this little solar system spins,
Their swept design's a mighty swell surprise.

Not one dog day in a Blue Ridge blue moon
Does a DODGE clipper with giant fins dock here:
A cyclops's toy dropped from a space cocoon,
Its wings so wide they're hard for the hose to clear

And reach the tank to slake its ancient thirst.
Do phantoms backfire? This gem's real as three
Bells on a one-armed bandit. Why was it cursed?
Those push-button gears confused the bourgeoisie.

The trick's inventor was CHRYSLER's all-time goat.
Thank heaven he fled to LENIN MOTOR WORKS.
NATION IN CHAOS if clowns like that could vote,
Spurring an exodus faster than Dunkirk's.

Gauguin felt driven to desert Paris
And moved to Tahiti: simply up and went,
Pursuing his star, his one-man Polaris.
That's not how the CHRYSLER kook's exile was spent.

The poor sap ended up in GULAG ice,
Eating rats raw and thawed mammoth meat
Just to survive, living to feed his lice.
More cruel hearts than his jailers' never beat:

Hard as a pounding hammer, stubborn as steel.
They'd leave a starving man on a dog chain
To die in a beast's despair for its last meal,
Mouth locked open for random drops of rain:

Expiring thousands of miles from home and hope
Of a better world, the brotherhood of man
Stalin sold as volcanic pumice soap
To scour the blood off every FIVE-YEAR PLAN.

Yet the wired world is getting weirder still.
FIAT acquired CHRYSLER in 2009,
And thus CHRYSLER paid its bankruptcy bill.
Then once FIAT revamped its product line,

It launched a bold model for 2014:
A push-button shifting, all-electric car.
Could a craze for retro vintage features mean
Design's next leap in the automobile bazaar?

The hitch is, the car has only one forward gear.
Choose between that and REVERSE, you're underway:
Scant reason to drop a sentimental tear.
Revival or not, no style is here to stay.

But the more things change, the more can seem the same.
Where have you heard such trenchant thought before?
Soon after a novel trend collects a name,
The public's ready to show it the EXIT door.

None of this has a whit to do with you.
A '59 DODGE *Royal*'s not a trend,
And neither is its grainy, weathered hue:
Just transport to an overwhelming end.

Your UFO may not be right but it runs.
Cruise through Roswell and watch their heads turn.
Tell them its fuel comes from a second sun's
Photons captured making the stars burn.

This space-age showboat sure looks hard to steer.
On Big Muddy, tack for a country mile,
But on land if headlights swerve to miss a deer,
Your downfall yawns like a Delta crocodile.

CXXIV *Gypsy Rings*

You're quite a sport to brook this filibuster.
Your patience strikes a sympathetic chord.
Before these words of warning lose their luster,
Let's close this tale of you and time's swift sword.

In all-fired haste, will most folks shoot the breeze,
From restful shade and a classy leather seat,
With Jesus Christ in EXXON dungarees?
Their destination must be a scarlet suite

At some go-to-hell spa down in the Keys.
One carload made my peaceable blood boil,
Squealing their monster tires like banshees.
Cracker in a CORVETTE adds to the turmoil,

Stops en route to a poodle show, of all things:
Shouts his travel needs like a trumpet blast,
Then leans back twirling his Georgia gypsy rings.
Some you cotton to, some you'd sooner see gassed.

In his lap was a pink ball of kinky fur
Named Fifi, whose constant, constipated yap
Would cause a living saint to throttle her:
Wring her neck with a clear, heartwarming snap.

Yours truly could have kicked her without a qualm.
The cracker stewed while nailed by this same speech,
But left as meek as the *23rd Psalm.*
By 3 A.M., he was pale as chlorine bleach.

Fifi? Somehow she left the scene alive,
Her hornet's heart heaving a powder-puff breast.
May she stick her snout in a killer beehive,
And get stung dead as fluff in a rat's nest.

Your hardy soul has great attention span:
A joy to jawbone with, you goofy ox.
This station attendant craves a true fan.
It compensates for the rudeness and the rocks

Thrown by crude persons who deeply offend
This honest, humble witness, whose simple wish
Would shield you sheep from wounds no salve can mend,
With the thin armor of angst. As a jellyfish

Is a Portuguese man-of-war in martial guise,
To gird for the end of time's Trojan assault
Is well advised for a sot with graveyard eyes,
And far smarter than stumbling drunk on malt

Liquor, mumbling words from *Jumpin' Jack Flash*:
"Raised by a toothless, bearded hag—uh—
Schooled with a strap across my back—*crash!*—
Crowned with a spike right through my head—duh . . ."

The song reveals a touch of your mental hash.
Among clouds of upbeat TV ads and trite
Lingo shrouding time's downbeat backlash,
Before carrion demonstrates its might

And seals your soul, this killjoy would focus
Your mind on your quiet niche underground,
And scrap the Pollyanna hocus-pocus.
It's hard to face the abyss when alarms abound

In all the trivial on-the-spot reports.
This reflex era's dazed by episodes
Fleeting as fizz in soda pop. When the courts
Are clogged with torts, and gambler's greed erodes

The fertile fields of craft's and custom's soil,
The balanced pitch of a well-conceived slant
Upon the agony and the glorious toil
Of those who ran the town baloney plant—

Then guess whose brief is the fundamental facts?
To clean the pulp and cyber grime on your brain,
Carve into clear relief what time exacts,
And accent living's full measure of pain.

It's pure folly preaching to impudent fools.
Thank you for being a cut above the rest.
Since words of wisdom aren't precision tools,
Thank you for taking this achievement test.

Don't change lanes on Dolorosa Drive,
As the beach teems with nearly naked stuff.
It's curtains if girls reject your antique jive,
So follow this sage advice: lay on, Macduff.

The beach Bunnies will tease you half to death,
And the real upshot isn't happy days.
When just to watch them leaves you out of breath,
The spirit moves you, yet the flesh decays.

CXXV *Iron Mask*

As dialogue now gets down to brass tacks,
Won't you consider swallowing smart pills?
God knows how many literary hacks
Need them to cure a slew of stylish ills.

Electric in expectation marking the start
Of any voyage, prepare to soon be gone.
With untried guns and campfire courage, depart
As the Big Dipper wheels around towards dawn.

You're much the Spartan, even dying to go.
Your stamina must be ultra-high octane.
Deference pleases a gracious host, although
You act stiff as a parson from northern Maine.

Could a symbol stand for this interlude
By solemn fitness yet a dash of spice?
A plain memento still caustic and crude,
To char your husk and plunge your heart in ice?

It ought to sit on your bare chest as a charm,
An emblem of mishaps, snafus, and blind descents.
Too edgy to cool your heels down on the farm,
You're damned intent to scale life's prison fence.

It's zero hour for this bucket of bolts.
The boss is almost ready to charge you rent,
And your budget barely keeps alive twelve volts
Of battery juice, you corn-fed malcontent.

Takes one to know one, bud? Maybe you're right.
Your soothsayer is hardly underage.
Big talk and fortune-telling never quite
Collect an obit on TIME's *Milestones* page.

And rhyming speech is a listed manic trait—
Of rapidly spreading psychic crownfire.
All unborn thoughts the tongue must animate,
Conscript the savage syllables they require.

A further warning sign is pressured speech.
That's when the chatterbox just won't shut up,
As if he holds a major message to teach,
Rattling on like rocks in a tin cup.

Logorrhea's probably indicated,
With 400 pages of printed proof.
The clinical aspect can be debated,
Unless this entire work's a gonzo spoof.

One critic terms it "the poetry of assault."
One says "atomic pentameter" makes more sense,
Where two colliding stresses bring a halt
To lines which inspire a taste for breath mints.

Assigning it BTU's that can singe hair,
Some swear it's published by the STERNO brand.
Inflammatory claims are not unfair:
Rare is the book taking a sterner stand.

Those line-end spondees aren't atomic fusion,
Yet multiply throughout as chain reaction.
For thus nailing down a line's conclusion,
Some may count it more like trash compaction.

Surely the guy's a nasty little nerd
Hiding behind a show of verbal menace;
Sneaking around like a snake for the worst word;
And mistaking liquid EX–LAX for draft GUINNESS.

Lines severe as thunder, jagged as lightning,
Sound intent as a predator on the prowl.
And his morbid sarcasm is plain frightening,
Enough to make the devil himself cry foul.

Worse still is to sit in the seat of the scornful,
Wisely expressed by the first chapter of *Psalms*.
You look so out of it, hangdog and mournful,
Does your fortune read the same in both palms?

You're burning moonbeams while you're idling here,
Marked for death and wasting travel time.
Accept a free six-pack of sour beer,
And sail off to the workingman sublime.

More can be said, but soon you need to drift.
"Who's the windbag running my life," you ask?
Is that how you greet an all too timely gift?
It's no way to treat a man in an iron mask.

CXXVI *Broken Dreams*

You yourself are barely a primate, Mick.
When did you last enter a human house?
Your head has half the sense of a clay brick,
Your honor half the class of a hungry mouse.

It's different if a man's an outright rogue.
You come off as a slob with a filthy mouth.
Your heavy accent's not a Boston brogue
But a vestige of the backwoods mountain South.

The pace here's too busy for long good-byes.
To stand a commentator's frank talk,
You've shown true grit. If full destruction lies
Behind time's watch vigilant as a hawk,

Accept its swoop, like a frog in its beak.
Don't cross the double yellow line and cruise
At forty-five till your future springs a leak.
Shun the rat race. Even its winners lose.

Forgetting this torture on the night before,
Miss the expressway to the cemetery.
Rehearsing for eternity still means more
Than holing up in a cold monastery.

The Age of Aquarius died much too quick:
Expect no Eagle Scout to lighten your load.
To guard against becoming carsick,
Clench your dentures driving unpaved road.

Don't know where to go but getting there fast?
The land of broken dreams is way out west.
All shook up for nothing, hopes downcast?
Try TOPLESS GIRLS OF GLITTER GULCH, the best.

Ask one to do the lap-dance limbo rock
And shove her mons veneris in your face:
A better bet than staring at the clock
To give your fractured ego breathing space.

The JAGUAR CLUB is always crawling with cops.
Good guys to be in a war with some day, but
Don't get caught there when the music stops.
They'll close your tab and pocket the prime cut.

Stop the world, you want to get off? Sure thing.
Freed for bad behavior, coming right up.
Would you block a spear or strangle in a string?
A drink of LYSOL from a plastic cup?

A six-gun cocked for instant death? Whatever.
The only time off you get is ninety-nine
Percent of half the square root of never.
Sorry to lay sad tidings on the line.

To wash and to wax till death do you part:
That's you and your prairie schooner, knothead.
The last thing you want now is a false start.
Add water when heat declares condition RED.

Bypass Arizona? You're welcome to try.
Its desert wildness finally hems you in,
Beyond the nameless gulf of earth and sky,
Where no pilgrim is what he was again.

The Superstition Range? Don't be silly.
They punctuate suburban badlands.
Follow terrain not mountainous but hilly,
Dodging the bomb targets of WHITE SANDS.

The Sangre de Cristo Mountains are the ones
To tackle if you're seeking altitude.
Their pinnacles have seen 10 million suns
Cross the sky perpetually renewed.

You meet Comanches boiling down the hills?
Probably laid-off extras from Hollywood.
Quick-flashing gossip, coupled with pep pills,
Has them racing to remake *Robin Hood*.

CXXVII *Visionary Treasure*

To travelers on a trail of blazing sand,
The secrets of the deep are not revealed.
Upon the ocean blue or dry land,
Those mystery doors remain forever sealed.

The truth of death's infinity will emerge,
Far more frank than fictive *Tales from the Crypt*.
Death's never-neverland is on the verge
Of coming true for you according to script.

Abbreviate Arizona AZ:
The alphabet from birth to death in one.
This is no game in which you hide or flee:
Time sticks to you like snot on a hot cross bun.

Die of navigating ineptitude,
Not finding AZ in *Rand McNally?*
Relax. All roads lead to Tombstone, dude,
Even if a sign reads PLEASANT VALLEY.

You can't evade the Tombstone CITY LIMITS:
The designated driver is yourself.
There you finish dead as Admiral Nimitz
Falling off the continental shelf,

Whence matter sinks to an abyssal plain,
Whose species numbers rival the Amazon
Basin's forest soaked in surface rain:
Such plenty anywhere to prey upon.

Destination TOMBSTONE isn't a place
You skip within the basic scheme of things.
It lies on life's far edge as open space,
Awaiting what the human highway brings.

Your dreadnought's a great destroyer, razorback.
Its dual exhausts roar like twelve-inch guns:
Double barrels that kick like a kilo of crack,
Squashing your skull in recoil of twenty tons.

Each dog has his day, yours no shorter than most,
So burn bright as smelters at BETHLEHEM STEEL.
Seeing double? Shift into neutral and coast.
If a trooper stops you, act like a big wheel:

"I love to ride my horse and shoot my gun.
That's a cowboy's work, if the sky's blue.
Playing with pistols is how the West was won!
I'm just a handsome stranger passing through.

"A lone wolf, I plan to eat the world,
Though hunger pangs pass like everything else.
If my replies sound both twisted and twirled,
They're too entangled with my engine belts.

"I need like a can of worms a change of pace:
Go fish in muddy water, snooze in the shade.
With so many chicks I charmed in Peyton Place,
My soul's ripe for a BILLY GRAHAM CRUSADE.

"Seeking a lost and visionary treasure
Right along my pilgrim journey, I
Can't refuse a little spell of pleasure,
Being an All-American kind of guy.

"Blazing DEAR ABBY a trail of broken hearts,
I motor onward, one town to the next.
It's funny I haven't visited these parts
Before, delayed because I'm oversexed.

"There's a limit to what a man can achieve
When women anywhere demand his time,
Implore him with grief and guile not to leave,
Then call his departure a tragic sex crime."

CXXVIII *Fifty States*

"As I ramble across my native land,
I mainly aspire to avoid Dead Man's Curve.
I wake up feeling a hatchet in my hand,
And think my arm has merely pinched a nerve.

"The arm seems numb, although I grasp somehow
An hour of truth has come and travel on.
Every now and then I butcher a cow,
And obey the daily rise of blood-red dawn.

"I never understand exactly why
I sense I can't stay long in the same place,
Having grown quite fond of wider sky,
And quit regular housing's paper chase.

"The more I roam, the more I want to roam,
As days become a need to buy more gas.
Riding the wind has stripped my car's chrome,
While desert dust storms sandblast its glass.

"I've always liked the smell of gasoline,
A taste acquired when only a small child.
What thrills the most is a spill's rainbow sheen
On concrete: a single whiff can drive me wild.

"Clearly this rush helps keep me on the move:
The sheer enjoyment rolling down the road.
Years fly by but I retain my groove,
Inspired so much I ought to compose an ode.

"Yet I'm a man of action, not a poet.
I couldn't bear the drag of sitting still.
If there's a story here, time can show it.
I happily deed the whole mess in my will.

"That hatchet often tingles my right hand.
I look, find nothing there, but even so,
It's like one side of me truly can't stand
Living with what it knows it doesn't know.

"Or words to the same effect. I wish I knew
The path I chose to get this far today,
Where I've been, then where I'm headed to.
Tell me, is Arizona thataway?

"One magic night in Texas I recall,
I helped a woman set herself on fire.
Jesus, did she have the wherewithal
To power the earth's whirlwind of desire!

"It happened back on down the dusty trail.
A swell memory, though, good for the heart.
Regardless how I hear she took the veil,
What triumph was left for her exquisite art?

"I had my role once in her passion play.
To meet the chance anew, I'd gladly trade
Tomorrow's women for her one yesterday,
And embrace her wondrous body heaven-made.

"To recreate the sweet, sustaining dream,
To cause the long-dumb dream again to speak,
I'd swap my DODGE for a single moonbeam
That lights her glowing flesh, and one more peek.

465

"Yet now I'd better simply look ahead,
Maintaining a clear square inch of windshield.
Time will give us this day our daily dread,
So I'll advance while keeping my eyes peeled."

Lay it on thick: John Law might let you skate.
Mix country corn with city-slicker bull.
Assuring him your future cannot wait,
Tell the copper you're late for a tractor pull.

He may not sense you're wanted in fifty states,
With a week's growth shading your pasty face.
The blank impression your homely puss creates
Could make him miss the chance to crack your case.

"Haulin' you in? Nope, lettin' you off," he'll say.
"Runnin' on empty won't get far, I'm afraid:
End of the line can surprise you any day.
Forget them parkin' tickets you never paid."

The next act on your program is to leave.
You get your fill of nature, time you're through.
Stick to back roads, stuff some cash up a sleeve:
When age turns ugly, remit the AMOUNT DUE.

The worst thing you can do is gather dust:
It's just a couple of hours to Knoxville.
Although your motor is showing signs of rust,
Your flesh is still not ripe for the landfill.

CXXIX *Dust Devils*

Hasta la vista, Pancho, happy trails.
So long, bowlegs, you tumbling tumbleweed.
Roam till you tip Big Sky Country's scales,
And a sneeze begins time's downhill stampede.

Head 'em up and move 'em out, cowpoke.
Longhorns on open range mean little talk,
So worry later, wreathed in campfire smoke,
Trying to duck time's whirring tomahawk.

It's heap big wages you blow payday, cowhand:
In Corpus Christi, Waco, Santa Cruz?
Swing far wide of curves in the Rio Grande:
The streets of Laredo aren't the path to choose.

Open fire if they ambush you at the pass.
Only REMINGTON speaks in your behalf,
Once their posse reaches critical mass—
In Provo, Cheyenne, Las Cruces, or Flagstaff.

You'd rather ride the stagecoach, buckaroo?
It's bound for glory via Jericho,
Carthage, Memphis, and Blown-Apart Bayou.
Stash your spurs then, drover, time to go.

Last stop is Arizona, Cactus Patch.
Cross yourself when the driver cries, "Tombstone!"
Dust reclaims you, the clock restarts from scratch,
Past the home goal line of time's end zone.

It was Arizonans captured San Juan Hill:
Rough Riders, manic Teddy's bully troops.
Life dumped them all with the years, a nasty spill.
Think about that, jumping through time's fire hoops.

A burning ring of fire cooked Johnny Cash,
Gave him a taste of forever near home:
In FOLSOM PEN where hell is prison hash,
Every day till the Pope abandons Rome.

HE DIED TO PUT A NEW STAR ON THE FLAG,
Says the gravestone of Major Buck O'Neill.
This horseman fell too soon for pride to brag
On Arizona's gaining a state seal.

REMEMBER THE MAINE! drew him to volunteer—
Plus other inflammatory headlines—
For ending Spanish arms in the hemisphere.
And heroism has its own designs.

Your motives not so high as his, hotspur,
Ride the purple sage whose thundering herds
That raised dust devils are dead as ancient Ur—
But hide your scalp from indignant desert birds.

Trot off into the sunset, the show's over.
Your double leaving you victor, smile and wave.
Travel west clutching a four-leaf clover,
Sure to wear your six-guns to the grave.

Where you're headed, Apaches prized the rite
Of fusing bloods for kinship here and beyond:
A steadfast, lordly gesture of deep delight.
What civilized cynic will mock such a bond?

Yet disease renders it dumb to run that risk,
No eagle feathers sweeping down your back.
Now whores can have the stare of a basilisk.
This candid chatter would serve up what you lack.

It's only a simple truck-stop tête-à-tête,
No motive but to shut your ego down,
And bring your vacant mind-set up to date;
A send-off to eternal Tarrytown:

Tombstone, Arizona, on any map.
The very end of the earth, where you're concerned,
More subtle than Pieter Brueghel's death-trap:
The Triumph of Death must always be relearned.

CXXX *Western Union*

This switchblade's worn too dull to break the skin:
Godspeed, blood brother. Time's evil spell,
As long as stone mints fossils, will toil and spin.
Till Gabriel's bugle blows last trump, farewell.

In perpetuum, ave atque vale.
The serpent coiled in the eagle's empty nest,
To suck the eggs of either is sheer folly.
Pursue the sun, whose course is ONE-WAY west.

This visit hurts your sense of manly worth?
None leaves the turning world's delights alive.
May you wander many moons on the broad earth,
And reach the finish raising a high-five.

If you find the fabled happy hunting ground,
Pity this medicine man you left behind.
Save him space in heaven's burial mound,
And dispatch him passage there, lame or blind.

This doesn't mean by telepathic trance.
You weren't enthralled here by Merlin's ghost.
Transfer the fare by WESTERN UNION finance
From a lucky 7–ELEVEN outpost

In the far country, which is anywhere
West of here that's reachable by car,
That has an atmosphere finer than air,
And disregards the hood you really are.

Don't call it underfunded paradise.
In future-friendly terms, what do you want?
Surely it beats damnation's awful price,
Good enough as a permanent place to haunt.

An artificial paradise or not,
Choose it over oblivion, if it's true.
Emptying Crazy Horse's chamber pot
Is better than finding nothing left to do.

Your arms outspread to the Great Spirit, send
Back pictures of you posed on a mountain top.
With magic marker inscribe the words THE END,
Confirming how your story came to a stop.

As you stand eagle-armed to fly away,
And breath takes wing yet flesh remains below,
If washed in glory's light as warm new day,
Be kind and let your loyal brethren know.

Lifted down like a cross and laid to rest
By ragtag hobo-trekkers chancing by,
Say you ate your spinach and tried your best,
But the son of man and woman is born to die.

EPITAPH *Double Cross*

Let time's cold hands ignore the cosmic laws
That stopped this lone wayfarer's clock of clay.
May life's installment plan omit the cause,
The perfect double cross he met halfway.

Soon may the falling guillotine of age
Stick in its runners and turn red with rust;
The sable grain of this cast-iron page
Wear down the scythe of death to fairy dust.

Let providence across the bar suspend
Our certain capital sentence served on earth;
Our half-lives burn like radium's, halve no-end,
And never close full-circle with their birth.

May the veil over all nations and the web
Clouding all eyes disintegrate in light;
The deep darkness feeding eternity ebb,
And end the old chaos of day and night.

Could the force holding a king's heart in its hand
Spare us the lowly fate of blood and bone;
Permit us to bypass doom in wonderland,
And liberate us at last from Tombstone?

Spurn the drift of a final episode.
Time's leviathan, spit us out like Jonah!
To honor all found dead beside the road,
This plaque speaks for the state of Arizona.

54234087R00286

Made in the USA
Charleston, SC
27 March 2016